DAN O. VIA, JR. is Professor of New Testament at The Divinity School, Duke University. He is the author of the widely influential *The Parables: Their Literary and Existential Dimension* (Fortress Press, 1967)—now in its fourth paperback printing. He has also edited volumes in the Guides to Biblical Scholarship series and Semeia Studies.

THE ETHICS
OF MARK'S GOSPEL—
IN THE MIDDLE OF TIME

THE ETHICS
OF MARK'S GOSPEL—
IN THE MIDDLE OF TIME

Dan O. Via, Jr.

FORTRESS PRESS　　PHILADELPHIA

COPYRIGHT © 1985 BY FORTRESS PRESS

Library of Congress Cataloging in Publication Data

Via, Dan Otto, 1928–
   The ethics of Mark's Gospel—in the middle of time.

   Bibliography: p.
   Includes indexes.
   1. Bible. N.T. Mark—Criticism, interpretation, etc.
2. Ethics in the Bible. I. Title.
BS2585.2.V45   1985   226′.306   84–48733
ISBN 0–8006–0746–5

1417L84   Printed in the United States of America   1–746

To
M. R. Cherry
and
W. D. Davies
Friends and Teachers

Contents

Preface

The purpose of this work is to interpret the ethic of the Gospel of Mark in relation to specific hermeneutical reflection and through the use of several hermeneutical methods. The scholarly context for this discussion is threefold: First, biblical scholars have been calling for a treatment of New Testament ethics that will make its results accessible to constructive ethics; second, others have called for the pursuit of ethical reflection on the basis of narrative; third, Markan scholarship itself has enhanced our ability so to proceed.

My interpretation raises two theoretical issues of importance: first, the relationship of phenomenological hermeneutics to structural analysis; second, the question of the truth value of narrative form. These problems are integral to the discussion, but the interpretation itself can be pursued without working them out. I have therefore dealt with them in appendices, and the reader who is interested in theoretical questions is invited to look at these at the appropriate points.

I should like to express my gratitude to the University of Virginia for giving me a semester off for writing, which greatly facilitated the completion of the manuscript. I am also grateful to James Childress, Nathan Scott, and W. D. Davies for their critical and helpful readings of all or parts of it.

In addition I want to thank John A. Hollar of Fortress Press for his constructive editing, and my graduate assistants, Virginia C. Barfield and Stephen Pogoloff, for their able help in preparing the bibliography and indexes. Finally I wish to thank the Society of Biblical Literature for permission to use substantial parts of a paper of mine which was originally published as "Mark 10:32-52—A Structural, Literary, and Theological Evaluation," *Society of Biblical Literature 1979 Seminar Papers II* (Missoula, Mont.: Scholars Press, 1979).

The Divinity School   Dan Otto Via, Jr.
Duke University

INTRODUCTION

1

An Approach to
New Testament Ethics
and Narrative

New Testament Ethics
and Constructive Christian Ethics:
A Hermeneutical Matter

This work is a study in New Testament ethics, an attempt to understand the ethical teachings of the Gospel of Mark, and particularly of Mark 10, in the context of the narrative of that Gospel. Mark is being examined because of its fundamental importance as a New Testament text and because its ethical import has been neglected, especially the complexity and problematics which it introduces into ethical reflection.

My interpretation represents an exegetical study that makes use of literary and historical criticism as well as other interpretive methods that are necessary and fruitful for understanding a text from the past. This effort therefore is to be distinguished—although the two overlap—from another approach to the issues involved, an approach that might be called the use of the New Testament *for* Christian ethics.[1] These two approaches will differ in focus, emphasis, and intention in their dealing with the New Testament, but they need not and should not differ in principle. Constructive Christian ethics will focus on a systematic statement of the nature of the Christian ethical life for the contemporary situation, and its use of the New Testament will be adjusted to that intention. But such use as it makes of New Testament texts should take account of their historical context and literary dimensions. New Testament ethics, on the other hand, will focus on New Testament texts themselves in the light of their formal literary features and historical setting, with a view to saying what the texts meant in their original context. But whether this is all that exegesis should or can do and whether it can do it "objectively" will depend on how one views the nature and necessities of the hermeneutical process, the process of interpretation.

I will not then pretend that I do not have in mind constructive theological-ethical concerns which require hermeneutical reflection. We all live in the midst of the time process, between what Frank Kermode has called "the *tick* of birth and the *tock* of death,"[2] between creation and apocalypse—the biblical view of world history. The middle of Mark's plot will symbolize for us the middle of time, and there is a very real sense in which Mark 10 is the middle of the middle. How does this chapter show itself to be the mid-point of Mark's middle, and how does this mid-point represent for us the nature of existence in the middle of time, the fabric of temporality in which we must enact our ethical responsibility? These are some of the questions to be pursued.

On what ground can it now be claimed that a given study wants to focus on the interpretation of a New Testament text and wants to have as its horizon constructive, contemporary theological-ethical interests? The ground to be cited for making such a claim is Wolfgang Iser's theory of two closely related phenomena: the literary work and the act of interpretation. The literary work has two poles, the author's text and the realization accomplished in and by the reader. The work itself is neither of these; rather, its actuality is the virtuality or interaction situated between them, between the text and the subjectivity of the reader.[3]

A text does not contain a formulated meaning but is a potential for meaning; the act of interpretation therefore is the production, performance, or assembling of this potential by the reader.[4] The text itself has various qualities which summon the reader's participation in the constitution of its meaning: (1) The text's images must be ordered and their meaning made explicit by the interpreter. (2) A narrative will typically contain a number of perspectives whose reconciliation is not formulated in the text but must be by the reader if the reader is to make the experience of the text his or her own. (3) A literary text will make the everyday unfamiliar, but unlike a philosophical statement it will not formulate an explicit alternative to the ordinary way of viewing things. The reader must find the motive for this questioning of everyday reality and in so doing participate in the production of meaning.[5]

Not only is the reader spurred to action by what is said, however, but he or she is also activated by what is not said. What is missing—the gaps in the text—stimulates the reader to fill in the blanks with projections from the imagination. The text then brings the reader to the standpoint from which he or she constructs its meaning. Therefore the text exercises some control, and the reader is not free to have it mean arbitrarily anything he or she wants it to mean. At the same time, the reader's subjectivity—experiences, decisions, and attitudes—comes to expression in the meaning he or she projects. One must expect, then, a multiplicity of possible meanings.[6] It is the constitution of meaning projected by the interpreter which completes the work—so far as it can be completed.

This view of things justifies my effort to give an interpretation of Mark that shares a common boundary between New Testament theological ethics and contemporary constructive ethics. Such an attempt *is* an interpretation of Mark, because the work that Mark is, or belongs to, embraces both the text and its realization in the subjective world of the interpreter with his or her constructive concerns (see further Appendix I).

Having briefly examined the hermeneutical ground for connecting New Testament ethics and constructive ethics, we need to review selectively the recent call for such efforts. Brevard S. Childs, writing in 1970, expressed the judgment that "there is no outstanding modern work written in English that even attempts to deal adequately with the biblical material as it relates to ethics."[7] Constructive and social ethicists, on the one side, have made relatively little use of biblical material, while, on the other side, the mid-century biblical theology movement did not deal with the Bible in such a way as to make its resources available for use by ethicists and pastors. The result has been that many of the most promising theological students have been attracted to ethics without having been seriously influenced by biblical studies. Over against this situation Childs called on biblical scholars to deal with their material in a theologically significant way, addressing questions that are compatible with the biblical subject matter, critically understood, but that also relate to the constructive theological task. Similarly he states that a new biblical theology must aid in the process of making difficult ethical decisions today.[8]

A few years later Bruce C. Birch and Larry Rasmussen voiced a similar concern. They reminded us that while Christians have always regarded the Bible as central for ethics, biblical studies and Christian ethical reflection have often gone their separate ways. For the most part the two disciplines have not influenced each other.[9] Ethicists, particularly in America, have usually addressed practical issues and have been learned in the social sciences, and in philosophy in recent years; but to the extent that they have used the Bible, ethicists have been relatively inattentive to the relationship of ethical thought to the problems of biblical scholarship.[10]

Most biblical scholars, on their side, have not been familiar with the categories of ethics and have had little concern to relate the findings of critical biblical scholarship to ethics at either the theoretical or the practical level. Moreover, Birch and Rasmussen believe that biblical scholarship in the 1960s and 1970s has moved even farther away from a real concern with the constructive tasks of theology and ethics,[11] this turn being marked by the oft-cited articles of Krister Stendahl,[12] which maintain a sharp cleavage between the historical and descriptive nature of biblical theology and the constructive and philosophical nature of systematic theology. Birch and Rasmussen[13] think that most recent work on New Testament ethics reflects the Stendahl perspective. If that is in fact the case, there are other hermeneutical outlooks on the problem, one of which is being pursued in this book.

Birch and Rasmussen attempt to connect biblical studies and constructive ethics in a way that brings into view the methodological issues at both the practical and the theoretical levels. How can the Bible be appropriated for ethical reflection both as a resource for shaping character or moral identity and as an aid in making decisions?[14] Three issues that Birch and Rasmussen discuss are worthy of mention here:

1. The hermeneutical circle. It is necessary to be critically aware of the dialectical relationship between the theological-ethical predisposition of the scholar and the biblical texts to be interpreted.[15] I have already touched on this matter.

2. The problem of the authority of the Bible. The Bible has a unique authority for Christian ethics which cannot be relativized so that it becomes simply one source among many. But since the Bible is not the only authority, the problem becomes that of deciding on the relationship of the Bible to other authorities. The claim of primacy for the Bible is confessional, not objective.[16]

3. The means for making the Bible available as an ethical resource. The Bible's own unique character must be critically understood, and one must not ignore the variety of its ethically pertinent material—law codes, prophetic oracles, explicit instruction, narratives, and so forth. The tools of both literary and historical criticism must be used in exegesis: meaning cannot be abstracted either from literary form or from historical context. Birch and Rasmussen follow Childs in stressing the authority of the canon as the framework for interpretation. Among the benefits of this principle are the following: First, we are reminded of the sweep and variety in Scripture on a given ethical theme and thereby prevented from absolutizing a single text or position. Second, attention to the whole of Scripture helps curb the selection of biblical texts on the basis of presuppositions.[17]

The relationship between constructive ethics and biblical studies is not as slight in the 1980s as it was in the 1970s, but there is still much to be done. I myself am not attempting to deal with the whole of the New Testament but to do New Testament ethics—in relation to one text—in such a way that it opens out toward constructive ethics. The methodological concerns of Birch and Rasmussen will be extended, but I will leave it to others to compensate for any tendency of mine to overstress the significance of one text.

The understanding of time is one cardinal point at which New Testament ethics and constructive ethics can meet. I will attempt to articulate Mark's understanding of the temporal state of human existence from an analysis of the plot of the Gospel narrative in relation to the world plot of apocalyptic. And throughout, the effort will be made to relate Mark's ethical teaching organically to its understanding of temporality, or more exactly, to show that Mark itself makes such a connection. This is a way of making one significant New Testament text available to constructive ethical reflection. Because "apocalyptic" is being dealt with in a demythologized way, it is being made available immediately for use in contemporary ethical reflection. And because ethics in a New Testament text is being displayed as inseparable from demythologized apocalyptic, it is being suggested that this connection between apocalyptic and ethics should also be maintained by constructive Christian ethics—a matter that could be substantiated from other important New Testament texts as well.

Carl E. Braaten has affirmed that the one normative starting point for constructive Christian ethics is the eschatological kingdom of God as Jesus proclaimed and enacted it. He states that if eschatology is the key to ethics, "most of the leading names completely ignore it, especially in America. . . . One must conclude that the most prominent thinkers in the field have not yet found the key."[18] While Braaten here uses the term "eschatology," which is broader than "apocalyptic," he means eschatology as portrayed in Jesus' teaching on the kingdom of God with its futuristic as well as its realized orientation. In Braaten's opinion the kingdom of God is not the product of ethics but is prior to it as ground and possibility. Just as the kingdom was proleptically present in Jesus' speech and action, so also the kingdom can express itself in human ethical action. At the same time, the future kingdom reveals the imperfect and tentative quality of all human achievements in the present.[19]

At this point it should be noted that I propose to base Mark's ethics on certain aspects of the Gospel's literary (narrative) *form*. I am also interested in theological and ethical *concepts*—temporality, ground of ethical action, and so forth. This means that I do not agree with the tendency in contemporary literary theory to reject the legitimacy of conceptualizing, or using discursive language, in literary analysis. An extreme version of this point of view may be seen in Susan Sontag's famous statement: "Interpretation is the revenge of the intellect upon art."[20] In her opinion the interpretation of literature and art, as it has usually been practiced in the West, is based on the mistaken notion that art is primarily a matter of content. Interpretation, then, is the translation of one thing, an item of content, into something else, a latent equivalent. Not only does this injure art, it also depletes the world by setting up a shadow world of meanings. Interpretation is, moreover, an attempt to overcome art's capacity to make us nervous by rendering it manageable and conformable. A proper approach would recognize that the merit of a significant work of literary art is not its meanings but the "pure, untranslatable, sensuous immediacy of some of its images." A fitting criticism, then, would pay more attention to form than to content. It would "reveal the sensuous surface of art without mucking about in it." It would therefore enable us to experience "the luminousness of the thing in itself."[21]

A more moderate statement of a similar point of view may be seen in a recent work by a New Testament scholar. Bernard B. Scott makes the claim that the first and most important clue for dealing with Jesus' parables in relation to the kingdom of God is to observe that Jesus did not define the kingdom in discursive language. A would-be interpreter of the parables may not impose or explain meaning but should rather provide an opportunity for meaning's disclosure by creating the necessary conditions for hearing. "We cannot state what a parable means, for it has no meaning separate from itself." Scott hopes that his critical agenda will not betray itself by reducing symbol and parable to discursive language. To do so would be to suffer a loss of potential meaning.[22]

I have a certain respect for the literary piety that does not want to violate the pristine separateness of image, metaphor, and parable, or narrative, by reducing these forms to concepts. But it is a piety I do not altogether share. I find much more compatible the Roland Barthes of *On Racine.* In this text he states that the literary work should be understood as a sign—a signifier (expression or vehicle of meaning) joined to a signified (mental image or conceptual content), with criticism then being a deciphering of the signification, the discovery of the thing signified. For one signifier several possible things are signified: the signs are ambiguous, and decipherment is a choice. It is not the case that one choice is as good as another, but one can choose only by taking a stand on the mental system in its entirety. Racine lends himself to several different languages for reading: psychoanalytic, existential, tragic, psychological; note that these are all *conceptual* categories. None of these is innocent, and we cannot finally tell the truth about Racine. The critic must make the wager of talking about Racine in one way and not in another. With Barthes I agree that the first objective rule is to declare one's system of reading, recognizing that no neutral system exists.[23]

I contend that there is a dimension of narrative art that cannot be translated, paraphrased, or reduced to concepts. But at the same time language used aesthetically does integrally have conceptual implications. Therefore it is not a violation of the literary work's nature to bring these implications to articulate expression. Paul Ricoeur has argued forcefully that the symbol gives rise to the occasion for thought.[24] There can be a kind of conceptual language which preserves the tensive character of symbol, and there is no interpretation not mediated by some philosophical position.[25] One wonders exactly what Sontag means by a non-conceptual interpretation when she cites Barthes's *On Racine* as an example of it.[26] Barthes here makes obvious use of both Freudian and theological concepts in interpreting the plays of Racine.[27]

The aesthetic or poetic function of language brings about in and for the reader the experience of rapt attention and the defamiliarization of the everyday world. When one turns from the stance of involvement in the life-world of the work, that is, the aesthetic stance in which conceptual awareness is only tacit, to the distancing of the critical stance, then something of the powerful immediacy of the work—"the luminousness of the thing in itself"—is lost. But this loss in immediate participation is worthily compensated for by a gain in conceptual clarity which is far more than the revenge of the intellect upon art. Both art and criticism of a conceptual kind are necessary, and neither is a substitute for the other, as I have contended previously.[28] There is a continuity between action, idea, and image or metaphor, and both this continuity and the distinctiveness of the elements that compose it are ingredient to the wholeness of life.[29] Idea is organically related to image and action but also has its own distinctive significance, which is why criticism should not try to avoid concepts and should not try to ape art itself. Even if one took the position that criticism should reject the quest for conceptual meanings and satisfy itself with describing the surface of the literary work, then it would still have to be acknowledged that the surface is organically connected with the depth, both conceptually and structurally. Thus there would always be a strong element of subjectivity in any judgment about whether a given piece of criticism was revealing the sensuous surface or "mucking about in it."

I do not contend that my way of drawing out the implications of Mark's narrative is the only way or the final way of conceptualizing it. I fully accept the polyvalence of narrative art and the propriety of multiple interpretation. My approach is one justifiable way among many possibilities.

Ethics and Narrative:
A Slender Tradition

Here I turn briefly to the question of the relationship between plot and reality, the correspondence, or lack of it, between the temporal structure of narrative and the temporality of the "real world," the way we experience time in our everyday lives. For my purposes this is not just an exercise in theorizing. In Mark the important ethical issues—what the believer ought to do and be and how he or she is able to—rest squarely on the quality and structure of the time in which the believer lives, and this temporal character and pattern are grounded in the plot and other narrative features. I would want to maintain, therefore, that a study of Mark's views on the life of Christian discipleship should not neglect such issues as the messianic secret.[30] Since Mark is an organic whole, all of the parts relate to one another. Thus a study of the Markan view of discipleship should pay attention to the messianic secret motif because it is expressed in both plot and discourse and is a constituent of the narrative world which undergirds and shapes Mark's understanding of ethical obligation and possibility.

The problem about the relationship between the plot and the temporal state of the real world is not, of course, whether the content of Mark's story is historically true but whether the ordering of the world which belongs to its plot corresponds to reality as we experience it. Ethical responsibility and possibility depend on the character of the time of the believer, the time of the coming of the kingdom of God, and this emerges from the plot in relationship to the narrative world. If, then, it should turn out that the temporal ordering of the world in the plot were a falsification of the real world, the relevance of Mark's ethic for the real world would be seriously compromised. A successful defense of the truth value of plot as such would not prove that Mark's ethic is true. But it would show that it need not be false.

My focus here is on the Markan middle; but the middle is integrally connected with the beginning and the ending, a comic or redemptive ending, even if problematically so. In view of the preceding considerations, I now need to scrutinize the validity of the three-part Markan plot, including the particular problem of the happy ending.

Two issues have just been raised: (1) the affirmation that narrative and ethics have a positive relationship; (2) the problem of the truth value of plot as an ordering principle. The first of these will be dealt with at this point and the second one in Appendix II.

Stanley Hauerwas has observed that the concept of narrative has received scant attention in recent moral theory.[31] While this is no doubt true, some scholars have paid attention to the significance and fruitfulness of narrative for ethical reflection, with Hauerwas's own work being an important contribution. Since my own effort belongs to this undeveloped tradition, it seems appropriate to review the contributions of certain predecessors.

In 1958 the British philosopher Ronald W. Hepburn discussed "parable" (which genre for him expansively includes the gospel story, the whole Bible, and dramas, poems, and novels) in its significance for both religion and ethics. Hepburn's concern was to define the category of the religious in a way that would satisfy the empiricist but which he candidly acknowledged would not do justice to the claims of historical Christianity. It is not necessary that Christ should have died if the story of his life—true or not—gives backing to the Christlike way of life. Problems about the meanings of words such as "God," "heaven," and "resurrection" are solved by showing the part these words play in delineating the practical way of life. For Hepburn, the religious person is one who is committed to a pattern of ethical behavior, but what distinguishes religious from moral discourse is that the former provides a tightly cohering, extended parable which vividly expresses the way of life chosen and inspires the believer to implement it in practice. The parable, with its associated pattern of behavior, legislates, not for a part of one's life, but for all of it, and determines one's total imaginative vision of the world.[32]

I am mainly concerned *not* with Hepburn's treatment of the strictly religious dimension but with what he implies about the relationship between narrative and ethics. Here there is an element of instability. It is not clear exactly how the ethical pattern is associated with the parable. Is it that narrative gives a total vision of life, an understanding of the reality in the midst of which one is morally responsible?[33] Or is the narrative simply an instance or illustration of a moral rule, the "fortifying of morality by parable"?[34]

New Testament ethics is one of several areas to benefit from the seminal work of Amos N. Wilder, who in 1964 suggested the close connection between a good story and the realization of what one ought to do. "The road to a moral judgment is by way of the imagination."[35] This became the point of departure for two articles of my own in which I tried to display the significance of the birth narrative in particular but also of the Gospel narrative as a whole for Matthew's understanding of Christian moral obligation.[36] Symbol, action, and theme coalesce to create a sense of ethical responsibility which challenges the authority of law, regardless of how much that may be in tension with Matthew's self-conscious devotion to the law. The ambiguities and openness in the plot of the Gospel make a disciple's ethical standing uncertain. While Hepburn tends to let the religious dimension, the impingement of God upon the human, be exhausted by the ethical, I have tried to show that an interpretation of Matthew makes it possible for us to consider that what a person ought to do and be is made radically but relevantly enigmatic and complex by the eschatological divine intervention. That will also be true for Mark in its particular way. Hepburn wants to solve theological problems by turning them into ethical ones rather than recognizing that the theological problematizes the ethical. His move assumes that the ethical is less problematic than the theological, but they may be equally so.

In 1981 Alasdair MacIntyre attempted to recover a much-criticized Aristotle for modern ethical reflection and to argue the necessity of narrative for ethics, a relationship having deep historical roots. But it should be observed that the connection which he and others posit between ethics and narrative is more far-reaching than the notion of moral education, which can be seen before Aristotle. Already in Homeric society, for instance, the chief means of moral education was telling stories. The poems and sagas of this culture portray the values of society, the various human roles, and the privileges and duties following upon a given status. What is important is actions, for human beings in heroic society have no hidden depth. Human life has the determinate form of a certain kind of story, and that story is believed to capture the form of life already present in society although the poet claims a special insight into this structure.[37]

Similarly for Sophocles there is an objective moral order, but our perception of it makes it impossible to harmonize rival moral truths. This situation is tragic in that the authority of both claims must be recognized and is different from modern pluralism in which no position has any real authority. The moral conflict is undergirded by the structure of the tragic drama which allows no resolution. Sophocles portrayed human life in dramatic narrative because he believed that life already had the form of a specific type of narrative.[38]

MacIntyre finds fault with Aristotle for locating the tragic flaw in the hero or in politics and for failing to see Sophocles' point, that the conflict between good and evil is prior to human choice.[39] But Aristotle's understanding of virtue, including the way in which it was developed beyond Aristotle, is praised. Virtues are those qualities which are manifested in actions and practices (complex and cooperative socially established activity) and the possession of which leads to the end, goal, or telos of *eudaimonia* —blessedness, happiness, or well-being. This end, or telos, of life is not something to be achieved at a future point but is the whole of life itself. And while in a sense virtue is the means to this end, it is a particular kind of means, for it has an internal relationship to the end. The end, and therefore life itself, takes its quality from the means, the virtues.[40]

MacIntyre has high praise for Jane Austen, who, he believes, combines Christian themes with Aristotle's teleological understanding of happiness. In making this turn from the eighteenth century's competing catalogues of virtues, she became the last great representative of the classical tradition of virtues. One of her main Christian themes is the self-knowledge which is achieved through repentance. Austen's narrative form, ironic comedy, coincides with her moral point of view. She writes comedy rather than tragedy, because she is a Christian, and for her the end of life is implicit in its everyday form. The irony is that her characters and readers see and say more and other than they intend.[41]

Why does MacIntyre think that narrative is necessary for ethical understanding? A virtue is a disposition of the self, and the self is a whole whose unity resides in the unity of a narrative that links birth-life-death as narrative beginning-middle-ending. To ask what is the good for me is to ask how I may best live out this narrative unity of life and bring it to conclusion. What is good for humanity is what all of these individual narrative statements of the good have in common. Moreover, I can answer the question of what am I to do only on the basis of the stories of which I am a part. We enter society with roles, and we have to know what they are in order to understand how others respond to us and how our responses to them are likely to be construed.[42]

Finally, I turn to the significant work of Hauerwas, portions of whose work antedate some of the scholarship I have already reviewed. For Hauerwas, we *are* as we *see;* therefore metaphor and narrative come to be of fundamental importance, an importance that has consequence for both religion and ethics in their inseparable relationship. It is through metaphors organized into a story that we receive our vision of the world and of our condition. This vision sheds light on what we are to do but also on what is for Christian ethics the more important problem of how to do it.[43]

For the Christian the story of Jesus is *the* story par excellence, and the most significant christological formulation is the gospel as narrative. According to Hauerwas, Jesus is the kingdom of God in person, and as such he meets us only in his story.[44] In Hauerwas's view, the narrative character of the gospel is integral to the affirmation that Jesus' mission has redemptive significance.[45] What, then, are the redemptive effects of the story?

It is redemptive in what it does *for* the one who responds. It reveals life as a gift, makes forgiveness possible, and provides the conditions necessary for being an agent.[46] The last point turns us toward the other side of the redemption—what it enables *us to do*. Jesus did not simply have a social ethic, but rather his story is a social ethic. It enables us to live coherently amid the conflicts and diversity of our moral existence, making possible our action which is appropriate to the gift.[47] Action does not stand in the foreground of Hauerwas's ethical reflection, but it is certainly not absent. Character or self, the focus of his thought, is constituted by metaphor, story, and rule; and what we can become in our character in turn influences our action.[48] Agents are responsible when they are true to the narrative that provides the conditions for them to be uniquely who they are.[49]

If it is the story of Jesus which accomplishes these effects, what are the specifically "narrative" features that, at least in part, account for its capacity to accomplish them? Narrative incorporates the past into an ongoing process, creating a continuity between past, present, and intended future. This continuity makes it possible for us to accept our past as our own, both as flawed and as forgiven, and that acceptance provides the coherence of self that is necessary for moral responsibility.[50] Story is a necessary form of knowledge because it makes contingent, non-necessary events intelligible by connecting them in their significance. Only in story do we catch the connection between contingent and particular actions and responses, an intelligible pattern which combines events and agents.[51]

The foregoing scholars affirm a positive relationship between narrative and ethics. Here I will briefly consider more theoretically the question of wherein the relationship lies by returning to an earlier theme: the organic connection between text and interpretation, which comprise(s) the literary work.

Ethics needs narrative because narrative provides a life-world that is both coherent and particular, a world in terms of which the self can be realized. Narratives will also offer in varying degrees content that is more or less explicitly ethical. Moreover, narratives, with varying degrees of power, will be able to realize themselves in the life of the reader-interpreter.

But narrative also needs ethics, both as reflection and as action. As Iser has pointed out, a plot does not exist for itself but for the sake of something that extends beyond itself—the *Gestalt* in which the reader articulates the significance of the action of the plot by combining the directions given by the text with his or her own subjective position.[52] One of the contributions of ethics to hermeneutics is what it tells us about the nature of that *Gestalt*.

The *Gestalt* is self-understanding, the open structure of self-understanding which continually emerges from the ongoing dialectic between pre-understanding and new understanding. I also assume that this self-understanding constitutes human being or the self. This is an elementary Heideggerian theme: "There is some way in which *Dasein* (being there, human being) understands itself in its Being. . . . Understanding of Being is itself a definite characteristic of *Dasein's* Being." The understanding of Being is a fundamental *existentiale*—a basic mode of *Dasein's* Being.[53] This position is also implied in the teaching of Jesus. The one talent man in the parable of the talents (Matt. 25:14–28) *is* a victim, unable to act significantly in the world, because he understands himself as a victim. But I suppose that Heidegger would not regard this as an *existential* or ontological construct—the articulation of one of the *formal* possibilities of human existence. Rather, it is an *existentiell* or ontic formulation, an understanding of how such a formal possibility is *actualized* in a *specific* instance.[54]

Paul, I believe, has a similar view of the situation of the believer. In Phil. 3:4–16, to know the significance of Christ and have the righteousness of faith which comes from God is to have a new understanding of oneself, the giving up of boasting. Throughout Rom. 9:30–10:21, faith and understanding overlap each other and are closely associated with righteousness. But in addition to Paul's "faith-understanding" language there is also what might be called his "being-participation" language. We who have been baptized into Christ participate in his death. The consequence of this is that our old self (*anthrōpos,* humanity) has died, and while Paul refrains here from saying that the resurrection self has emerged now in the present,[55] he does say that it is assured in the future and already we walk in new life (Rom. 6:1-6). In 2 Corinthians he is somewhat less reticent in his language about the present fullness of salvation, although he still does not use *explicit* resurrection language. If anyone is in Christ, that person *is* a new creation (2 Cor. 5:17). But the person also is in the process of *being* changed into the likeness of the Lord (2 Cor. 3:18), and the inner person is *being* renewed day by day (2 Cor. 4:16). Thus it is that salvation is a new self-understanding given by God—that God is the ground of our well-being and not we ourselves—an understanding which if accepted confirms, or is, a new relationship with God. And salvation is new being achieved by participation in Christ sacramentally. Now what is the connection between this language of "faith-understanding" relationship and the language of "being-participation"?

E. P. Sanders thinks that the real thrust of Paul's theology is the "participation" language. Paul uses "faith-relational" language to express participation meanings, but not vice versa.[56] Sanders's view seems to be that, while there is an inescapable incompatibility between the two sets of terms, Paul nevertheless imposed participation meanings on relational language. Sanders does not know what category can be used to make the participation motif intelligible to us, but it cannot be reduced to the existential construct of new self-understanding creating a new relationship.[57]

Using somewhat different terms, I argued several years ago,[58] and would still want to do so, that "faith-understanding" language and "being-participation" language in Paul have a dialectical relationship. The new relationship becomes a change of being. A change of being is necessary in order to accept the new relationship. Each leads into the other, though they remain different in magnitude. But one could also argue, in direct opposition to Sanders, that in at least some texts Paul understands the new humanity or creation (being) as constituted by new self-understanding. In 2 Corinthians 3—5, Paul interweaves the two languages. Those who are perishing do so because their *minds* are hardened, veiled, or blinded (2 Cor. 3:14, 15; 2 Cor. 4:4). The new humanity or creation (2 Cor. 2:18; 4:16; 5:17), on the other hand, is one whose *mind* has been unveiled so that one can see the revelation of the Lord and be changed (2 Cor. 3:16-18). Paul uses the metaphor of the letter to speak of the Corinthian believers. They, or their hearts, are a letter (*epistolē*) written by the Spirit (2 Cor. 3:1-3). Writing suggests language, a connection borne out by the contextual references to the reading of Moses (2 Cor. 3:14–15) and the preaching of the gospel (2 Cor. 4:5). The work of the Spirit, metaphorically described as writing, lifts the covenant above the level of the letter (*gramma*): the covenant does not rest on the *gramma*, the law as the demand for good works. But the metaphor of writing does associate the Spirit closely with another language. The Spirit is the power of the language of the gospel to change a person at the core of his or her being, to rewrite the heart (2 Cor. 3:3). It is the power of this language, written or spoken, to remove the veil from the mind (2 Cor. 3:16–17) and bring the light of the knowledge of God into the heart (2 Cor. 4:5–6). The heart is the seat of will and understanding (see chapter 7). In sum, the Spirit writes with the language of the gospel (2 Cor. 3:3; 4:5), changing the heart (2 Cor. 3:1–3; 4:5–6) and unveiling the mind (2 Cor. 3:14, 16–17), giving a new self-understanding, and thereby brings about new being (2 Cor. 3:18; 4:16; 5:17). I therefore see Paul to be doing here tacitly what Heidegger does explicitly, interpreting being *as* the understanding of being. Or to be more exact about Paul, he interprets the new being (*anthrōpos*, creation) in Christ as constituted by faith's new self-understanding mediated by the gospel. This is all the more the case since Paul interprets his participation in Jesus' death and life (resurrection) as the rhythm of upset and recovery occurring in his everyday existence, a rhythm *understood* as sharing Jesus' death and resurrection. That is, Paul interprets participation as an understanding of participation (2 Cor. 4:7–12; 6:1–10).

Thus whether the relationship between human being and self understanding is one of dialectical interaction or identity, I take it to be a principle grounded in New Testament thought that human being or the self is constituted in significant part by self-understanding, the understanding of the self in its extended social and communal connections. A narrative text is completed when it realizes itself in the new vision or understanding of the interpreter. New Testament ethics then needs to remind hermeneuticians that self-understanding is not merely internal; it manifests itself in action: the interpretation in which the narrative is realized is completed only in the acts of the interpreter. The self which has character also acts in accordance with, or against, that character. Character is comprised of continuing ethical dispositions or attitudes, will (the resolve to act on these dispositions), power, feelings, conscience (the capacity of the self to react in judgment against itself when it violates what it takes to be a norm), and self-understanding (the mind's grasp of the other constituents in their *interrelationships* and *in relation to* the whole of reality). Self-understanding is paradoxically one constituent in and the structure of the whole, and ethical *reflection* is a strand in self-understanding. If the self is a *Gestalt* composed of character and action, and if interpretation involves the constitution of the self through self-understanding, then interpretation is complete only when the interpreter engages in responsive decisions and *acts* which are appropriate to the story. Interpretation is completed in the living interaction between character and action.

Mark 9:43-48 displays this interaction. Here Jesus tells his disciples: if your hand, foot, or eye causes *you* to stumble or sin, *you* cut it off or pluck it out. It is better for you to enter life maimed than to be thrown into hell with all your members. Character, the dimension of coherence and continuity, is represented by the personal "you," manifested in both the second person pronoun and in the verb endings of the second person imperative. Specific actions or directions are represented by the parts of the body—hand, foot, eye. The self is comprised of both character and act, but character comes closer to manifesting the whole self than does act, for character finally has more power. Thus I tend to use "character" and "self" interchangeably.

The hand or eye concretizes the tendency of the whole self—you!—to sin. The whole self is involved because it is *your* hand or eye. The concrete organs suggest the specific acts or directions through which the whole self goes wrong, or character is negatively modified. Conduct affects character, and character, or the whole self, is present in the act or direction: your hand (act) causes *you* (self) to sin, but it is you who do the sinful act. In context the act envisioned is ethical, or more accurately unethical, because it is the act of leading another person astray (9:42). This ethical misdirection, if pursued, can lead to the utter ruination of the self, the utter deformation of character: *you* can be thrown into hell.

As disastrous as this ethical misdirection can be, the text attributes to the self power over its acts. The self is put under the imperative (9:43, 45, 47): *you* cut off your hand or foot, pluck out your eye. That is, the self is to recover itself by reversing the specific wrong ethical direction in which it is being lost. Character has power to transform conduct. It should be observed that the intention or purpose that directs the reversing of the wrong conduct here is the preservation of the self: it is better to enter life having renounced certain cherished acts than to go into hell having done it all without restraint. The Markan text definitely presupposes that the whole (the self, you) is a *Gestalt,* more than the sum of its parts.[59] You (self) can enter life with parts missing. But you can be destroyed with all parts present. So *you* are more than all of your parts (acts). Thus for Mark the self is clearly a *Gestalt,* a whole.

Hauerwas has observed the similar circularity in Aristotle. One must be excellent in character to perform excellent deeds. On the other hand, one can become just in character by acting justly. But one cannot act justly unless one has the requisite character, and so goes the circle. Hauerwas finds the circularity instructive but denies that Aristotle had a conception of the self that would enable me to claim my actions as my own.[60] I hope to show that Mark does have an adequate view of the nature of human being and a grasp of the redemptive process that keeps the circle from being vicious.

In sum, the interpretation of a narrative text involves the re-creation of the human self through the new self-understanding which emerges in the dialectical interaction between the directions in the story and the pre-understanding of the interpreter. And it involves the further dialectic between character and action in the self of the interpreter as this one seeks to respond appropriately to the story being interpreted. This view of things, then, means that action is part of the new self-understanding which interpretation is. And action, along with the events of recent social history, is also an ingredient in the pre-understanding which gives us access to the text. Pre-understanding is not simply subjective reflection. It has been suggested that only our committed action vis-à-vis the *modern* history of oppression enables us to see the depth and scope of the Bible's concern about the poor.[61]

The method to be pursued, then, in this book is dominantly a phenomenological one, making some use of phenomenology of reading, but even more basically it is a phenomenological method in the existential mode with an orientation to ethical issues. That is, I will try to *describe,* being critically aware of the *circular* relationship between the subjective concerns of the reader-interpreter and the clues in the text, Mark's understanding of *existence* in a *social* and *cultural* world. The phenomenology of reading will be seen at work in that elements of both plot and theme which are unconnected in the text will be given coherent connection through the interaction between the textual clues, on the one hand, and the categories and synthesizing moves of the interpreter, on the other hand. The existential mode will be manifested in the attention given to such anthropological motifs in Mark as hardness of heart, hearing, and understanding. The existential question will focus on the ethical dimension of existence: what the disciple of Jesus is to do, why he or she is to do it, how (or whether) he or she can do it, what kind of communal structures he or she moves from and into. Posing these questions to Mark represents the Gospel as *concretely* manifesting such ethical categories as character versus action, norm, motive, intention, enablement, and so forth, which are modern in their formulation and which belong to the interpreter's frame of reference and are not *formally* announced as such in Mark.

These questions will be put to the Gospel understood as a unified (literary) narrative structure, not as an (uneasy) combination of tradition and redaction.[62] Both literary-critical and structuralist (see Appendix I) tools will be used for dealing with the text. At the same time, it will not be possible to ignore the historical meaning of Mark's text, and at points psychological and sociological questions illumine the ethical concerns. These various approaches—existential, ethical, literary, historical, and so forth—are elicited by the Markan text itself, and they also belong to the subjective stance of the interpreter. They are given a certain unity in that they all are made to bear on the ethical question. They are also interrelated by the method employed, that is, they all belong to the concerns and questions of the reader-interpreter by means of which he or she interprets the text and turns it into a work meaningful to his or her own situation. We would expect the interpreter's position to contain a variety of components because it derives from his or her varied cultural experience.

NOTES

1. For this distinction, see James M. Gustafson, *Theology and Christian Ethics* (Philadelphia: Pilgrim Press, 1974), 121–23.

2. Frank Kermode, *The Sense of an Ending: Studies in the Theory of Fiction* (New York: Oxford Univ. Press, 1966), 58.

3. Wolfgang Iser, *The Act of Reading: A Theory of Aesthetic Response* (Baltimore and London: Johns Hopkins Univ. Press, 1980), 21, 92.

4. Ibid., 22–25, 27, 38, 141.

5. Ibid., 35, 36, 38, 47–48, 74, 141.

6. Ibid., 17, 21, 24–25, 38, 85, 92, 123, 141, 168–69.

7. Brevard S. Childs, *Biblical Theology in Crisis* (Philadelphia: Westminster Press, 1970), 124.

8. Ibid., 58, 92–93, 124–25.

9. Bruce C. Birch and Larry Rasmussen, *Bible and Ethics in the Christian Life* (Minneapolis: Augsburg Pub. House, 1976), 11–12, 19. Two recent works that fruitfully present the mutual interaction of biblical scholarship and constructive ethics are Thomas W. Ogletree, *The Use of the Bible in Christian Ethics* (Philadelphia: Fortress Press, 1983), and Allen Verhey, *The Great Reversal: Ethics and the New Testament* (Grand Rapids: Wm. B. Eerdmans, 1984).

10. Birch and Rasmussen, *Bible and Ethics*, 20–21.

11. Ibid., 30, 35–36.

12. Krister Stendahl, s.v. "Biblical Theology, Contemporary," *The Interpreter's Dictionary of the Bible*, idem, "Method in the Study of Biblical Theology," in *The Bible in Modern Scholarship*, ed. J. P. Hyatt (Nashville: Abingdon Press, 1965), 199, 202, 204–5.

13. Birch and Rasmussen, *Bible and Ethics*, 37.

14. Ibid., 12, 19, 37, 47, 104, 112.

15. Ibid., 57–59.

16. Ibid., 145, 149, 150, 152.

17. Ibid., 174–82.

18. Carl E. Braaten, *Eschatology and Ethics* (Minneapolis: Augsburg Pub. House, 1974), 105. Ogletree (*The Use of the Bible*) and Verhey (*The Great Reversal*) both recognize the importance of eschatology for Christian ethics.

19. Braaten, *Eschatology*, 13, 105, 107, 110–11.

20. Susan Sontag, "Against Interpretation," in *Against Interpretation* (New York: Dell, 1966), 7.

21. Ibid., 5, 7, 8–10, 12–13.

22. Bernard B. Scott, *Jesus, Symbol-Maker for the Kingdom* (Philadelphia: Fortress Press, 1981), 11, 15, 17.

23. Roland Barthes, *On Racine*, Eng. trans. R. Howard (New York: Hill & Wang, 1964), 163, 165, 171, 172.

24. See Paul Ricoeur, *The Symbolism of Evil*, Eng. trans. E. Buchanan (Boston: Beacon Press, 1969), 348–57. This is elaborated in *De l'interprétation* (Paris: Éditions du Seuil, 1965), 45–50.

25. See Paul Ricoeur, "Biblical Hermeneutics," *Semeia* 4 (1975): 36, 129, 139.

26. Sontag, *Against Interpretation,* 12.

27. See Barthes, *On Racine,* 8–9, 38–39, 44–49, 63–65, 72–73, 77–80, 107, 124, 126–28, 130, 136.

28. See Dan O. Via, *The Parables: Their Literary and Existential Dimension* (Philadelphia: Fortress Press, 1967), 79–88, 93–94.

29. On this matter, see James Hillman, *Re-Visioning Psychology* (New York: Harper & Row, 1975), xiii, 44, 115–17, 120, 122–23, 127, 130, 132, 142, 145, 156.

30. *Contra* Ernest Best, *Following Jesus: Discipleship in the Gospel of Mark,* Journal for the Study of the New Testament, Supplementary Series 4 (Sheffield, England: JSOT Press, 1981), 13. See Gustafson (*Theology and Christian Ethics,* 126, 129) on the position that Scripture has a role in interpreting the structure and meaning of the historical process for ethical reflection.

31. Stanley Hauerwas, *A Community of Character* (Notre Dame, Ind.: Univ. of Notre Dame Press, 1981), 133.

32. Ronald W. Hepburn, *Christianity and Paradox* (New York: Pegasus, 1966 [first published, 1958]), 193–95.

33. Ibid., 195.

34. Ibid., 192–93.

35. Amos N. Wilder, *The Language of the Gospel: Early Christian Rhetoric* (New York: Harper & Row; London: SCM Press, 1964), 68; revised edition (Cambridge: Harvard Univ. Press, 1971), 60.

36. Dan O. Via, "Narrative World and Ethical Response: The Marvelous and Righteousness in Matthew 1—2," *Semeia* 12 (1978): 123–49; idem, "Structure, Christology and Ethics in Matthew," in *Orientation by Disorientation,* ed. Richard A. Spencer (Pittsburgh: Pickwick Press, 1980), 199–215.

37. Alasdair MacIntyre, *After Virtue* (Notre Dame, Ind.: Univ. of Notre Dame Press, 1981), 114–15, 117–18.

38. Ibid., 124, 133–34.

39. Ibid., 147, 148, 153.

40. Ibid., 115, 139, 140, 163, 172, 175, 178, 183.

41. Ibid., 223–26.

42. Ibid., 191, 201–3.

43. Stanley Hauerwas, *Vision and Virtue* (Notre Dame, Ind.: Fides Publishers, 1974), 2, 3, 30, 34; idem, *A Community of Character,* 131.

44. Stanley Hauerwas, "Story and Theology," *Religion in Life* 45/3 (1976): 340, idem, *A Community of Character,* 37, 45.

45. Hauerwas, *A Community of Character,* 44.

46. Ibid., 135, 147–48.

47. Ibid., 37, 135, 144, 148.

48. Hauerwas, *Vision and Virtue,* 62, 74; idem, *A Community of Character,* 147.

49. Hauerwas, *A Community of Character,* 135.

50. Ibid., 147.

51. Hauerwas, "Story and Theology," 343–44.

52. Iser, *The Act of Reading,* 123–29. Note Hans-Georg Gadamer's "fusion of horizons" in his *Truth and Method,* Eng. trans. and ed. G. Barden and J. Cumming (New York: Seabury Press, 1975), 304, 350, 357.

53. Martin Heidegger, *Being and Time,* Eng. trans. J. Macquarrie and E. Robinson (New York: Harper & Row, 1962), 32, 78, 182–83.

54. Ibid., 33.

55. Note Ernst Käsemann's "eschatological reservation" in his *New Testament Questions of Today,* Eng. trans. W. J. Montague (Philadelphia: Fortress Press; London: SCM Press, 1969), 125, 132–33.

56. E. P. Sanders, *Paul and Palestinian Judaism: A Comparison of Patterns of Religion* (Philadelphia: Fortress Press; London: SCM Press, 1977), 502, 503, 506, 507, 520.

57. Ibid., 507–8, 519–22.

58. Dan O. Via, "Justification and Deliverance: Existential Dialectic," *Studies in Religion/Sciences Religieuses* 1/3 (1971): 204–12.

59. For this definition of *Gestalt,* see Maurice Merleau-Ponty, *The Visible and the Invisible,* Eng. trans. A. Lingis (Evanston, Ill.: Northwestern Univ. Press, 1968), 204.

60. Hauerwas, *A Community of Character,* 137–40.

61. See J. Severino Croatto, *Exodus: A Hermeneutics of Freedom,* Eng. trans. S. Attanasio (Maryknoll, N.Y.: Orbis Books, 1981), vi, 2–3, 11; L. John Topel, *The Way to Peace: Liberation Through the Bible* (Maryknoll, N.Y.: Orbis Books, 1979), 151–53. On the shaping of pre-understanding by praxis in liberation theology hermeneutics, also see Anthony C. Thiselton, *The Two Horizons* (Grand Rapids: Wm. B. Eerdmans; Exeter: Paternoster Press, 1980), 110–12.

62. I have earlier dealt with the relationship between literary and structuralist approaches, on the one hand, and redaction-critical approaches, on the other. See Dan O. Via, *Kerygma and Comedy in the New Testament: A Structuralist Approach to Hermeneutic* (Philadelphia: Fortress Press, 1975), 71–78, 90–103; and the Editor's Foreword in Daniel Patte, *What is Structural Exegesis?* (Philadelphia: Fortress Press, 1976), iii–iv.

PART ONE

THE PLOT OF MARK, APOCALYPTIC, AND TEMPORALITY

2
Apocalyptic and the Markan Narrative

The Christian Bible as a whole is a story stretching from the creation of the universe to a point which the author of the Book of Revelation takes to be the eve of the historical and cosmic end. While we will take a quick look at Jewish apocalyptic and the place that it gives to beginning and end, we need to remember that in other than a literal reading of transcendent events these ultimate terminal points ought not to be thought of as happening in time. What, then, is to prevent time from being an indeterminate middle without pattern or structure, without beginning or end? One way in which this outcome is prevented is that during "the middle," people create narratives of various kinds—epics, histories, biographies, novels, short stories, gospels—with less ultimate beginnings and endings. How does beginning relate to ending in biblical apocalyptic? How do the finite terminal points of individual stories, such as the Gospel of Mark, relate to the ultimate terminal points—creation and apocalypse? What is the status of the terminal points with respect to the temporal reality which we experience? And what is the character of the middle?

Jewish Apocalyptic

A theme in Jewish apocalyptic, as well as in certain strands of Oriental thought outside of Judaism, is that the end will involve a new creation, a new beginning (Isa. 65:17; 66:22; 1 Enoch 91:16–17). One important motif connected with this is that the end should in some way correspond to the beginning, a point that had already come to expression in the Old Testament (Isa. 11:6–8; Ezek. 34:25–27; see also Barn. 6:13; 2 Esdras 6:1–6).[1] In pursuing this theme, I should like to consider two "proto-apocalyptic" works in the Old Testament.

1. Zech. 14:6–8. Paul D. Hanson has pointed out that pessimism about the existing structure and redeemability of this world was the germinating element for speculation about a new creation. In the Priestly creation

story God brought the cosmos into existence by making certain separations and thereby creating binary oppositions: sea and land, day and night, cold and hot, summer and winter (Gen. 1:3–10; 8:22). But for apocalyptic thought, this order had become corrupted and needed to be replaced by a new creation.[2] Zechariah 14:6–8 portrays the eschatological return to paradise: the living water of Eden (Gen. 2:10) from which Adam and Eve had been expelled (Gen. 3:23–24) will now flow from Jerusalem. Hanson thinks that the restoration of the paradise motif in the eschaton seriously threatens the prophetic linear view of history, but it stops short of identifying *Urzeit* and *Endzeit*. That which prevents the reduction of history to a circle is that the history of Israel intervenes between beginning and end.[3]

The presence of the living water in both paradise and eschaton does suggest some element of identity between the two terminal points, but the intervention of the history of Israel is not the only thing that prevents complete identity. The imagery indicates difference as well as likeness, which Hanson himself notes.[4] The primordial opposition day/night will give way to continuous day in the eschaton, and the original separation between summer (dry) and winter (wet) will be resolved in favor of an eschatological ever-flowing stream. Unity replaces opposition.

2. Isa. 51:9–11. For Second Isaiah, God is the first and the last, the one who declares the end from the time of the beginning (40:10; 48:12) and also acts in the middle (51:10b–11). The divine purpose (46:10) extends from creation (44:24; 45:18) through history (42:6; 43:28; 45:1; 46:3, 11) and beyond (51:6). Thus there is a divine continuity which transcends history and also expresses itself in the particularities of the temporal process. The prophet believes that he stands on the eve of the saving event (45:14–25; 46:13; 51:5–8), which is at once the historical deliverance of Israel from Babylon (43:14; 44:26–28) and the eschatological event (48:6; 46:10).[5]

Hanson observes that Second Isaiah was the first to place the myth of the primordial conflict at the center of the prophetic message. In Isa. 51:9–11 he combines the cosmic (creation) with God's historical victory at the Red Sea and with the eschatological future. Thus, according to Hanson, the entire development of prophetic Yahwehism is recapitulated.[6] In a similar way, Walther Eichrodt[7] states that God in Second Isaiah commands the entire development of the world. I want to add that while the prophet surely is interested in historical development, that does not fully get at what he says in 51:9–11. Here the prophet metaphorically connects the time (event) of creation with a spatial element—the appearance of dry land, brought out of the primeval chaos waters by the arm of the Lord. This coordination of time and space, this space-of-creation-time, is then predicated of later times—the exodus of Israel from Egypt and the return of the Jews from Babylon to Jerusalem. Each of these is seen as the others. It is not simply that three distinct times or events are connected with the same place, which would not be an extraordinary or tensive statement. It is, rather, that three widely separated moments of time—the primordial past, the salvation-historical past, and the salvation-historical-eschatological future—are made simultaneous with one another by being connected to the same fusion of time and space, the dry land way brought from the primordial waters. The way of Israel from Egypt to Canaan and from Babylon to Jerusalem is identical with the *first* land to appear. The prophet creating the metaphor makes all of this synchronous with himself. We might say that the power and meaning of the first time is predicated of all times, but the temporal structure is maintained, as we have seen, in many other texts in Second Isaiah; and the chronological distinctiveness of beginning, middle, and end is not surrendered. The diachronic reality of different moments of time is upheld, but their synchronicity is also expressed in the metaphor, a tension to which we will return in various ways.

The Theological Significance of the Relationship Between Beginning and End

What is the point of the correspondence between beginning and end in apocalyptic? We may find a clue to an answer in a brief comment by Gérard Genette, who is not talking about apocalyptic as such and who has no explicit theological interests. The first time—first kiss, first sight of the sea, first evening at a particular hotel, first dinner with certain friends—"to the very extent to which one experiences its inaugural value intensely, is at the same time always (already) a last time—if only because it is forever the last to have been the first, and after it, inevitably, the sway of repetition and habit begins."[8] Genette has spoken of a kind of lastness or eschatology of the first time. The first time is the last time that newness, spontaneity, life, and intensity are experienced. After that, sameness has set in. If the first time is the last time, then the role of the last time is to be once again the first time. How are apocalyptic and the more "ordinary" stories that Genette is talking about related?

Genette has bespoken the degradation that takes place in various individual stories or micro-histories. Nicolas Berdyaev has stressed the

congealing or coagulation of freedom, the objectification, which charac-
terizes being or history on a larger scale. After Francis of Assisi came the
commonplace routine of the Franciscan order. After Luther came the
rationalism and moralism of the Lutheran Church. And after Christ came
the history of Christianity.[9] Apocalyptic, for its part, in various ways
portrays the deterioration of world history as a whole (Dan. 4:31–45;
7:2–12). One may acknowledge a certain measure of objective reporting
in Berdyaev's observations, and even apocalyptic writers may have used
some historical sources. But apocalyptic thinking writes history from a
mythological standpoint.[10] And I take it that apocalyptic myth is genuinely polysemous and that the anthropological (existential) level of meaning is as integral to it as the cosmological is. If that is the case, then there
is a connection between the stories of individuals and the world history
portrayed by apocalyptic. The fact that individuals fall into habit and
emptiness after the first time would seem to be a part of the existential
basis for apocalyptic—the individual, as creator of apocalypse, projects
his or her own sense of loss onto the cosmos and history, and then, as
reader-recipient, reads it back from macro-history onto himself or herself.

The purpose, then, of the correspondence between beginning and end
is to say that what the beginning has lost in the middle is recovered in
the end. Let us assume provisionally the linearity of the biblical outlook
on history and grant that since specific and different things happen, the
content of times does change. The repetition of the beginning in the end,
then, is not the literal repetition of events but the restoration of the
vitality and power of the first time that had been lost. As we have seen
from the discussion of Zechariah 14 and Second Isaiah, the end is both
like and unlike the beginning in content, and the purpose of the predicated likeness is to affirm that both are equally immediate to God. The
end is no improvement in principle on the beginning, for the latter is not
something that could be improved upon. The end is rather, in mythological terms, the re-actualization of the beginning. In demythologized terms,
there are no ultimate terminal points of the world historical process. But,
to anticipate our discussion of Mark, the narrative, in its threefold form,
creates a new beginning and end for the world of the reader. By connecting the middle to both beginning and end it also creates a new middle.
I have tried to suggest that apocalyptic logic implies the recovery of the
beginning in the end even if there is no explicit correspondence between
the two terminal points. Therefore, since the middle in Mark is the
anticipatory actualization of the ending, it is also the actualization of the
beginning. The "good news" is that the vitality and newness of the
beginning can overcome the repetitiousness of habit in the middle.

Second Isaiah and Mark's
Narrative World

I enter the discussion of Mark by referring back to Second Isaiah. However much Mark may have agreed with Second Isaiah's faith in the unbrokenness of God's purpose in history, for Mark that purpose only *recently* began to be eschatologically realized and has not yet been completed. It is still unknown to the mass of human beings, including Israel, for Second Isaiah's time turned out not to be the eve of the eschaton when God's salvation would become universal (Isa. 42:6; 45:22-23; 49:6; 51:4-5; 52:10). For Mark, the hardness of heart which has prevailed in the human world since shortly after creation (Mark 10:5) still continues, so that his audience is no less in need of the good news than was Second Isaiah's (Mark 1:1). To present this good news as he saw it, Mark found it necessary to dissolve, at least relatively, the elements in Second Isaiah's metaphor in their synchronicity and to establish a new diachrony, however much he may have used metaphorical language to do it. Although Mark, like Second Isaiah, believed in some sense that he lived on the edge of the eschaton (Mark 9:1; 13:30), the historical process is still taken seriously (see chapter 11).

In constructing his narrative world—the totality of events referred to or assumed, as distinguished from the plot, the structure of events narrated[11]—Mark pushed the primordial creation back to an indeterminate point in the past (Mark 10:6), and the time of the prophets is pushed back less far and made a time of prediction (1:2-3; 7:6-7; 14:21). Prophetic language can be used to define the negativity of the present (4:12) as well as its redemptive elements. Mark introduces between the prophetic time and his own time a new *archē*, the beginning of a new story. Through the discourse of the narrative the eschatological kingdom—the end—is both projected into the future and seen as realized in the present (1:15), a point that requires further discussion later.

In affirming that the eschaton began with the *archē* of Jesus' story but is yet to come, Mark is positing a synchronicity between his own time, a segment of world time, and the time of the kingdom of God, but this synchronicity is a sequence rather than a point. That is, Mark does not state it with the same metaphorical intensity that Second Isaiah does (Isa. 51:9-11). But in claiming it at all for his own time he in effect denies that the synchronicity avowed by Second Isaiah's metaphor had actually occurred. Since Mark presents synchrony as the time of the kingdom's overlapping a narrative sequence, he allows that chronos passes and the content of times changes, even in the kingdom. However, the newness of

the first-last time is always there as a possibility and is sometimes actualized—in healings and exorcisms, in forgiveness and new community.
There is tension between the synchronicity of Second Isaiah's metaphor
and the character of Mark's narrative synchronicity. While Second Isaiah can and does distinguish the moments of history, his metaphor suggests that all times participate equally in the power of the first time.
Mark knows that is not the case. It may well be that every segment of
the Markan story is defined in some way by the presence of the kingdom
of God. But sometimes the kingdom manifests itself by redemptively
transforming the situation, and at other times it is met by rejection and
misunderstanding. And while Mark can affirm the overlapping of history
and the kingdom, he can also distinguish this age and the age to come
(Mark 10:29–30). By failing, or refusing, to synchronize all times completely in a comprehensive metaphor Mark preserves temporality—the
chronological and diachronic—more securely, and more realistically, than
did the prophetic metaphor. Had Mark wanted to affirm the synchronic
as radically as did Second Isaiah, he would not have had Jesus oppose
divorce by saying: "But from the beginning of creation, 'God made them
male and female' " (Mark 10:6). He would rather have had Jesus say,
"But now is the beginning of creation when 'God made them male and
female.' " This understanding of the relationship between temporality
and the eschatological kingdom should be kept in mind as the horizon for
further discussions of this topic.

The Markan Plot and
Apocalyptic Literary Strategy

Now I want to consider how Mark has ordered and shaped certain
events and elements from his narrative world into a plot. According to
the apocalyptic tradition, which is a part of Mark's context and heritage,
world time is a threefold plot composed of creation, history, and end.
Mark has taken the eschatological end, the third segment of the world
plot, and turned it into the tripartite story of Jesus and his disciples. This
end expresses itself in Mark's plot in both mythological and nonmyth-
ological ways and also extends into the narrative world of the Gospel as
the future coming of the kingdom and the return of the Son of man. Thus
the plot as a whole is eschatological time. The first segment of the world
plot, the creation of the cosmos, is not a part of Mark's plot, although it
is part of his narrative world; and his plot overlaps only a small part of
the world-historical middle. Despite what Mark owes to apocalyptic, I
would still not abandon my earlier claim that Mark is not generically an
apocalypse.[12]

Before moving further I want to consider here Howard Clark Kee's view of the relationship of apocalyptic to Mark's narrative. Kee presents the literary mode of apocalyptic as having a beginning-middle-end which he apparently identifies with narrative of past history-present crisis-eschatological denouement. He then says that Mark also has an apocalyptic literary strategy.[13] That seemingly would have to mean that Mark's beginning-middle-end takes the form of past history, i.e., story of Jesus (beginning)—present community crisis (middle)—eschatological denouement (end). The obvious problem with this is that the present of the community does not appear in the story as an identifiable middle, nor is the eschatological cosmic end a part of the plot, the narrated story, but is rather a part of the narrative world. Since apocalyptic is basically mythological in its language, it is consistent to make transcendent events, like the eschatological end, an integral part of the story. But in a story as realistic as Mark, ultimate terminal points get pushed out of the plot.

Kee tacitly recognizes these problems when he states that while the present crisis is Mark's main interest, he speaks of that crisis as under the guise of the past history or story of Jesus.[14] And Kee goes on to speak of the eschatological vision of Jesus' exaltation (9:2–9) as the center of that narrative.[15] But then he really does not deal clearly with the beginning-middle-end of the story. And when he tacitly acknowledges that the Jesus narrative is Mark's whole story, it can no longer be claimed that its structure parallels the apocalyptic literary strategy as he has defined it.

One of the basic problems here is that Kee seems to have mixed up synchronic and diachronic elements in portraying the apocalyptic literary structure of beginning-middle-end as historical antecedents-present crisis-eschatological denouement. Historical narrative and ending are, or may be, synchronic elements, parts of the same narrative meaning system. But the community's crisis is a historical or diachronic element, external to the narrative. As I have observed, it does not appear in the plot as the middle. This mixing of the synchronic and diachronic has deflected Kee's attention from a clear look at the story itself. So far as Mark's sense of a community crisis affects the story, it is not as a discrete segment of the plot but appears in discourse and in the way the story as a whole is told and interpreted. The author's stance is transformed into a strand in the synchrony of the story.

In my depiction of the apocalyptic world plot as creation-history-cosmic end and in dealing, as I will, with the Markan beginning-middle-end, the representation is consistently synchronic. In each case the three

segments are parts of the narrative *as narrative,* parts of the same meaningful construct. At the same time, within each story there is an internal
diachrony or chronology which is a part of the synchrony, part of the
system of meaning.

The Denial of the Validity of the Happy Ending in Recent Criticism

Mark ends with the announcement that Jesus has risen from the dead
(16:6), and however problematical the resurrection in Mark turns out to
be, it is still in some way a happy ending. Mark is comedy, even though
tragicomedy. As I have contended, the motif of death and resurrection
is the foundation of comedy.[16] But we have seen in recent years a questioning of the validity or believability of the happy ending, a denial that
it can represent our experience of reality. I should like to take a brief look
at that position.

According to Joseph Campbell, the happy ending is a misrepresenta-
tion of the real world of inescapable brokenness and death.[17] Or at least
that is the case in literature that pretends to be realistic. But in myth,
fairy tale, and the divine comedy of the soul we have the happy ending
which does not contradict reality; rather, it transcends it. That is to say,
it is not that objective reality is changed, but a shift within the subject
causes the subject to behold it as transformed. The hero's triumphs are
psychological rather than physical.[18]

John Dominic Crossan views tragedy as saying that there is death and
tears, while comedy responds that there is death, supper, tears, and
sleep.[19] Crossan then adopts the position that Christian comedy leaves
the world (birth, struggle, death) to tragedy and establishes comedy only
in another, later world. Moreover, resurrection is itself divided into hell
and heaven, which means that tragedy and comedy are securely located
elsewhere and frozen into unchanging actualities. By contrast, Crossan
wants to see tragedy and comedy as two different viewpoints on birth-
struggle-death, and the comic viewpoint would be called resurrection. He
prefers this view over having resurrection as another plot episode following death, for that leads to the difficulties of otherworldliness described
above.[20]

But does "Christian" comedy necessarily put resurrection in another
world? When the New Testament writers speak mythologically, they do
put resurrection in another world, but they do not always speak that way.
Paul understands his life in this world as a sharing in Jesus' death and
resurrection (2 Cor. 4:7–12; 6:1–10), which is the form of the new being

(2 Cor. 5:17). And John's Gospel speaks of rebirth (John 3) and resurrection (John 11) in this life. There is no reason why, in a story, this quality should not be manifested as an event, as it surely is in the parable of the prodigal son (Luke 15:11–32). The prodigal's resurrection (my son who was dead is alive) is not a viewpoint on his degradation but the event of his reception at home, a this-worldly transformation of a this-worldly desperate situation.

Why would Crossan, speaking as a theologian, resist this characteristic New Testament pattern? Perhaps a gnostic orientation would explain it. For Gnosticism, victory (resurrection) is not attainable in this world but only by getting out of the world. Thus resurrection, or the only resurrection one can have in the world, becomes, not an event, but another viewpoint—*gnōsis* ("knowledge"). If it is argued that *gnōsis* for at least some Gnostics conferred real liberation in this life, it must be said that that was not freedom to be involved in the transformation of society but freedom to be detached from it.[21]

David L. Miller in his illuminating discussion of the problem of the happy ending seems to deny that the happy ending can belong to other than fantasy—fairy tale, myth, dramatic comedy—and to deny it on the ground that none of us has ever literally experienced anything like unadulterated happiness.[22] But neither do we know whether anyone has ever experienced unadulterated tragedy. Yet Campbell,[23] for example, is prepared to grant to the tragic ending a kind of validity he is not willing to accord to the comic ending. It could be that while some critics regard any ending at all, along with the whole temporal structure of narrative, as wishful thinking which falsifies reality, Miller is only saying that certain kinds of happy endings falsify the world and our experience of it. One must, however, examine this position further.

Miller observes that biblical eschatology as interpreted by Christian theology posits an infinite qualitative distinction or contradiction between God and human beings at the eschaton. Given this contradiction, which is a denial of immanentism, the only way to distinguish unhappy and happy endings is to attribute to the happy ending a sentimental absence of pain and suffering.[24] Miller holds that Western reflection on comedy has tended to perpetuate this point of view. But in view of counter cases, he wants to reconceive the happy ending as contradiction having given way to realistic congruity with suffering remaining.[25]

In myth, humanity suffers the terror of plurality and the many-sidedness of reality. Apparently in comedy the suffering becomes more intense, but the suffering plurality, if deep enough, may be without contradiction.

There is rather a many-faceted congruity. Miller wants to replace a final infinite distinction between humanity and one God, which is experienced painlessly, with a final congruence between humanity and many gods (archetypal possibilities) in which suffering continues.[26]

With the increasing emphasis on pain one wonders wherein resides the happiness of the happy ending. Perhaps it is in the congruity between the hero and the many deities or archetypes. What, then, is the ground for holding that the colliding archetypal forces may in fact be congruent? Perhaps it is the power of metaphor to create correspondences among dissimilars.[27]

It appears to me probable that Miller finally denies that the happy ending of narrative can be a redescription of the world—of intersubjectivity, history, and nature. He cites the statement of Heraclitus that "in a circle the beginning (*archē*) and the end (*peras*) are the same."[28] He then goes on to point out that Heraclitus used a cognate word for "end" in speaking of the "end" of the soul. He said that one cannot discover the end of the soul, because it is too deep. The end for Heraclitus is not the horizontal extremity of Aristotle and Plato but the depth whose up and down are the same, like the beginning and end of a circle. And for Miller the locus of the ending of the narrative is finally the endless depth of the psyche.[29] The world apparently is not changed for the better.

In Defense of the Happy Ending

What is now to be said to the claim that the happy ending is a falsification of the real world? We find a view quite different from that of Campbell, Crossan, and Miller in Robert M. Polhemus's recent study of the British comic novel in the nineteenth and early twentieth centuries. For Polhemus's purposes a work qualifies as comic if it seeks or tends to be funny and if it has a happy ending, an ending of which a normal audience would say, "This should be." A happy ending represents the successful conclusion of a given segment of time and stands as a metaphor for the success through time of human life and will. Although comedy has often been at odds with idealistic philosophy and orthodox religion, the comic imagination is itself a mode of religious consciousness, for it deals in miraculous transformations and the instantaneous casting off of burdens and suffering. Polhemus thinks it plausible to assume that a basis for believing in the value and regenerative process of life can be found in the fact of comic expression itself.[30]

Later (in Appendix II) I will try to construct a convincing argument that both subjects (knower, interpreter) and object (world of reality) inevitably leave their imprint on all acts of perception and interpretation. If that conclusion may be assumed here, it would mean with regard to narratives that the broad structure beginning-middle-ending and the happy ending more particularly are not just the imposition of the mind on the experience of a radically different kind of reality, although the literary form undoubtedly gives our sense of the world and time a greater clarity than they would have without it. We know what both tragedy and comedy are, in large part, from literature. But these forms, since they raise up reality to truth,[31] are not alien to that reality; rather, they are prompted by it. If *word* and *world* are dialectically related to each other, we would not have the word of the happy ending if that phenomenon were not experienced in some way in the world. But what it might be in the world may be greatly transformed and enlarged by narrative art.

One would not want to deny that the comic ending does in fact express a subjective transcendence of an unchanged tragic world in some cases. But if language and reality inhere in each other, it may also be the case that the comic ending can represent the possibility of the amelioration of historical reality. If Campbell were to take seriously his own statement that in myth the inexhaustible resources of the *cosmos* (my italics) pour into cultural manifestation,[32] how can it also be said that the hero's victory is only psychological and subjective? And if the word of God is active in the historical process as well as transcendent, then it is reasonable for the believer to hope for movements toward the improvement of the human social community in history. But the belief, even in demythologized form, that the kingdom of God *will* come and is therefore *beyond* forbids the belief that it has fully come.

In conclusion I suggest that the failure to hold language and reality together in dialogue leads to the situation which Samuel Beckett's "Unnamable" experiences with such desperation: "The words are everywhere, inside me, outside me . . . a minute ago I had no thickness . . . I'm in words, made of words, others' words . . . the place too, the air, the walls, the floor, the ceiling, all words, the whole world is here with me, I'm the air, the walls, the walled-in one . . . nothing ever but me . . . I'm all these words . . . with no ground for their settling, no sky for their dispersing."[33] "If only there were a thing somewhere, to talk about . . . but . . . there is not . . . they took away things . . . they took away nature, there was never anyone . . . anything but me."[34]

NOTES

1. D. S. Russell, *The Method and Message of Jewish Apocalyptic* (Philadelphia: Westminster Press, 1964), 280, 282.

2. Paul D. Hanson, *The Dawn of Apocalyptic: The Historical and Sociological Roots of Jewish Apocalyptic Eschatology* (Philadelphia, Fortress Press, 1975), 376–78.

3. Ibid., 398, 407.

4. Ibid., 377–78.

5. See Gerhard von Rad, *Old Testament Theology,* Eng. trans. D. M. I. Tasker (New York: Harper & Row, 1965), 2:245; Hanson, *The Dawn of Apocalyptic,* 127, 310–11; Walther Eichrodt, "In the Beginning," in *Israel's Prophetic Heritage,* ed. B. W. Anderson and W. Harrelson (New York: Harper & Row; London: SCM Press, 1962), 5–6.

6. Hanson, *The Dawn of Apocalyptic,* 310–11.

7. Eichrodt, "In the Beginning," 5.

8. Gérard Genette, *Narrative Discourse,* Eng. trans. J. E. Lewin (Ithaca, N.Y.: Cornell Univ. Press, 1980), 72.

9. Nicolas Berdyaev, *The Beginning and the End,* Eng. trans. R. French (New York: Harper & Row, 1957), 99, 111, 113, 169, 187, 203.

10. See Hanson, *The Dawn of Apocalyptic,* 312–13.

11. See Norman R. Petersen, *Literary Criticism for New Testament Critics* (Philadelphia: Fortress Press, 1978), 40, 47. Petersen identifies the narrative word with the fabula. I use the latter term in a different sense.

12. Via, *Kerygma and Comedy,* 78–90.

13. Howard Clark Kee, *Community of the New Age: Studies in Mark's Gospel* (Philadelphia: Westminster Press, 1977), 66.

14. Ibid., 67–68.

15. Ibid., 75–76.

16. For my argument that Mark is tragicomedy, see my *Kerygma and Comedy,* 45–46, 98–101. Gilbert G. Bilezikian has argued that in tragedy itself the drama usually ends with the intimation that, in spite of appearances, the hero and his cause have triumphed. I doubt that that is the case in tragedy, and Bilezikian himself sometimes seems to contrast tragedy with victory. See Bilezikian, *The Liberated Gospel* (Grand Rapids: Baker Book House, 1977), 53, 96.

17. Joseph Campbell, *The Hero with a Thousand Faces* (Princeton: Princeton Univ. Press, 1968), 25–26.

18. Ibid., 27–29.

19. John Dominic Crossan, *Raid on the Articulate* (New York: Harper & Row, 1976), 21.

20. Ibid., 22–23.

21. See Walter Schmithals, *Gnosticism in Corinth: An Investigation of the Letters to the Corinthians,* Eng. trans. J. E. Steely (Nashville: Abingdon Press, 1971), 218–45.

22. David L. Miller, "Images of Happy Ending," in *Eranos Yearbook 1975* (Leiden: E. J. Brill, 1977), 61, 64.

23. Campbell, *The Hero with a Thousand Faces,* 27–28.

24. Miller, "Images of Happy Ending," 62–63.

25. Ibid., 65–66.

26. Ibid., 84–85.

27. Ibid., 76, 80–81. Mark C. Taylor has declared that proponents of polytheistic theology (such as Miller) have lost sight of the fact that the form of human self-consciousness presupposes the simultaneous maintenance of plurality and unity. If unity does not accompany plurality, we are not able to be aware of plurality as plurality, and if there is no inner difference, we are unable to recognize our self-identity. See Mark C. Taylor, "Toward an Ontology of Relativism," *Journal of the American Academy of Religion* 46/1 (1978): 56.

28. Miller, "Images of Happy Ending," 86.

29. Ibid., 83, 87.

30. Robert M. Polhemus, *Comic Faith* (Chicago and London: Univ. of Chicago Press, 1980), 3, 7, 17, 20.

31. Gadamer, *Truth and Method,* 101–2.

32. Campbell, *The Hero with a Thousand Faces,* 3.

33. Samuel Beckett, *Molloy, Malone Dies and the Unnamable,* Eng. trans. P. Bowles (New York: Grove Press, 1959), 537.

34. Ibid., 549.

3

Beginning, Middle, and End in Mark

Here we turn to the Markan beginning, middle and end to consider more carefully the relationship of each to the other and to the beginning, middle, and end of apocalyptic world time. It is certainly true that the ultimate beginning and end of apocalyptic world time cannot be contained in historical time. But it is no more an "illusion"[1] to project the experience of the eternal backward and forward than it is to speak of the source of eternity as depth or height. Both the temporal and the spatial terms are symbols of the transcendent on which the world depends, and the images of unspoiled primordial time and redeemed eschatological time are natural for a people who experience divine activity in history as purposeful. The following excursus on method may aid in understanding the discussion of the Markan plot but it is not necessary for it.

Structuralist Tools

Before proceeding to the Markan narrative, I want to comment on the structuralist categories that I will use and subordinate to phenomenological hermeneutics.

First we turn to the test sequence of A. J. Greimas. For Greimas, just as there is a sentence syntax which governs the relationships between the parts of the sentence, so there is a narrative syntax, an orderly arrangement which transcends the sentence in principle and which identifies the units of a narrative and states the nature of their interrelationships. The narrative syntax is composed of deep structures, which are relational networks or systems of abstract units that are relatively empty of meaning content. Let me illustrate with the example of the test sequence, which is a deep structure composed of five functions: (1) Mandating; (2) Acceptance (or Rejection) of the Mandate; (3) Confrontation; (4) Success or Domination (Win or Loss); (5) Consequence, Attribution, or Communication. This structure is deep in that its units (functions) and their relationships are abstracted from the particularities of narratives in general. A function is the constant abstract class to which all of the variable actions or occurrences of a particular kind belong. For example, the function confrontation is abstracted from all of the conflicts, wars, and struggles (physical, military, social, doctrinal, psychological, etc.) that occur in all of the narratives that have been or may be written or told. At the same time, such a structure is thought to account for the organization of the surface structures that appear in the particular stories that concretely manifest the deep structure. The test sequence is useful for my purposes, because in Greimas's opinion these five functions comprise the irreducible diachronic—chronological and developmental—element of a narrative. Moreover, its focus on confrontation is especially applicable to the Markan narrative where conflict is such an important element in the plot. On the other hand, Greimas can say not only that this sequence is *diachronic* but that the scheme is a *logical* consecution.[2] This apparent tension leads us to note the distinction between plot and fabula.

The fabula is a deep structure of narratives, or of their plots. It is a series of functions whose order is determined by narrative syntax, that is, by "natural logic" or by probability as determined by the expectations of a literary genre or of a certain culture. A plot, on the other hand, is a series of motifs (specific elements which in a given narrative manifest functions) whose order is determined by the choices of the author from an indeterminate number of possibilities.[3] Thus Greimas's test sequence is fundamentally a fabula. If the plot motifs in a particular story happen to have the order of the functions in Greimas's test sequence, that is a matter of chance or stylistic choice. Actually it seems to me that the order of the fabula, test sequence, is a fusion of logic and chronology. It would not be *logical* to have a victory (Success) before a battle (Confrontation), because *chronologically* the battle must precede the victory. The logic is a matter of chronological necessity. But in a particular narrative plot it would be perfectly possible to begin with the victory or even the consequences of victory and then later narrate the battle, and its antecedents, which led up to the victory.

It should also be noticed that Greimas distinguishes three kinds of tests: qualifying, main, and glorifying. All three have the same five functions, but they are differentiated in that the consequence or attribution function differs in each of them in content with regard to the object communicated. In the qualifying test, power or a helper is attributed to the hero; in the main test, a good or value, liquidation of lack, is communicated to him; and in the glorifying test, recognition, or a message, is attributed to him.[4] Obviously, in order to distinguish the three tests it was necessary to give the fifth function a more specific semantic content than it has in the test sequence *per se*.

Some use will also be made of Daniel Patte's adaptation of Greimas's system. The broad deep structure of an ideal narrative would contain at least three sequences: an initial correlated sequence, a topical sequence, and a final correlated sequence. The first relates a social rupture or a failure to carry out a contract. The second deals with a new contract, the carrying out of which would be the means for or a contribution to the repairing of the initial breach. The third narrates the reestablishment of the social order. Any character, thing, or place in a sequence may be more fully dealt with in a subsequence.[5]

Sequences are composed of syntagms, syntagms of statements, and statements of functions and actants.[6] An actant is a sphere of action (helping or opposing, for example) usually manifested in a character. My interpretation will make some use of sequences and functions. Therefore I present the functions as listed by Patte:[7]

arrival vs. departure
      departure vs. return
conjunction vs. disjunction
mandating vs. acceptance (or refusal)
confrontation
domination vs. submission
communication vs. reception
attribution vs. deprivation

Finally, one should note Claude Bremond's articulation of the deep structure of an elementary narrative. His position is quite appropriate for the interpretation of biblical narrative because he does not separate deep structure from temporality. His basic question is, "What are the minimal conditions necessary in order that any temporal segment . . . be completely given in a narrative?" And his answer is that it is both necessary and sufficient to grasp the narrative as a process with three moments.[8] There must be (1) origin: initial state as potentiality; (2) development: process actualized, or simply process; (3) conclusion: goal or result (final state). The initial (or the final) state may be one of disequilibrium: a *surplus* of good (satisfactory state) or a *lack* of good (deficient state). Or the initial state may be a balance of good and bad. Any one of these states is a potentiality for change and thus the source of a process. A satisfactory state can be degraded, extended, or even improved. A deficient state can be improved, extended, or even made worse. And a balanced state can be unbalanced for either good or evil. Thus the process in the middle can be one of amelioration or degradation, or it can be a complex intertwining of the two.[9]

Here I will state my position briefly (see Appendix I). Structuralist interpretation is defined by the analytical movement away from the text toward those abstractions from the concrete text which are the deep structures. Phenomenological hermeneutics in the existential mode, on the other hand, moves from the text toward the world as the reader-interpreter tries to understand himself or herself in the light of the way of being in the world which the text projects. A given interpretation cannot give equal weight to these opposite interpretive moves. Therefore I will subordinate structural (existence) analysis to phenomenological hermeneutics, but the former is a useful way of grasping the surface content so that hermeneutical questions can be put to it.

The Plot as the Manifestation
of Process

The end is a different event from the beginning, but it recovers in part the power of the beginning, which has been attacked in the middle and threatened with loss. I make the formal assumption that the narrative can be understood as a three-part process. The beginning, the initial state, is a potentiality for extension or change, and in Mark it manifests both a fullness and a lack (Mark 1:1–13). Emptiness is seen in the sin of Israel (1:4–5), the absence of the Spirit from the people (1:8), and the assault of Satan (1:12-13) on Jesus. But power and sufficiency express themselves in the opening of the heavens and the descent of the Spirit (1:9-11), and in Jesus' victory over Satan (1:13b), although the latter is no more than hinted at until 3:27. God will be newly present among his people. Whether the positive and negative simply balance each other or one is more powerful than the other is not revealed until the end of the story—if then.

The middle of Mark (1:14—14:52) is composed of processes that actualize the possibilities offered by the initial situation. A process of amelioration or redemption is manifested in Jesus' mission. A new time is opened up (1:14-15) because Jesus came out to do and to preach (1:38). He begins to call a new community into existence (1:16-20) and offers forgiveness (2:1-17), healing (1:29-31; 5:21-43), deliverance from the law (2:23-28; 3:1-6; 7:1-23), and freedom from the demonic power that alienates one from self and society (1:21-28, 32-34; 3:20-27; 5:1-20; 9:17-29). The redemptive process is the extension of the initial fullness and the amelioration of the initial lack. The process segment also manifests a process of degradation in the opposition of the Jewish leaders who consistently attack Jesus because they interpret his iconoclastic actions as a violation of the will of God (2:1—3:6; 7:1-23). The increasing misunderstanding of the disciples (Mark 8—10) is also a strand in the process of degradation. This process is the extension of the initial emptiness and the degradation of the initial fullness.

The result segment (14:53—16:8) manifests the apparent victory of the process of degradation in Jesus' death, which ironically brings about the real victory of the process of amelioration in the resurrection. The irony of life out of death occurs (8:35) because God reverses human intentions (12:10).

In the beginning, life comes down in the Spirit. In the middle, it becomes actual in the temporal process and is opposed. In the end, it is put to death but reasserts itself with qualification.

What I have said and will say here is akin in a nontechnical way to the *deductive* method of Erhardt Güttgemanns. He argues that a narrative poet begins with a basic outline, a plot kernel, a coherent structural framework which is comprised of beginning, middle, and end. The poet develops the plot by inserting episodes into the kernel.[10] Such an approach is inherent in the structuralist method. If the poet begins with the plot kernel, it is at least *one* legitimate approach for the critic to begin his or her analysis at that point. I am taking process—composed of the three moments, potentiality, process actualized, and result—as the plot kernel, and I am looking at enough episodes to discern the thematic content of each part of the plot and the concrete interrelationships of the parts to each other. I am not trying to give a full analysis of the plot but to conceptualize it as a process and to grasp the motif of its temporality — the interpenetration of redeemed (eschatological) and fallen time. The ending will disclose both a continuation and a modification of this paradoxical overlapping.

This procedure differs from the *inductive* approaches of such scholars as Werner Kelber, Norman Petersen, David Rhoads, and Donald Michie, who begin with the particularities of the text. Kelber argues that the nature of the kingdom of God in Mark provokes antagonism, dividing the audience into insiders and outsiders. This generates a story that is essentially that of the conflict between Jesus and the Twelve, whose result is the Twelve's utter failure to grasp finally the nature of Jesus' mission and their permanent exclusion from the new manifestation of the kingdom in Galilee.[11] Kelber also has spoken of the ruling motif in Mark as paradox or reversal. This controls both the theology and the action.[12]

According to Petersen, prediction (and the related anticipation) is the major, but not sole, plot device in Mark's narrative, and prediction creates suspense with regard to whether the predictions will come true. The dominating question raised by the plot is whether the disciples will ever overcome their ignorance about Jesus' identity, and in Petersen's view they do in the time of the narrative world beyond the plot.[13] Petersen deals in detail with how this and other plot devices are worked out in Mark.

The treatment of the plot by Rhoads and Michie is substantively similar to that of Kelber in that they see Jesus' affirmation of the kingdom as a challenge to every other claim to power. This challenge brings Jesus into the various kinds of conflict — with demons, with nature, with other human beings (Jewish and Gentile officials and the disciples), with himself — which constitute the plot. Each of the types of conflict is treated separately and in detail by these scholars, though they believe that the conflicts are interwoven into one artistic whole.[14]

The inductive approach gives focal attention to the matter of the story but is tacitly aware of such formal narrative constructs as conflict and testing. The deductive approach focuses on the coherent plot kernel but also pays attention to specific events and themes. The advantage of the inductive method is that it stays closer to the concrete particularities of the narrative, while the deductive procedure better facilitates the conceptualization of the whole in relation to the parts.

The Parts of Mark's Plot and the
Apocalyptic World Plot

The parts of Mark's plot—beginning, middle, and end—manifest internal relationships with one another and also relationships to apocalyptic world time. These two kinds of connection will be treated separately, but they will not and should not be completely separated, because they interpenetrate. Each part of Mark's plot is related both to the apocalyptic world plot and to the other parts of its own internal order. I begin with the relationship of the Markan plot to the apocalyptic scheme.

It can hardly be doubted that the *archē* of Mark 1:1 has a paradigmatic or metaphorical relationship to the *archē* (LXX) of Gen. 1:1, especially since Mark speaks of the *archē* of creation in 10:6. The Markan beginning is seen as the beginning of the world, the never-to-be-repeated first time which the Gospel narrative nevertheless recovers. It should also be pointed out that Mark 10:5-9 presupposes, although paradoxically, the continuation of the unspoiled primordial time. The very beginning of the story, even before Jesus actually appears in his public ministry, is the advent of the newness of creation which is also the eschatological time. There is another first time despite the fatigue of world history.

The middle of Mark's plot overlaps the middle of the world-historical plot, not only in the literal chronological sense but also qualitatively. Mark sees hardness of heart as the condition of humanity throughout the course of world history. He does not speak explicitly of a fall but implies that hardness of heart, which has obtained since before the time of Moses, was not there at the beginning when marriage was established. But it is here now, and it still qualifies the human condition (10:5). It manifests itself concretely in the Markan middle in the opposition of the Jewish officials to Jesus' iconoclasm (3:5) and in the misunderstanding which is characteristic of the disciples (6:52; 8:17-21). The disciples' hardheartedness finally leads to their abandonment of Jesus (14:50), but earlier in the plot they are presented in a more favorable light. In Mark 2:13-28 they are joined with Jesus in the context of three specific issues: sin, fasting, and the Sabbath. Here they seem consistently to follow Jesus' initiative and to engage in behavior characteristic of the kingdom: they eat with outcasts, do not fast, and ignore Sabbath requirements. And, like Jesus, they are brought into conflict with the Jewish opponents.[15]

In the last part of Mark's plot, history and myth are fused. The end of the story brings the end of world history into history, for resurrection belongs to the apocalyptic end of the world. Therefore the power of the end is predicated of an epoch in time. But this epoch is at the same time kept securely *in time* by reference to the disciples and Peter and to the fear of the women and their failure to report what they had seen (Mark 16:7–8). And the discourse also makes reference to the apocalyptic end which is still to be realized (8:39—9:1; 13:24–27). Mark obviously makes the apocalyptic orientation explicit by the use of myth. But the apocalyptic recovery of the lost primordial time is relatively and indirectly present in any plot that first falls and then rises. The initial decline shows that the beginning was the last (relatively) uncorrupted time, while the subsequent ascent leads to its reclamation.

The Beginning of the Story

Mark's first word, *archē* ("beginning"), is the term that Aristotle uses for the first part of a dramatic plot, and Gilbert G. Bilezikian[16] seems to think it not impossible that Mark could have been aware of that. At any rate, Mark's beginning seems to fit Aristotle's requirements: it narrates something that does not necessarily come after something else, though something exists or comes about after it.[17]

How much of Mark's narrative is included in the *archē*, the beginning? The material in 1:1–13 distinguishes itself from 1:14–45. In 1:14 Jesus begins his public ministry. Prior to that we have the Old Testament prophecy of the forerunner and of the Lord and then the preparation of the Son for his mission. All of this is before the first announcement of the gospel by Jesus and before he begins to enact his mission in relation to Israel. But it is integrally related to the gospel as preached and enacted by Jesus. The Old Testament defines the mission of the forerunner (1:2–3) and of the Son of man (8:31; 14:21), and it is through the mission of the forerunner that the Son receives his mandate. Thus the Old Testament and the mission of John the Baptist *are* the beginning of the good news about *Jesus*. And Jesus' mandate from God to be the Son is tied "immediately" to his baptism by John (1:10), and the temptation is "immediately" connected to the mandate (1:12). Before the public ministry, which begins at 1:14, however, there is a temporal break: "after" John was arrested, Jesus came. Moreover, Jesus' messianic status is explicit (for the reader) in 1:1–13 but not in 1:14–15, and we are in a more mythological world in the former passage. The most obvious meaning of the *archē*, then, in 1:1 is that it is the introduction comprised of 1:1–13.

But Mark also projects a narrative world chronologically beyond his plot: the history of the church in the world which will run until the return of the Son of man (8:38—9:1; 13:26). In the light of this projection beyond the plot the whole plotted narrative could be the *beginning* of the good news about Jesus.

The Middle: Process as the Movement and the Formal Staying of Time

The Markan middle is related to the end. In it we see redemptive acts which anticipate the victory of life in Jesus' resurrection and the eschatological salvation of the elect. We also have opposition to and misunderstanding of Jesus which anticipate his trial and crucifixion in the plot ending and the rejection of him which will continue until the end of time. We have seen that the ending of the Markan plot anticipates the end of the world, and the Markan middle anticipates both of these endings. It is both the time in which eschatological expectations are already fulfilled and the time in which they are awaited (1:15).

The middle is also related to the beginning. It is the actualization in process of the dual potentialities of the first part of the plot, as we saw above. And since the Markan *archē* is a tacit reinstitution of the primordial *archē* in the midst of the hardness of heart and the process of redemption actualizes the potential in the beginning of the plot, the middle of the plot is also connected to the primordial beginning; therefore it is not surprising that at one point the Markan middle itself is seen by implication as a continuation of the unfallen creation situation. I have reference to the Markan teaching on marriage (10:2–9). Because the fulfillment of time is the leitmotif of the whole Gospel (1:14–15), it must be assumed that the call for the permanence of marriage is grounded on the belief that the kingdom—a new kind of situation—is a present reality. But in 10:2–9 the appeal is not made directly to the ground that the eschatological kingdom is already present by anticipation; rather, the appeal is made to creation. From the *beginning,* marriage has been a one flesh union which is indissoluble so that *now* divorce is forbidden. Jesus calls on his listeners to live now as if they were in the primordial time before hardness of heart set in and made divorce (apparently) necessary. Since Jesus calls on his hearers to live both in the eschatological kingdom and in the primordial time, the former must be the recovery of the latter. The kingdom which dawns in the mid-time is the actualization, with qualification, of both ultimate terminal points. The middle of the plot actualizes the primordial beginning directly by making it the ground for permanent marriage, as we have just seen, and indirectly in that it (the middle) anticipates the eschatological time which is a recovery of the lost vitality of the beginning. And because the new time in the middle is *not* just the continuation of primordial vitality but even more emphatically the anticipation of the eschaton, we should speak of the *continuity* between creation and mid-point in a guarded way. The power for life has been there in human history, continuing from the time of creation into the mid-time, but it has been so submerged under hardness of heart that its reinvocation by Jesus is a qualitatively new event activated by the impingement of the eschatological future on the present. To sum up, Mark 10:5-9 refers far more directly to creation than to eschaton; but because Mark generally is much more thoroughly oriented to the end than to the beginning, the new beginning affirmed for the middle of time should be seen more as an anticipation of the eschatological new creation than as a continuation of the primordial creation.

Here we may raise the question whether Mark's plot has unity or coherence. John Meagher has denied that it does. In commenting on Mark 1:32-34, for example, he criticizes Mark for a lack of clarity about why the demons are not to speak. He seems to think that the reader could not be expected to make a connection between the silencing in 1:25 and the reason for it in 1:34 and also that the reason is too sketchy and not an example of good technique. He praises Luke for his greater explicitness. Similarly he finds great fault with Mark for not clearing up what the leaven of the Pharisees means in 8:14-21 and praises Matthew for making clear that it means teaching. Meagher feels that the individual units in Mark 1 are faulty and that the sequence lacks any unifying principle—thematic, cumulative, rhythmic, or other—that would give it a coherence that transcends the parts.[18] Bilezikian, on the other hand, feels that Mark's plot has a unity that would satisfy Aristotle.[19]

Frank Kermode has also argued that Mark is not a well-formed narrative but jostles us from one puzzle to another with its frequent use of "immediately" and "again," as if its purpose was not to provide a comfortable sequence but to pile up crux upon crux. Yet Kermode knows that Mark has some kind of profound unity even if its meaning remains mysterious.[20]

It is true that Mark has gaps and is a jostling kind of narrative. But some will think that these gaps are superior to the greater explicitness of Matthew and Luke, for it is these that call the imagination of the reader into play. It is up to the interpreter to find types of coherence that are not explicit in the *text* as the *work* is completed by him. It appears to me that the events in the Markan middle can be grasped as manifesting processes of amelioration and degradation, and the connections of these processes can be seen to display the unity of the story.

The ameliorative or redemptive process extends and actualizes the fullness of the beginning—the opening of the heavens, the descent of the Spirit, the appointment of Jesus as divine Son, and his victory over Satan. Moreover, it elusively continues the unfallen creation time. At the same time, it amelioratively challenges the emptiness manifested in the sin of Israel, the absence of the Spirit and the first appearance of Satan (1:5–13). Looking in the other direction, the process of redemption antici- pates the saving effect of Jesus' death and the victory of the resurrection of Jesus in the ending. Resurrection, as well as apocalyptic discourse, suggests the end of the world, which the middle also therefore antici- pates. That is, the middle of the plot anticipates the end of the world. In its own temporal space the redemptive process is interwoven with the process of degradation or opposition which produces a sequence of conflicts.

The process of opposition degrades the fullness of the beginning and extends the emptiness of the beginning. It also continues the hardness of heart which has conditioned human existence in world time through- out its course. And looking in the other direction, the process of degrada- tion anticipates the death of Jesus as the apparent victory of the opposition and the continuing rejection of Jesus' mission throughout the course of history (8:38). The two processes are interwoven and both point forward and backward. And once Jesus emerges as the suffering Son of man, the one who saves by suffering, and the reversing irony of God is taken into account (12:10–11), the two processes are not simply interwoven but rather coalesce. The intention of Jesus to redeem becomes confluent with the intention of his opponents to kill him.

The time in the middle has the quality that it has not only because it comes after a certain kind of beginning and before a certain kind of ending but also because beginning, middle, and end interpenetrate each other in the middle. We see chronological movement from beginning to end, but we have seen the correspondences among the parts which create a kind of circularity. The beginning returns to itself, so to speak, in the middle and in the ending. The coming down of the Spirit on Jesus in the beginning (1:10) corresponds to the rising up of Jesus presupposed in the end (16:1–8), and the coming down of Moses and Elijah and the voice in the middle (9:2–8) correspond to both. Murray Krieger has pointed out that the creation of narrative form by means of repetition, juxtaposition, and other forms of having the narrative refer to itself has the effect of transforming chronological order into logical. Teleology is added to time. This move also results in spatializing the chronological movement. There- fore we must read a narrative in two ways at the same time. We see it

reflecting the running course of our own lives as we move through beginning, middle, and end as a series of irreversible and unrepeatable events.
At the same time, we sense the staying of this movement in that a
simultaneous system of meaning is created by the logical relationships
among the parts.[21]

The Ending: A Reconstitution of
Revealed/Concealed

The ending begins at Mark 14:53 when Jesus has fallen into the hands
of his captors and no longer takes initiatives or countermeasures. The
ending includes the trials, the crucifixion, and the resurrection; but for
my purposes, attention will be confined to the last of these components
in its Markan theological context. What kind of closure does the resurrection story in 16:1–8 confer on the narrative? In what way does it satisfy
expectations generated by the text and thereby give the reader a sense
that the narrative has reached a goal and been completed?[22]

I take it that 16:8, the last verse of the Gospel in the reliable Greek
text,[23] is where the story originally ended. The women in fear fled from
the tomb and did not report the announcement of the resurrection to the
disciples. No one has ever been able to make clear how an original longer
ending relating resurrection appearances could have been lost and not
immediately restored.[24] Nor do the traditional arguments from internal
evidence for an original longer ending amount to much of a case. To the
argument that the predictions of resurrection appearances in 14:28 and
16:7 require a fulfillment, it may be said that the resurrection is in fact
implicit in 16:1–8[25] and that the whole Gospel presupposes the resurrection.[26] These points are true, but Matthew and Luke also presuppose the
resurrection throughout and still narrate resurrection appearances. We
must see why the absence of resurrection appearances in Mark is congruent with his theology as a whole.

It has been pointed out that the rules of Greek syntax make it difficult
to end a book or even a sentence with the word *gar*. But many recent
studies have pointed to the stylistic possibility of such an ending.[27] Yet
it is unusual. Kermode has raised the question why Mark should have
chosen to end the gospel of Jesus Christ with the least forceful word he
could find. The conclusion is either intolerably clumsy or incredibly
subtle.[28]

And then, would it not have been too strange to end the story of the
good news on the note of fear? It may be responded that the women's fear
is really a religious awe which is appropriate to the revelatory experience

of the resurrection.[29] Or it may be argued that the fear and flight of the women are culpable and must be interpreted in the light of the scandalous flight of the disciples (14:50) and the shame of the young man who fled naked when the chief priests' men seized him (14:51–52).[30] The same verb, *pheugō* ("flee"), is used of the disciples, the young man, and the women at the tomb. I incline to the second of these two views. In what way is the culpably fearful flight and silence of the women congruent with Mark's theological position?

Recall that David L. Miller wants to replace the traditionally Christian happy ending, which posits a lack of suffering despite an infinite qualitative distinction, or contradiction, between human beings and God, with a reconceived happy ending, which realistically retains suffering but posits a new congruence between human beings and a multiplicity of deities. *What* actually seems to be the case in Mark—making use of these categories? I will argue that in Mark suffering is overcome in part, and the divine-human contradiction, which is more complex than it may appear to be, is also overcome in part. I say "in part" because Mark's view is that the end both has and has not come.

Suffering in some way must have been overcome, because the women who witnessed Jesus' death (Mark 15:40–41) and who because they belong to the end of the story must have absorbed the pain of the whole narrative are told that he has risen (16:6). But this does not give them unambiguous equanimity and peace, for the news of the resurrection fills them with such fear and astonishment that they do not report it to the disciples and tell them about Jesus' expected appearance. And this irresolution regarding the response of the women and the future of the disciples undoubtedly causes the reader anxiety. Because of the nature of the *response* in the end the happiness is certainly qualified. What about the nature of the *revelation?* This entails a discussion of the divine-human contradiction.

The text itself suggests that we need to analyze this contradiction. I will distinguish between ontological difference (difference in being) and religious alienation (the absence of effective revelation) and ask, how are these related in Mark? In the Bible, ontological difference is assumed and is not regarded as a problem because it is mediated by the word of God. C. H. Dodd had long ago remarked that revelation by the word in the Bible preserves the ontological distance between human beings and God while affirming that God chooses to deal with human beings in a way they can understand.[31] Mark seems to assume the ontological difference without being concerned to say much about it. In the resurrection, human beings will be like the angels in heaven (12:25), but that does not make them equal to God in being, because the angels do not have God's knowledge (13:32). In this case the lack of knowledge is not due to a failure of revelation but to a difference in level of being. In 10:27 the human lack of power in comparison with God might be thought of as ontological. But in context the lack of capacity in human beings to be saved is not based on their level of being but is based on the fact that they tend to walk away from the call of Jesus and toward their possessions (10:22).

Notwithstanding a partial exception to be noted below, Mark generally does not regard ontological distinction as a problem, as a source of alienation. The source is religious and moral deviation. Mark probably regards ontological distinction as mediated by the word. The word for Mark is intended also to overcome religious alienation. If religious alienation is conquered, then ontological distinction is not alienating. Jesus' word has authority and power to give healing, life, and forgiveness (1:22, 41; 2:5, 11; 5:8, 13, 41–42; 7:34; 9:25–26), and it does not pass away (13:31). But is it actually effective in the lives of the disciples? The disciples finally abandon Jesus (14:50) without having grasped the message of the death and resurrection of the Son of man (9:32). The reason they do not grasp it is that they do not themselves want to take the way of the last and the lowly (9:34–35; 10:35–45). The word is not effective, because the disciples will not accept its meaning for them.

But is that the whole story? Jesus conceals his message from the crowd, from outsiders (1:34; 3:12; 4:10–12; 8:30). He gives the secret of the kingdom (4:11) to the disciples and repeatedly confronts them with the word about the death and resurrection of the Son of man (8:31–33; 9:31–32; 10:32–34), and there is a sense in which the word makes the event present because the word is powerful. Yet it is also a Markan principle that the real truth about the Son of man cannot be known until his resurrection in the future (9:9). And that resurrection which is so often anticipated (8:31; 9:31; 10:34; 14:28) never occurs as an actual appearance. It is only proclaimed to the women that it has occurred, and they do not report the proclamation to the disciples, who have been off the scene since they abandoned Jesus (14:50). Thus the suggestion in 9:9 that the disciples will be able to tell others who Jesus really is—what they have seen at the transfiguration—is made ironical to a degree by the way the resurrection is narrated. Revelation, then, is ineffective, not only because it is refused by the disciples but because the revelation which is given is *concealed* by the revealer. Alienation is therefore not totally a matter of the religious and moral deviation of the disciples; but *is* the problem, from God's side, one of ontological distance? It is true that the disciples do not know in part because they cannot. What they need is withheld by God. This is akin to tragedy: there is an inevitability. It is reminiscent of the situation of the classical tragic hero who because of the ignorance of his *finitude* commits hybris and as a result suffers nemesis. But Mark does not fall into tragedy, because ignorance here is not caused by finitude, and there is a wealth of redemptive imagery in the Gospel. The confession of the centurion (15:39) represents the hope for a believing community in the future. To the extent that revelation is ineffective, this lack is in *part* caused by the disciples' rejecting it. The other part is not ontological, due to the incommensurability of the being of God and human being, but is a function of eschatology and of the mysterious personal nature of God. God has decided to reserve full revelation for the future.

Will revelation ever be given fully enough to overcome religious alienation? Is there a point at which the human situation vis-à-vis God changes qualitatively? To pursue this question further we need to take another look at the ending in the light of several recent interpretations. According to Theodore Weeden, the women did not execute the angel's command, because cowardly fear incapacitated them. The disciples therefore never heard the message, never met the risen Lord, and were never made apostles. Mark's narrative totally discredits the disciples.[32]

Norman Petersen has reacted against Weeden's literal reading of Mark 16:7–8 by arguing that we should read 16:8 ironically. We should not take the narrator to mean what he says but rather deliteralize the behavior of the women. This provides a satisfactory closure from which the story can be read. Mark 16:6–7 tells the reader that while the women are "muddling about," Jesus, having arisen, is on his way to Galilee, where the disciples will see him. The reader is then directed to provide the closure, which is actualized when the reader supplies from his or her imagination the meeting of the disciples with Jesus—satisfying the expectation generated by the prediction (16:7) that such would occur. This resolves the plot, for now the eleven come to understand what they had previously misunderstood. The ironic reading of 16:8 is the bridge between the expectation generated by 16:7 and the imaginatively created meeting with Jesus. Before the resurrection the disciples are on the wrong side of the question as to whether Jesus is a political, this-worldly Messiah or the dying-rising and apocalyptic Son of man, but afterward they are on the right side. The continuity between the two periods is the persistence of this question, while the discontinuity is the move of the disciples from the wrong to the right answer. Thus the message of Mark is not so much the dullness of the disciples as God's overriding it.[33] In a similar way, Thomas Boomershine has argued that the ending of Mark resolves the tension between disclosure and concealment which is resident in the messianic secret. The audience is called on to repent of its fearful silence and proclaim Jesus' messiahship after his resurrection. Secrecy is reversed.[34]

According to James M. Robinson, Mark seems to be making the effort to push back the hermeneutical turning point—the point at which an earlier obscure revelation is made clear—from Easter to a time in Jesus' public ministry when he begins to speak plainly (8:32). In Mark 8 the surprised question (8:17, 21), the fate-laden character of understanding (8:17–18), the healing of the blind man (8:22–26), and the prediction of the passion (8:31) followed by a saying on cross bearing (8:34–37) all point toward a shift from the enigmatic, coded teaching in parables, which prevailed earlier (4:11, 34a), to the open teaching in terms of the church's kerygma about the death and resurrection of Jesus (8:31, 32). Robinson thinks that this change may have been occasioned by an emergent orthodoxy's effort, against Gnosticism, to validate Jesus prior to his death as a source of ultimate interpretation.[35]

First of all, Robinson may be right that Mark's composition—placing kerygma in Jesus' mouth at 8:31–33—is to be explained, in part, by the theological polemics of Mark's historical situation. But the effect of introducing the remark about plain teaching is to generate a cutting irony. The early enigmatic teaching was to *outsiders* (4:11) and already in Mark 4 the *disciples* were receiving plain or open teaching in the form of explanations (4:14–20, 34). In what sense, then, is the open teaching of 8:31–32 a new departure? There *may* be a shift in content (I say "may" because we do not know what was in all the explanations), but is there any shift in clarity or understandability? The explanations referred to in Mark 4 were apparently ineffective, since in 6:52 and 8:17–21 the disciples were sadly uncomprehending. The "explanations" turn out to be ironical. In this context we have some reason to think that the plain teaching in 8:32 will enhance the effectiveness of the explanations; there will be a new departure, a new clarity. But the result of the open teaching is the repeated failure to understand (8:32b; 9:32; 10:35–40). Thus the really new thing beginning at 8:31–32 is a deepening or doubling of the irony: the explanations did not really explain and the open teaching was not really open. This directs us to read 8:32 in the light of 4:34. However "open" Jesus' words, they are still parables, enigmas. Mark 4:34 over-

comes 8:32. Jesus spoke only in parables—truly without an enigma he did
not speak to them—right down to the end of the story.

In the second place, does the resurrection remove the incomprehen-
sibility of the revelation? Is the messianic secret dispelled? I myself argue
that for Mark the paradox of concealed revelation is never resolved,
although he envisions a change in its constitution. Petersen, for example,
does not really deliteralize the behavior of the women. His statement
regarding their "muddling about" is a summary but not a deliteralizing
of their being afraid and not saying what they were told to say. Moreover,
I am not convinced by his argument—nor do I think a convincing one can
intrinsically be given—that the muddling of the women is a bridge between the prediction of the disciples' meeting with Jesus and the reader's
imagined fulfillment of the prediction.

As a matter of fact, the fear and silence of the women should be taken
literally, and that can be done in such a way that it will not feed into
Weeden's position but will point to the consistency of the total narrative,
the continuity between plot and narrative world, between the time before
the resurrection and the time afterward. The resurrection story joins
these two times. It shows that both of them are qualified by the opposition revealed/concealed. The announcement of the young man that Jesus
has risen is concealed revelation: it is revelation in that the resurrection
is declared, but the revelation is concealed in that the resurrected Jesus
is *not there in the story* as he is in Matthew and Luke. The fear and
silence of the women portrays the concealed element in the church's
proclamation of the resurrection. We will see that the resurrection is
effectively proclaimed, but the note of fear and silence qualifies its power
and suggests its ambiguity.

Revelation is *given* during the time of the plot. That the light breaks
through from time to time is seen in the healed Gerasene demoniac's
proclamation of Jesus (5:18–20), in the restoring of sight to the blind
(8:22–26; 10:46–52), in the faith of the Roman centurion (15:39). These
events do qualify the time of the plot, however much their description
may have been colored by the resurrection faith of the church. But the
final inconsistency of the crowd (15:11–15) and the pervasive opposition
of the authorities and misunderstanding of the disciples mean that during the time of the plot concealment dominates in the revealed/concealed
opposition.

After the resurrection, concealment still diminishes the effect of the
resurrected Jesus upon his followers and the world. The failure of Jesus'
disciples to understand his teaching about the death and resurrection of

the Son of man belongs to the plot. But because this teaching is given in terms of the church's proclamation, the time of the disciples and the time of the church are assimilated to each other. There will be failures to understand *after* the resurrection. The revelation is not so clear that believers or potential believers cannot be led astray by false claimants to be the Christ (13:5-6, 21-22).[36] The situation of the church is also reflected in 4:14-20. The effectiveness of the word will be limited by Satan, the attractiveness of the world and situations that produce danger and hence fear. The presence of Satan here gives a kind of transcendent inevitability to the threat of the this-worldly phenomena: wealth and suffering.

Yet Mark does lead us to expect that the resurrection will make a difference. His strong emphasis on the hope that it will happen (8:31; 9:31; 10:34; 14:28), his suggestion that it will enable the disclosure of Jesus' true identity (9:9), and his obvious acknowledgment of the continuing history of the church show that Mark believes that something happened. And what happened changed the disciples, and Petersen is right about that. During the plot the disciples did not understand Jesus and they abandoned him when he was arrested. But in the situation that Jesus projects into the future, Peter, Andrew, James, and John represent the believing community. They are the ones who will suffer for Jesus' name (13:3-5, 9-11, 13). Revelation during the time of the church, after the resurrection, is still concealed, but the transformation of the disciples shows that disclosure has begun to dominate in the revealed/concealed opposition.

In Mark the word of Jesus has authority (1:27). It is effective in human life (2:5, 10-12) and has power over the cosmos (4:39). This word embraces the kingdom of God (1:14-15, 38), the cross (8:31-32), and the ethical demand (7:12-13). It also includes the word about Jesus' powerful deeds (1:45). It is this word which for Mark provides the continuity between the time of the disciples and the time of the church, for Jesus' words will not pass away (13:31). But we have seen that this continuity is also supplied by the persistence of the opposition revealed/concealed. The resurrection does not introduce a radically new departure, and the redeeming kerygmatic word and the demanding ethical word will never be made unambiguously clear. The continuing word is disclosed/concealed.

But something has happened; there is also a discontinuity. Will the revelation ever be fully given so as to overcome religious alienation? It will not be given fully enough to overcome it completely. If we recognize along the way that the narrative renders ironical both Jesus' explanations of enigmas and his plain words, we will not expect to get complete illumination. We get as much in the ending as the narrative gives us reason to expect. In the time of the plot, concealment dominates in the revealed/concealed opposition. The resurrection does not completely expel the concealed element, but it brings about the dominance of disclosure. This is the discontinuity.

In sum, throughout Mark's plot and into the time after the plot, events are governed by the theme that the eschatological reality has both come and not come: revelation is both given and withheld. In fact, it is because the kingdom has both come and not come that revelation is both given and concealed, that the Son of God–Son of man is manifested but his identity is concealed. This raises a fundamental question about the realizability and nature of Mark's ethical norms (see Part Two).

NOTES

1. As claimed by Berdyaev, *The Beginning and the End*, 207.

2. See A. J. Greimas, *Sémantique structurale* (Paris: Larousse, 1966), 196–97, 205; Jean Calloud, *Structural Analysis of Narrative*, Eng. trans. D. Patte (Philadelphia: Fortress Press; Missoula, Mont.: Scholars Press, 1976), x–xii, 3–5.

3. See Lubomir Doležel, "From Motifemes to Motifs," *Poetics* 4 (1972): 58–61, 65, 67.

4. Greimas, *Sémantique structurale*, 197, 202–3, 206; Calloud, *Structural Analysis*, 28.

5. Patte, *What Is Structural Exegesis?* 38, 51. More recently Patte has substituted the term "program" for "sequence," but I will retain "sequence." See Daniel Patte and Aline Patte on exegesis of Mark 15 and 16 in *Structural Exegesis: From Theory to Practice* (Philadelphia: Fortress Press, 1978), 117.

6. Patte, *What Is Structural Exegesis?* 39–40.

7. Ibid., 41.

8. Claude Bremond, "The Narrative Message," *Semeia* 10 (1978): 33.

9. This scheme is a synthetic adaptation of several related constructions. See Bremond, "Narrative Message," 33; Claude Bremond, "Morphology of the French Folktale," *Semiotica* 2 (1970): 247–52; Tzvetan Todorov, *The Fantastic*, Eng. trans. R. Howard (Ithaca, N.Y. Cornell Univ. Press, 1973), 163–66; Doležel, "Motifemes," 62; William O. Hendricks, "The Structural Study of Narration: Sample Analyses," *Poetics* 3 (1972): 101, 105.

10. Erhardt Güttgemanns, *Semeia* 6 (1976) 29–31, 128, 185. Gerd Theissen's treatment of the miracle story genre is similarly deductive. The stories have a broad fourfold structure, each of whose four parts can be filled out with a variety of individual motifs. The narrator decides which motifs to actualize in each of the four major parts of the story and is free to put a motif in a part where it is not usually found. See Gerd Theissen, *The Miracle Stories of the Early Christian*

Tradition, Eng. trans. F. McDonagh (Philadelphia: Fortress Press; Edinburgh: T. & T. Clark, 1983), 73–74.

11. Werner H. Kelber, *Mark's Story of Jesus* (Philadelphia: Fortress Press, 1979), 15, 87–90.

12. Werner H. Kelber, "Conclusion: From Passion Narrative to Gospel," in *The Passion in Mark,* ed. W. H. Kelber (Philadelphia: Fortress Press, 1976), 178–80.

13. Petersen, *Literary Criticism for New Testament Critics,* 52, 56, 61–63, 78–79.

14. David Rhoads and Donald Michie, *Mark as Story: An Introduction to the Narrative of a Gospel* (Philadelphia: Fortress Press, 1982), 73–75, 100.

15. See Joanna Dewey, *Markan Public Debate: Literary Technique, Concentric Structure, and Theology in Mark 2:1—3:6* (Chico, Calif.: Scholars Press, 1980), 125–27.

16. Bilezikian, *The Liberated Gospel,* 121.

17. Aristotle, *Poetics* 7.

18. John C. Meagher, *Clumsy Construction in Mark's Gospel* (New York and Toronto: Edwin Mellen Press, 1979), 46–50, 53–56, 77–79.

19. Bilezikian, *The Liberated Gospel,* 55.

20. Frank Kermode, *The Genesis of Secrecy: On the Interpretation of Narrative* (Cambridge: Harvard Univ. Press, 1979), 139–41, 143–44.

21. See Murray Krieger, *Theory of Criticism* (Baltimore and London: Johns Hopkins Univ. Press, 1976), 156, 157, 208, 211, 240–41.

22. See Norman R. Petersen, "When Is the End Not the End? Literary Reflections on the Ending of Mark's Narrative," *Interpretation* 34/2 (1980): 152.

23. Among the most reliable textual authorities supporting the ending at 16:8 are ℵ, B, Sinaitic Syriac, Clement, Origen, Eusebius, and Jerome.

24. See W. G. Kümmel, *Introduction to the New Testament,* Eng. trans. H. C. Kee (Nashville: Abingdon Press, 1975), 100.

25. R. H. Lightfoot, *The Gospel Message of Saint Mark* (Oxford: At the Clarendon Press, 1950), 93–96.

26. Willi Marxsen, *Introduction to the New Testament,* Eng. trans. G. Buswell (Philadelphia: Fortress Press, 1968), 141.

27. Kümmel, *Introduction to the New Testament,* 100–101; Lightfoot, *The Gospel Message of Saint Mark,* 86; Bilezikian, *The Liberated Gospel,* 137; see the thorough investigation in Thomas E. Boomershine and Gilbert L. Bartholomew, "The Narrative Technique of Mark 16:8," *Journal of Biblical Literature* 100/2 (1981): 213–23.

28. Kermode, *The Genesis of Secrecy,* 66–68.

29. Kümmel, *Introduction to the New Testament,* 101; Lightfoot, *The Gospel Message of Saint Mark,* 85, 87, 90.

30. Thomas E. Boomershine, "Mark 16:8 and the Apostolic Commission," *Journal of Biblical Literature* 100/2 (1981): 229–30, 237.

31. C. H. Dodd, *The Interpretation of the Fourth Gospel* (Cambridge: Cambridge University Press, 1953), 263.

32. Theodore J. Weeden, *Mark—Traditions in Conflict* (Philadelphia: Fortress Press, 1971), 48, 50.

33. Petersen, "When Is the End Not the End?" 160–63, 164–66.

34. Boomershine, "Mark 16:8," 225, 233, 237–38. Ernest Best also suggests that at the resurrection the disciples achieved full understanding (*Following Jesus,* 123–37), and Bilezikian declares that the resurrection illumines all things (*The Liberated Gospel,* 56, 75, 86, 96–97, 123).

35. James M. Robinson, "Gnosticism and the New Testament," in Robinson, *The Problem of History in Mark and Other Markan Essays* (Philadelphia: Fortress Press, 1982), 46–48, 50–52. Quentin Quesnell had also suggested that the open teaching at 8:31–32 marks a new beginning in the Gospel (*The Mind of Mark* [Rome: Pontifical Biblical Institute, 1969], 128, 133).

36. I am aware that in this discussion I am dealing with two related but not identical themes: the concealment of revelation and the disciples' failure (refusal) to understand. In the discussion of the messianic secret (chapter 12) I will try to show that these two themes necessarily co-implicate each other.

4

Theological Reflection on Mark's Gospel

The Kingdom of God and Chronological Time

In the Bible there is a dialectical attitude toward both time and eternity, and there is a correlation between the two dialectics. Let me illustrate from Mark. Time with its human possibilities is both the expression of and matrix for the divine intention, and it is fallen as, for example, in Mark 10:2-9. Marriage is intended by God, and it is supposed to continue in time—it takes time. At the same time, human beings in time have contracted hardness of heart, and that is the condition in which marriage has to be lived out. Eternity or the kingdom is also viewed dialectically. It is the *goal* or *end* of the historical process—understanding *end* in a nontechnical teleological sense. This is seen in all of Mark's references to the future coming of the kingdom of God or the Son of man. The end draws out the consequences of action in time (8:38—9:1). But the kingdom is also the *means* or the enabler for significant occurrence in historical time. The kingdom's intersection with time is the means which enables all of the liberating and redemptive acts of Jesus: new community, forgiveness, freedom, and so forth. The kingdom occurs in the present through significant events—by anticipation. Therefore it must be consummated in the future. There is temporal tension and movement.

Time as both intended by God and fallen is correlated with the kingdom as both present in history and future goal in that the kingdom as the means for significant temporal happening is explanation in part for the positive evaluation of time. That the kingdom does intersect time, that the eschatological event can be presented as a three part plot, shows that time may well be the matrix for the divine intention. On the other hand, that the kingdom is the goal of history, and thus is not yet here but is still to come, is correlated to the fact that hardness of heart still prevails.

As we contend, time has positive moments, not only because the eschaton is anticipated but because the creative intention continues (Mark 10:6-9) despite hardness of heart (10:5). Mark's formulation here reveals a biblical basis for Paul Tillich's position that "essential being," while never existing in purity at a literal, primordial time or place, is present as distorted under the conditions of existence in history.[1] "Essential being" comes to expression in Mark's terms in the expectation that human beings should live their marriages in vitality and without separation after the time of creation, that is, throughout the course of history. But this potentiality for newness is encased in hardness of heart, the distortion of existence. Beginning and end are joined in Mark, not only because of slight verbal correspondence but also because both are present in the middle as the basis for ethical action.

The Emergence of the Eschatologically New in Mark's Narrative: Chronos and Kairos

Nicolas Berdyaev has spoken of the emergence of the new (the kairotic), the existential, in history, which breaks up the cosmic cycle and the determinism and objectification of the historical process. And he understands the appearance of Jesus as the metahistorical or existential event par excellence.[2] But Berdyaev has not related his philosophical reflections to the narrative language of the Gospels (see Appendix II). How, for instance, does the "new" emerge in the Gospel of Mark? For the narrator the new emerges through the telling of the story—he offers a new beginning to the reader in and through the story. That the story itself is seen as an effective event is not just a matter of evaluating it in the light of a modern hermeneutic, for the Markan text reveals an awareness of the power of narrative to create faith. The word *logos* ("word") occurs for the first time in Mark at 1:45. This is a characteristic New Testament term for the Christian preaching. Paul, for example, refers to the *logos* of the cross (1 Cor. 1:18), and also in Mark the *logos* is, among other things, the word of the cross (8:31-32). In Mark 1:45, however, the *logos* is the story of Jesus' miraculous activity, and interestingly the characteristic New Testament word "to preach" (*kēryssein*) is also used here. The healed leper preached freely and spread the word about Jesus' healing activity. The result was that the people thronged to Jesus (1:28; 3:7-12). Both the woman with the hemorrhage and blind Bartimaeus heard about Jesus, heard his story, and as a result came to him (5:27) or sought him (10:47). This seeking of Jesus is interpreted as faith (5:34; 10:52), a faith to which Jesus' story had brought them.

James M. Robinson is right that having faith or understanding the mystery of Jesus is fate-laden in Mark. Understanding is a gift given to the one who already has it (4:24-25).[3] When one hears it, if one does not already understand it, one will not understand what is heard. On the other hand, if one brings understanding to the hearing, one's understanding will be increased. Mark's view of the possibility of becoming a true disciple, as we know, has its dark sides. But in the context of the effectiveness of the story motif we see a brighter side. One must "have" in order "to be given," but the story about Jesus has the power to break into the vicious circle that not-having produces more not-having, and by this inbreaking the story generates faith.

I observed in chapter 3 that Jesus' special explanations to the Twelve (Mark 4:34) and his open teaching to them (8:31-32) were rendered ironical by their failure to understand. That special teaching is made ironical from another angle: the woman with the hemorrhage and blind Bartimaeus, who had received no special explanations but had only heard the story of Jesus, came to faith. But when one considers the nature of faith in Mark, the darker side presents itself again.

When we look *within* Mark's story, we see that the new life in Jesus manifests itself in several ways. The narrator can speak mythologically of the direct intervention of the transcendent, the intersecting of the horizontal by the vertical. At the baptism the heavens are opened and the Spirit descends on Jesus (1:9-11). And at the transfiguration Jesus is glorified, and the divine voice audibly identifies him as "beloved Son" (9:2-8). The new is also seen nonmythologically in that Jesus announces a new time (1:15), the time of celebration rather than fasting, which makes old ways inadequate (2:18-22). And Jesus enacts this newness by contravening convention, law, cult, and doctrine (2:1—3:6). And there is a third way. Mark, and the other Gospels, do not understand the event of Jesus to be as radically and directly the intervention of the vertical as Berdyaev does. Nor would Mark agree with Berdyaev that the existential or metahistorical, once it intersects history, does not at all shape history.[4] We have noted that the direct intervention of God is one element in Mark, but Jesus is also who he is because of Old Testament prophecy, something in his past which affects his present (1:2-3; 8:31; 14:21). Mark undoubtedly thought of the prophetic word as word of God, but the word of God works through as well as into the historical process. The prophetic tradition does help to shape Jesus' destiny, but he also gives the tradition a new meaning.

In view of the dichotomy which Berdyaev posits between chronological and existential time it is difficult to see how he could account for the fact that Christianity attaches meaning to history and time, which he does acknowledge.[5] It is also hard to see how he avoids contradicting himself when at points,[6] against his dominant tendency,[7] he himself holds to some kind of positive relationship between chronological and existential time. In any case, we have seen that in Mark, and I think in the Bible generally, existential or kairotic time and chronos are meaningfully correlated and not antithetical. Berdyaev tends to speak as if existential time is of another dimension than the chronological. It comes into chronos from the outside and intersects it but has no extension in the horizontal. Is it not nearer the truth to say that kairos or the existential is the quality or content of chronos, what it is time for? It does not exist in some other "place" than chronos but is the imprint of the transcendent on chronos. The chronological without the existential is empty, but the existential without the chronological has no "place."

The Flow of Time and the Well-Being of the Psyche

I do not contend that the chronological is the only important element in the biblical understanding of time, but that it is an indispensable element, that chronos and kairos are fused, that chronos is shaped and modified by plot and that this plotting of time is not a falsification of the real world (see Appendix II). The really significant thing about the chronological is not that it is measurable but that it moves from past to future, from anticipation to fulfillment. Again, chronos and kairos are fused. It is the kingdom of God, occurring by anticipation in the present (1:15) but also pointing into the future (8:38—9:1; 13:24-27) which keeps time moving.[8] In terms of the plot the movement is from possibility through process to goal. If the eschatological element in Mark were seen simply as a vertical irruption intersecting time at a point but not shaping it, or if the temporality of eschatology were denied, then in my judgment Mark's point of view not only would have been misinterpreted but we would also have an interpretation that is psychologically less healthy.

Henri Ellenberger points out that in depressive patients the basic symptom is that time is no longer experienced as a propulsive energy.[9] The future is experienced as blocked, attention is directed to the past, and the present is experienced as stagnating. The most immediate, subjective experience of time is the flowing of life experienced as spontaneous, living energy, while the most disturbing experience in depression is the slowing down, arresting, or reversing of the flow of time. Flowing time is automatically structured as the irreversible sequence of past, present, and future. For the normal individual the future is open, but for the depressed it is inaccessible and blocked.

Eugene Minkowski raises a fundamental question in discussing the causal relationship between a particular delusion and the view of the future in a case of delusional schizophrenic depression.[10] Minkowski argues that the patient did *not* have a hopeless future, *because* he mistakenly believed, every day, that he was going to be executed the next day. Rather, the basic disorder is the distorted attitude toward the future of which the delusion is a manifestation: he believed every day that he was going to be executed the next day *because* he had lost his sense of the future. This can be seen in the way in which the man experienced time. Each day was experienced as like every other, as independent and not immersed in a perception of life continuity. This is a consequence of a sense of the future as blocked.

In a study of the world of the compulsive, V. E. von Gebsattel observes the usual distinction between the compulsive's phobia—of dirt, pollution, odor, and so forth—and his compulsive defense reaction, two aspects which the subject experiences as a whole.[11] The compulsive never has any peace; something must always be analyzed, inspected, repeated, or washed. His life has a rule-ridden unchangeability. But regardless of how scrupulous he is, the pollution, or whatever, persists; and this persistence is the equivalent of being nailed to the past at the cost of the future. In von Gebsattel's view, the inability to get rid of the past pollution is the real meaning of the pollution. The fundamental problem is the blocking of becoming, the fixation of the past, the inability to let one's energies stream into task-oriented self-development. This fixation can be experienced as pollution, but the contamination or the odor is a symbol of a life deprived of one of the possibilities of purification—orientation toward the future.

The representation of temporality in the Gospel of Mark speaks to this problem. The psychological is one, but probably not the only, category for interpreting the demonic. To be demon possessed is to suffer psychological distortion and victimization, to suffer the blockage of time. That is what has happened to the demoniac in Mark 5:1-20. Although literally alive, he was already dead, living among the tombs (5:3), alienated from society and from himself. In Mark, a person must be delivered from the demonic in order to be ethically responsible, in order to be able to respond to the demands of the kingdom for living in the world. In psychological and ontological terms, that is to be put into free-flowing time which has a future. And that is what happens for those from whom the demons have been exorcised. The man in Mark 5:1–20 is enabled to tell what Jesus has done for him (5:19–20). He becomes a part of Jesus' story, a redemptive story with a future, and he has a story of his own to tell, the one Mark has just told. It is a dramatic story about the movement from life-in-death through death to life-in-death and on to life itself.

If Mark is right that the very reading or hearing of the story can catch the reader or hearer up in the story itself, then it will point her or him to the kind of open, redemptive future needed. The Markan plot points to the victory of eschatological life over death in the resurrection of Jesus. Mark's narrative world is finally bounded in the future by the ultimate manifestation of God's power and glory in the coming of the kingdom (9:1) or the return of the Son of man (13:26). The expected future is thus qualitatively different from the present and can summon one out of the sameness of undifferentiated days and toward something new and different. The import of these eschatological and cosmic symbols is expressed at the psychological and existential level, although still with some use of myth, in the deliverance of the demoniac from the legion of demons.

But the Markan narrative is not an empty form into which preconceived psychological content can be pressed. It makes its own claim about how the fulfilled life can be achieved. One moves toward the promising future by following Jesus in his way, and that means finding *all* by losing *all* (8:34–37; 10:21, 43–44). One enters a plot constituted by the conflict between the forces of life and the forces of death. The conflict is seen in the larger story in the opposition to and misunderstanding of Jesus. It is seen in the story of the demoniac in that he experiences Jesus' will to liberate him as a tormenting threat which he resists (5:7–10). It is frightening to be compelled out of the miserable security of life-in-death and into the risk of an open future in the world. The delivered one lives with a sense of the indeterminate future for which there is the promise of the victory of life over death. By preserving the movement or flow of time into the future, by representing discipleship as movement along a way, Mark provides a narrative basis for the kind of psychological and existential posture that is requisite for ethical responsibility.

NOTES

1. Paul Tillich, *Systematic Theology* (Chicago: Univ. of Chicago Press, 1957), II:33.

2. Berdyaev, *The Beginning and the End,* 166–67.

3. James M. Robinson, "Gnosticism and the New Testament," 47.

4. Berdyaev, *The Beginning and the End,* 155.

5. Ibid., 207.

6. Ibid., 229–30.

7. Ibid., 231–32.

8. For more details on the movement of time in Mark, see Via, *Kerygma and Comedy,* 81–82.

9. Henri Ellenberger, "A Clinical Introduction to Psychiatric Phenomenology and Existential Analysis," in *Existence: A New Dimension in Psychiatry and Psychology,* ed. R. May, E. Angel, and H. H. Ellenberger (New York: Simon & Schuster, 1958), 100, 103, 104, 105.

10. Eugene Minkowski, "Findings in a Case of Schizophrenic Depression," in *Existence,* ed. May, Angel, and Ellenberger, 132–33.

11. V. E. von Gebsattel, "The World of the Compulsive," in *Existence,* ed. May, Angel, and Ellenberger, 174, 176, 185.

PART TWO

TIME AND ETHICS:
MARK 10 IN ITS CONTEXT

5

Introduction to Mark's Ethic

This chapter will deal with three issues that are preliminary to the ethical discussion proper and to the interpretation of Mark 10 in particular.

Jesus as Teacher in the Gospel of Mark

Mark 10 begins on the note that Jesus was teaching the crowd as was his custom (10:1). Except for the miracle story in 10:46–52, which itself has theological import, the material in Mark 10 is teaching or brief narrative which occasions teaching. Paul J. Achtemeier has pointed out that neither Matthew nor Luke regards "teacher" as an adequate christological role, but it is quite otherwise with Mark. The latter identifies Jesus as a teacher, describes one of his activities often as teaching, and includes long teaching sections. In addition to Mark 10, we may note 4:1–34; 7:1–23; 9:30–50; 11:27—12:44; 13:1–37. Contrary to the scholarly impression sometimes given, one of Mark's intentions was to establish the idea that Jesus was preeminently a teacher.[1]

If we except the initial programmatic statement about Jesus' preaching of the kingdom (1:14–15) and the call of the first disciples (1:16–20), then the first specific practice of Jesus that Mark mentions is teaching (1:21–29).[2] But it is the authority of the teaching in contrast to the habitual teaching of the scribes, rather than the content, which comes to expression. It is the power of Jesus' teaching as the power to overcome demons which is the manifest content of this pericope. Mark wants to subordinate miracle-working to teaching and establish Jesus as a teacher whose power is made visible in his miraculous acts.[3]

Some aspects of the teacher image may be explicated pursuing several ideas of David L. Miller. In Mark 1:15 the time is fulfilled, as Jesus preaches the gospel of God and begins to be portrayed prominently as a teacher (1:21). The time's being full of content and the occurrence of good teaching co-implicate each other. Jesus both preached (1:14, 39) and taught (1:21; 2:13; 4:1; 10:1), which implies that in great teaching, in the fullness of time, when one is full of one's subject matter and has the appropriate words, teaching and preaching are one.[4]

Miller has provided a conceptual framework for connecting the fullness of time, Jesus as teacher and the theme of life through death (fullness through emptiness). In Mark the time is full because Jesus has appeared, and what he brings as the fullness of time is the actualization of the truth that life comes through death (8:31, 35; 10:45; 14:24). And this theme is reinforced by the teacher archetype as Miller interprets it.

In the *Symposium,* Plato recalls Alcibiades as saying that the greatness of Socrates' philosophical teaching is that he is like the mythical god Silenos. Silenos is the tutor of kings and other gods, and he is represented by fat, little statuettes that are empty in the middle; but the emptiness contains little images of other gods and goddesses. The emptiness is full of divinity, and this provides the archetypal image of the great teacher.[5]

Two things are universally said about Silenos in the classical writers: (1) He was a drunk. (2) He taught that the best thing for all men and women is not to have been born and that the next best is to die as quickly as possible. It may be, however, that the dying he spoke of was not literal but rather referred to the death of childish ego perspectives. And the drunkenness is an intoxication in which certain inhibitions and roles of the persona, the public personality, fall into oblivion. The death and drunkenness are an emptiness, an in-between, which is the necessary vessel for filling. They are a forgetting which is the necessary precondition for the remembering of truth. Forgetting is *lēthē,* and *lēthē* is the river that leads into the underworld of the soul where *a-lētheia* ("truth") is disclosed. It is a forgetting of certain perspectives of the everyday consciousness of the ego, which enables the remembering of the deep truth that has been obscured by the ego's ideas, opinions, fancies, and feelings.[6]

The teacher leads into emptiness, into the death or forgetfulness of the ego's ideas and values, so that the depth of truth (fullness) might become manifest. One need not strain to find echoes of this in Mark. Jesus eats with sinners and is known for his feasting rather than fasting (2:15–17, 18–19). He also teaches the necessity of dying (8:34–37). The archetypal idea of fullness through emptiness comes to expression in Mark in the principle that one can find life only by passing through death. Jesus teaches this principle to his disciples (8:34–37). But he does not just teach it; he enacts it for them (8:31; 9:31; 10:33–34, 45; 14:24). And this pattern of existence also takes on the specific content of an ethical demand (10:42–44).

The Markan Community

Mark 10 tells us some rather definite things about what the Christian community *ought* to be. But what do we know about the *actual* community, historically and sociologically, that Mark was writing to and/or in? And how much do we need to know? The more we know about the historical context, at least in broad terms, the better we can understand Mark's language and the phenomena, historical and conceptual, to which he refers. And it would satisfy our historical curiosity to know how much tension or distance there was between what the community was and what Mark wanted it to be. But we do not need to have precise and detailed knowledge about the historical connections and social formation of the Markan community in order to understand, so far as it can be understood, what Mark thought it should be and how he believed its members should behave. That knowledge is available in the text as a coherent *Gestalt,* a narrative world. And there is a very good question about how much we *can* know about the historical Markan community, other than what comes from the text itself.

Here I will consider two recent works that have made interesting and important observations about Mark's historical situation. According to Werner Kelber, Mark speaks for a northern, Galilean Christianity and to (and against) a southern, Jerusalem Christianity. His community is composed of both Jews and Gentiles, and a number of its specific characteristics emerge from the conflict stories in particular. These believers have a freedom grounded in the authority of the Son of man to forgive sins and dispense with Sabbath observance. On the basis of this freedom, human beings exercise the authority to forgive sins, and there is a positive, inclusive attitude toward Gentiles. Friday, the day of Jesus' crucifixion, is now the day of fasting, and the Sabbath has become unhinged.[7]

The Jerusalem Christianity that Mark opposes must have traced its origins to Jesus' relatives and considered itself to be standing in the unbroken tradition of the Twelve led by Peter. It advocated a faith so Jewish in nature that it was indistinguishable in Mark's eyes from the position of the scribes and the Pharisees, who in the conflict section (2:1—3:6) really represent the Jerusalem Christian community that Mark opposes.[8]

Kelber's presentation of the eschatological position of the Jerusalem community and therefore his presentation of Mark's own eschatological

message, which is supposed to correct it, are rooted in some real obscuri-
ties. On the one hand, the Jerusalem group seems to be without hope or
fulfillment because it tied its hope for the arrival of the kingdom to the
fall of the temple, and the temple has been destroyed without the con-
summation of the eschaton, without the coming of the kingdom.[9] On the
other hand, the Jerusalem community, or at least its leaders, so far from
being hopeless, is guilty of a prematurely realized eschatology. Mark's
theological opponents have claimed identity with Messiah Jesus and
have maintained that his eschatological parousia is being enacted in
them.[10]

One must question how a Christian community with an over-realized
eschatology could also have been devoted rigidly to a Pharisaic commitment to Sabbath, fasting, and so forth. Realized eschatology is the natural enemy of fixed traditionalism.

When it comes to Mark's own message, Kelber's view is that Mark
offered the kingdom already realized in Galilee to the failed hope of
Jerusalem.[11] But against the excessively realized eschatology of the Jerusalem group Mark maintained that the kingdom is still future and near
but is not tied to a specific event such as the fall of Jerusalem.[12]

It is not clear to me how Kelber understands the dialectic between
realized and futuristic eschatology in Mark's message, and it is less clear
what he sees to be the relationship between the hopelessness and over-
realized hope of the opponents. Perhaps Kelber's view is that from *Mark's*
standpoint the fall of Jerusalem has rendered the opponent's hope empty
and futile.[13] But as Kelber has defined the situation and as he tacitly
acknowledges, the opponents themselves would not feel that way. If the
fall of Jerusalem is past, as Kelber says,[14] and the opponents still believe
that Christ is appearing eschatologically in Christian prophets, then they
must have reinterpreted the parousia, which failed to occur with the fall
of Jerusalem, as now occurring in the prophets. Thus the opponents
would have a positive understanding of salvation and it would be as free
from a literal tie to Jerusalem as Mark's is. Therefore, in order to disengage them from their position Mark would have to penetrate the issue
more deeply than simply to affirm that the kingdom is still future, but
so far as it is realized, it is occurring in Galilee. In fact, Mark has done
far more than that, as Kelber knows.

In the view of Howard Clark Kee the disciples are the model for the
Markan community. They are summoned to abandon their families, busi-
nesses, and means of support in order to follow Jesus. This produces a
transformation in the social and economic structures so that the natural

family is replaced by a new community devoted to the will of God (3:20–35). The disciples live off of the generosity of others, but they are also to strip themselves of all possessions (10:17–22, 23–31).[15] Jesus has a position of authority for this community similar to that of the Teacher of Righteousness in the Qumran literature. But while the Teacher of Righteousness made the law more stringent than Moses, Jesus set the claims of the law aside in favor of those of the kingdom and the gospel. And while Qumran was a community carefully delineated in numbered ranks, Mark gives almost no evidence of organization.[16]

The Markan community saw its activity reflected in Jesus' travels in Gentile regions (3:8; 7:1–30). Its mission included preaching, healing, and exorcism (3:14–15; 6:13); and the refusal to take money, along with the concomitant dependence on local hospitality, reflects the practice of the itinerant Cynic-Stoic charismatic preachers. This mission produced an open community which included Gentiles and women, which cut across social, economic, sexual, and ethnic barriers.[17]

In its political stance the Markan community was similar to the later Hasidic position. It rejected force (10:42–45) and did not support the rebellion against Rome (12:13–16).[18]

According to Kee, there were four main options open to Jews under Roman domination: (1) full collaboration with the Romans (Herodians); (2) passive acquiescence while preserving ethical and cultic purity (Pharisees); (3) withdrawal from society (Essenes); and (4) insurrection (Zealots). In Kee's view, Mark did not take any of these ways. His open community would have offended both Pharisees and Essenes. He warned against the leaven of Herod (8:15), and his political stance would have enraged the Zealots.[19] Yet Kee clearly sees the Markan community to have been closer to the Hasidic-Essene apocalyptic tradition than to any of the others. Like the Jewish apocalyptic communities, Mark's church was an alienated group activated by a charismatic prophetic figure to hope for the ultimate political and social transformation of the world.[20]

It is Kee's judgment that a lack of detail about the fall of Jerusalem points to a time of writing before A.D. 70. Greek was the spoken language, but of a low cultural level; and Aramaic thought patterns were current (5:41; 14:36; 15:34). Galilee is a possible provenance, but although the author knows Galilean place names, he does not really have an accurate knowledge of the topography. These factors could well suggest Syria, but Mark's preference for villages and open spaces over cities points away from Antioch.[21]

There are a couple of problems about Kee's approach that should be noted. His programmatic position is that we cannot understand Mark except in the light of its social and historical context. The lines of meaning run from the context to the text.[22] In actual practice, however, Kee moves in the opposite direction. He deduces the nature of the community from the text. On the basis of certain miracle stories (1:23–26; 1:40–45; 1:29–31; 2:1–12), he concludes that the Markan community regarded Jesus as an eschatological agent who had come to defeat the powers of Satan. A community that believed that Jesus was successfully challenging Satan's hold on the present order must have been informed by Jewish apocalyptic views.[23] Kee has deduced the setting from the text, and the only contextual evidence that he gives is from Jewish apocalyptic—a context of ideas, not of social setting. Similarly he derives the community's view of its mission from the text's description of Jesus' mission.[24] Kelber tacitly acknowledges that he moves from text to setting,[25] and Achtemeier acknowledges it explicitly.[26]

In addition to moving from text to context, at some variance with his stated intention, there is also a problematical aspect to Kee's treatment of the text, namely, that he does not always clearly distinguish between statements about what the community was and statements about what the narrator thought it ought to be.[27] This gives the impression that he sees the community to be what the text thinks it ought to be, but that, as we shall see, may not be the case.

I turn now to John Gager's explicitly historical and sociological, or social-scientific, approach to the New Testament[28] in order to deal with two matters. Gager notes that a sociological approach to early Christianity takes what redaction criticism tells us about the beliefs, practices, and presuppositions that shaped the Gospels and understands this information as sources for re-creating the social world of the Christian community. It takes it as evidence for how early Christianity constructed and maintained its world, as evidence for the community's effort to give sacred grounding to the human social world of values, truth, reality, duties, roles, and so forth.[29] It seems to me that one can in fact do this. But even if one regards early Christianity's sense of meaning, reality, and truth as a product determined by the social order, as Gager apparently does,[30] then a study of the beliefs and meanings on which the community grounded its world is still more like a theological or religious approach to the New Testament than it is like an empirical analysis of the social formation of early Christian communities, despite Gager's effort to make a sharp distinction between a theological and a social-scientific approach.[31]

But Gager also draws conclusions about the social character of the community itself. For example, he states that, given passages such as Mark 10:25; Luke 6:20; Matt. 5:3; and James 5:1–3, there can be no mistaking a clearly formulated ethic of poverty. This in turn reflects the fact that early believers came primarily from disadvantaged groups and in return were rewarded with the promise that poverty and not wealth was the key to the kingdom.[32] One ought to say that these passages do suggest an ethic of poverty *in some sense*. But they do not necessarily reflect the sociological phenomenon that the communities involved were from disadvantaged groups. They, or some of them, may have been from advantaged groups that had been brought by the gospel to believe that they should relinquish their advantages.

Elements in a narrative that are history-like or society-like do not refer *directly* to history or to society. Rather, such elements are recontextualized by the narrative form and given a new meaning. They become a part of the narrative world, the world shaped by the informed content of the story. Therefore, even if such an element was an empirical phenomenon, it is transformed by its inclusion in the narrative. Take, for example, the teaching cited by Gager (Mark 10:25) that it is easier for a camel to go through a needle's eye than for a rich man to enter the kingdom of God. This enforces the statement in 10:23 that it is hard for the rich to enter the kingdom. But in between (10:24) Jesus remarks about the difficulty of entering without any mention of wealth. Therefore 10:24, as well as the development of the story, turns a saying about the difficulty of the rich entering the kingdom into a statement of the general impossibility of one's saving oneself, without regard to economic status. The words of the text refer first of all to the narrative world, the world of meaning shaped by the form of the story. To think that they refer directly to the real social world is to commit the referential fallacy,[33] to ignore the interposition of the (ideal) narrative world (signified) between the language of the text (signifiers) and the real world. But surely the Markan narrative does refer in some measure to the social world of the Markan community (as well as to Jesus in his own world); however, we cannot know how exactly it refers if we do not have other sources dealing with that community with which we could compare the Gospel. Since we do not have such sources, we will have to be satisfied with indirect and general knowledge of the community.

If we do not have direct, ostensive reference to phenomena in the real world, or if the passage of time has made ostensive reference irrelevant,[34] that does not mean that all significant reference has been vitiated.

Discourse has to be about something, so once a text is disengaged from a direct connection with a specific situation of origin, its reference is to an existential project. It points to a new way of being in the world for the reader, a way of being in his or her own world which is, nevertheless, shaped by the form of the narrative.[35] Mark's ethical point of view is at least in part a strand in his existential project. But to what extent are references to required modes of behavior descriptive of the community's actual social intercourse? Was the Markan community in actuality generally forgiving and inclusive of all, or is that what Mark thought it should be? Was the community composed of people who had really given up all of their wealth, even if they had almost none to begin with (12:41–44), or is that a part of the existential posture which Mark projects as the community's obligation and possibility? If Mark spoke of a community that had actually renounced all private wealth, why did he tell the story about a man who was unwilling to give up everything and then generalize about the impossibility of entering the kingdom? We learn from the Gospel more directly and clearly what the community should and might be than we do what it was.

The Place of Mark 10 in the Gospel

Mark 10 is closer to the end than to the beginning of the middle (process function) of the narrative as a whole, but it is still, broadly speaking, in the middle of the middle. And the interweaving of ameliorative (redemptive) and degrading (oppositional) processes which constitutes this function is manifest in Mark 10.

The text begins on the note of redemption: and he was teaching them as was his custom. We have seen that, for Mark, Jesus' teaching is the occurrence of power. Opposition appears as the Pharisees put Jesus to the test regarding divorce, but amelioration is seen as he beats them in debate and in the creation of a new beginning through his word. Redemption is presupposed in the bringing of the children to Jesus but is opposed in the disciples' effort to keep the children from him. Redemption reasserts itself in Jesus' taking sides with the children and in his word about the kingdom and his blessing of the children. Amelioration continues in the approach of the rich man to Jesus and in Jesus' call to him to renounce his wealth and follow, but it is opposed in the rich man's refusal. There is another recurrence of redemption in Jesus' implicit call to the disciples to forgo dependence on wealth and in his promise of divine aid. Peter's claim that the disciples have left all to follow Jesus appears to be a positive response to the redemptive possibility, but in the light of the whole narrative this claim becomes ironical. Another word of promise, however, both for this age and for the age to come follows Peter's statement. Jesus' announcement of the suffering and death that await him in Jerusalem (10:33–34) is a redemptive moment, both as promise of salvation (10:45) and as a call to follow in his way (10:42–44). The Twelve fail to get his point (10:35–41)—degradation—but blind Bartimaeus receives sight—understanding—and follows Jesus in the way (10:46–52) —redemption. The chapter, having begun on the note of Jesus' redemptive power, ends with the appropriation of that power by a disciple.

I have reviewed the surface content of Mark 10 as the manifestation of an elementary narrative structure. Now I should like to extend this synopsis, with a view to pointing out the centrality of Mark 10 by a closer look at its themes. Mark 10 presents the transition from the Galilean to the Judean ministries of Jesus, the transition from the place of revelation, where Jesus is already threatened, to the place of final attack. This transitional chapter is not simply a continuation of the discipleship theme which Mark has been pursuing throughout and to which he has given a new turn in 8:31–33 with the introduction of the suffering Son of man motif. The theme of discipleship is intensified and developed in meaning, and it, along with other significant topics treated in the chapter, points both backward and forward, illuminating the whole.

The kingdom of God, which is the presiding theological motif of the Gospel (1:14–15; 9:1; 12:34), appears in this chapter in both its realized and futuristic expressions (10:14–15, 23–24, 29–30). The conflict with the Jewish authorities, which began early (2:1—3:6; 3:22–30; 7:1–22) and led to his death (11:18; 12; 14:1–2), is present in 10:2–12 in the argument about divorce. And 10:29–30 alludes to and develops the conflict between Jesus and his family (3:19b–21, 31–35). The miracle-working theme appears in Mark 10 in the healing of blind Bartimaeus (10:46–52). The hardness of heart metaphor, which has a close relationship to Mark's ethical outlook in 10:5, is connected with the opponents (3:5), the disciples (6:52; 8:17), the parable theory (4:10–12), and the overall view of the human condition which Mark both generally presupposes and explicitly expresses (7:14–23).

The suffering Son of man Christology and the consequent discipleship of self-denial and taking the last place, which receive focal attention in Mark 8 and 9, come to expression for the third time in 10:32–34, 35–45. But discipleship receives fuller treatment here than in either Mark 8 or 9. The note that Jesus teaches the crowd, as well as the already called disciples, about the meaning of following him (8:34) is repeated (10:1, 13,

46) and given greater force by the fact that two concrete individual persons from the crowd approach him about discipleship, one of whom finds the way too hard and goes away (10:17—22) but the other of whom follows in the way (10:46–52). In addition, the interpretation of discipleship is enlarged by having the suffering motif expanded by the image of childlikeness (10:13–16).

Discipleship is deepened in meaning in that its possibility is understood as a miracle. That has been suggested by the restoration of sight to the blind man in 8:22–26, immediately preceding the first Son of man and discipleship passage; but it becomes more explicit in Mark 10. Salvation is impossible for human beings left to their own resources but is altogether possible with God (10:24–27). Mark 10:45 presents the concrete and objective salvation-historical ground for entering the kingdom: the Son of man gives his life as a ransom. Then the following story (10:46–52) identifies in other terms the objective side of salvation—Jesus' powerful healing word—and also dramatizes the occurrence of salvation in the human subject—the reception of sight.

And finally some ethical concomitants of discipleship are indicated by reference to two or three specific issues. Discipleship involves a way of dealing with the natural family (marriage and divorce, 10:2–12), with one's possessions (10:17–25), and with a new community (10:29–30).

Quentin Quesnell has suggested that the most significant difference in Mark after 8:27 is the extraordinary extent to which Jesus' universal moral teachings have been gathered into one section (8:27—10:52).[36] This may be broadly true, although I regard some of the material that Quesnell identifies as moral imperatives as faith imperatives. And I have tried to show that Mark 10, although a part of the flow of opposing processes, is a relatively self-contained unit. It is the transition between Galilee and Jerusalem, beginning with Jesus' departure (10:1) from Capernaum (9:33) and ending with his arrival near Jerusalem (10:52—11:1), beginning with the activity of Jesus' powerful teaching (10:1) and ending with the actualized effect of that power in bringing a man to follow in his way with sight, that is, understanding (10:52). And I have tried to show that Mark 10 contains a concentration of ethical and other related materials which make it a microcosm of the Gospel. It narrates an in-between time, so it is not a completed story, since more comes after it. But it is a whole story, which moves from potentiality (Jesus' teaching) through conflicts to a redemptive conclusion. There is a sense, in fact, in which Mark 10 with regard to its own content is more complete in terms of plot than is the Gospel as a whole. In Mark 10, Bartimaeus receives insight and follows

Jesus in the way of suffering. Within the plot of the whole Gospel the Twelve do not do that.

Our interpretation of Mark 10 will point to various interconnections among the themes. One cannot find a more concentrated fusion of dominant and subdominant Markan motifs elsewhere in Mark. In both formal and material terms Mark 10 may be regarded as the mid-point of the Gospel.

NOTES

1. Paul J. Achtemeier, " 'He Taught Them Many Things': Reflections on Markan Theology," *The Catholic Biblical Quarterly* 42/4 (1980): 472–76. A similar point is made by Bilezikian, *The Liberated Gospel,* 72. Best (*Following Jesus,* 15) sees the whole quite differently in affirming that Mark's view of discipleship emerges not from an understanding of Jesus' teaching but from an understanding of Jesus himself and his way. A recent work by Vernon K. Robbins assesses Mark's presentation of Jesus as teacher in the light of both Jewish and Greco-Roman religion and literature. See his *Jesus the Teacher: A Socio-Rhetorical Interpretation of Mark* (Philadelphia: Fortress Press, 1984).

2. Fernando Belo, *A Materialist Reading of the Gospel of Mark,* Eng. trans. M. O'Connell (Maryknoll, N.Y.: Orbis Books, 1981), 103.

3. Achtemeier, " 'He Taught Them Many Things,' " 478, 480–81.

4. David L. Miller, *Christs: Meditations on Archetypal Images in Christian Theology* (New York: Seabury Press, 1981), 107–9, 119.

5. Ibid., 125–26.

6. Ibid., 128–29, 146–48, 151–53.

7. Werner H. Kelber, *The Kingdom in Mark: A New Place and a New Time* (Philadelphia: Fortress Press, 1974), 21–22, 51–53, 59, 62, 64–65, 129–32.

8. Ibid., 22, 64.

9. Ibid., 1, 14, 113, 138–39.

10. Ibid., 115–16.

11. Ibid., 11–14, 45, 113, 129–32, 139.

12. Ibid., 115, 124–25, 127.

13. Ibid., 127.

14. Ibid., 1.

15. Kee, *Community of the New Age,* 87, 88–90.

16. Ibid., 88, 151–52.

17. Ibid., 89, 92, 96–97, 104–5.

18. Ibid., 93–94.

19. Ibid., 97–98, 100.

20. Ibid., 78–81, 83, 86, 93–94, 100.

21. Ibid., 101–5.

22. Ibid., 2–3.

23. Ibid., 34–38.

24. Ibid., 97.

25. Kelber, *The Kingdom in Mark,* 21–22.

26. Achtemeier, " 'He Taught them Many Things,' " 465.

27. Kee, *Community of the New Age,* 87–90, 96–97, 105.

28. John G. Gager, *Kingdom and Community: The Social World of Early Christianity* (Englewood Cliffs, N.J.: Prentice-Hall, 1975), 2, 4–5, 7, 12.

29. Ibid., 8–10.

30. Ibid., 9.

31. Ibid., 4, 5, 10.

32. Ibid., 24. Robin Scroggs points out a new consensus among sociologists of early Christianity that the movement drew from various social classes and not just from the poor. See Scroggs, "The Sociological Interpretation of the New Testament: The Present State of Research," *New Testament Studies* 26/2 (1980); 169–70.

33. On the referential fallacy, see Petersen, *Literary Criticism for New Testament Critics,* 39–40, 47. If the sociologist of the New Testament is dependent on the data produced by the historian in order to do comparative, synchronic studies (as claimed by Scroggs, "Sociological Interpretation," 167–68), then, at least when dealing with narrative texts, the sociologist shares with the historian the task of having to reconstruct the real world from the narrative world of the text. If there is no external data, this cannot be done with any exactness. If, on the other hand, the sociologist takes the sociology of knowledge approach and is content with talking about the symbolic world of early Christianity, he or she is not far from the literary critic who stresses the poetic or self-referential character of the text's language, but is quite a ways from talking about the social dynamics of the actual community.

34. See Étienne Trocmé, "Why Parables? A Study of Mark 4," *Bulletin of the John Rylands University Library of Manchester* 59/4 (1977): 468.

35. See Paul Ricoeur, *Interpretation Theory* (Fort Worth: Texas Christian Univ. Press, 1976), 34–37.

36. Quesnell, *The Mind of Mark,* 134, 138.

6

The Kingdom, Faith, and Conduct: Mark's Non-Autonomous Ethic

Six Ethical Categories

Here we turn to faith and conduct in Mark. A strictly autonomous ethic would have no place for religious faith or God in human life, would not think of human life or its ethical dimension as a gift from God or as directed by him. An autonomous ethic would be concerned to guide life in such a way that the human being as human would be fulfilled and society would be healthy.[1] Mark's ethic, too, is concerned about the fulfillment of the individual and the well-being of society, but it is dominated by an orientation to the working of God in the world, and its understanding of human being and of the community is governed by its view of God's initiative in human affairs.[2] It is proper to say that Mark has an ethic, because central ethical categories come to manifest expression in the Gospel, although they are obviously not formally announced as such.[3] Ethical *norms,* statements about *what* the disciple *ought* to do or be, are articulated both as principles (love the neighbor, 12:31; be last of all and servant of all, 9:35; 10:43–44) *and* rules (no divorce, 10:2–12; renunciation of property for the poor, 10:17–22).[4] *Intentions* are statements about why something ought to be done, statements of the purpose or effect for the sake of which it should be done. They are forward-looking reasons for acting (to secure life, 9:43–48, or forgiveness, 11:25). *Motives* are backward-looking reasons for acting (on the ground that the other belongs to Christ, 9:41).[5] Mark is also concerned about *how* a norm can be carried out, which I refer to as the category of *enablement* (God's eschatological activity)—a statement about what makes a proposed action or disposition possible. Ethical actions are carried out in certain *circumstances* (under the pressure of persecution, 13:9–13) and with *consequences* (eschatological reward, 9:41; new community, 10:29–30).[6] It should be said that intentions, motives, consequences, and enablement are not categories with firm boundaries. They may coalesce with one another, and they do in Mark. Thus my analysis tends to suggest that the distinctions are finer than they really are.[7]

Consequences: Pertaining to God,
the Other, and the Subject

The consequences of unethical acts in Mark as they pertain to God, the ethical agent or subject, and the ethical other or object, now need our attention. The disciple of Jesus is one who does the will of God (3:35), and God's will so far as it pertains to the disciple's relationships with other people is that one love the neighbor/other as oneself (12:31). One who loves the neighbor as oneself and God with one's whole being (12:28) is not far from the kingdom of God (in this case a scribe, 12:34), which is Mark's encompassing theological motif (1:14–15). Since God wills love for the neighbor, loveless acts or dispositions are an offense against God. They violate his right as king to obedience. That unethical acts offend God himself is only an implicit consequence in Mark. What is explicit is God's reaction against this rejection of his revelation of the way to life (8:34–38). Judgment, then, is the connecting link between two consequences of lovelessness: it offends God and it causes the ruination of the ethical agent (9:43–48). Judgment is the manifestation of the divine governance of the world in the loss of self which devolves upon one who acts against love. Lovelessness, however, is also an offense against the neighbor/other. This particular consequence rarely comes to expression in Mark, but it does in the divorce section. A man who divorces his wife and marries another commits adultery *against her* (his wife, 10:11). Here the preposition *epi* with the accusative can mean "against" with hostile intent.[8] Beyond that, immoral acts or thoughts are also an offense against the person who commits them. The ethical subject is defiled by the evil thoughts and actions that stem from his or her own heart (7:14, 20–23). Thus the act against the will of God has three consequences, against three different but closely related objects. The violation of love is simultaneously and inescapably an offense against God, the other, and oneself. But Mark's ethic does not give the same kind of attention to these three foci of the ethical situation.

Intentions and Motives

These three consequences of lovelessness may *imply* three corresponding intentions for action in love: to honor God, to secure the well-being of the other, and to obtain salvation for the agent. How does it actually work out in Mark? It is everywhere assumed or stated that one ought to obey God. God figures prominently in the expression of norms, but never does honoring God become a specific intention in itself for obedience, as in Matt. 5:16—the light is to shine before people in order that they may see your good works and glorify your Father in heaven. However, *motives* that invoke *Jesus* do come to expression in Mark. In Mark 9:41 one who gives a disciple a cup of water *because* the disciple belongs to Christ (motive)[9] will not lose one's reward (consequence). In 9:37 if "in my name" (*epi tō onomati*) modifies child, it defines the object of the act as a believer or a representative of Jesus. But if it modifies the verb, "receives," it expresses the motive of the ethical agent: the agent acts in Jesus' name, because Jesus wills it. The meaning could be either of these,[10] and, as we shall see, it is probably both. It is frequently and emphatically stated in Mark that the other ought to be loved or served: the other is mentioned in the statement of norms (9:37; 10:44; 12:31). But rarely does the other figure in a statement of consequence (the other does in 10:11 and possibly 9:42), and never does the well-being of the other become a specific intention of love. It may be implicitly suggested as an intention in 2:27–28. If the Sabbath is for humankind, then the Son of man must exercise lordship over it for the sake of humankind. And if disciples are to follow in the way of the Son of man, then they too should be intentioned by the desire to contribute to the well-being of others. This is also supported by 3:1–6, where Jesus' action is for the purpose of improving the quality of a person's physical existence.

In relation to the ethical subject both consequences and intentions come to expression. The loss of salvation is a consequence of lack of love (Mark 9:42–48; 10:21–26), and lack of faith (3:28–30; 8:35a, 36–37; 8:38). Or, alternatively, salvation is the reward for serving love (9:37, 41). What about intentions? Perhaps the most explicit statement is 11:25: the subject is to forgive *in order that* the Father in heaven might forgive the subject. But let us look also at two other passages. It appears that the consequence of the rich man's walking away from the command to give up his wealth is that he will not enter the kingdom (10: 21–26). But it was his intention to inherit eternal life—what must I do? (10:17)—that prompted his approach to Jesus in the first place. Jesus does not rebuke him for that but rather loves him. In 9:42–48 the loss of oneself in hell is clearly a consequence of taking the wrong ethical direction. But the threefold reminder that it is *better* to enter life maimed than to be thrown into hell with all of one's members surely means that gaining the better thing is an intention, a reason for acting. The subject acts ethically with the intention of securing his or her own salvation.

Overall we might say that Mark is quite concerned about what the disciple ought to do and be and how the disciple is enabled to. With regard to consequences and intentions the Gospel is expressly interested in the subject of ethical action, but is less explicitly interested than we might have wished in intentions toward and consequences for the other.

God: The Enabler of Faith and Action

It is now appropriate to pay closer attention to the place of God and of the ethical subject, beginning with God. In the discussion of marriage and divorce we will note the importance of God's eschatological saving act as the enablement for ethical action. I will treat this theme by analyzing the interrelationships among faith, ethical obedience, and the kingdom of God. There are clear indications that Mark understands faith as an attitude or posture toward God and/or Jesus which is distinguishable from ethical dispositions and acts—the posture toward one's fellow human beings. There are specific references to faith in such passages as 2:5; 4:40; 5:34; 9:23; 10:52; 11:23–24. This is faith as a sense of Jesus' power to work miracles. But faith in Mark is also "in the gospel" (1:15), and what this means can be grasped by looking at what for Mark is the heart of the gospel: the death and resurrection of the Son of man (Mark 8—10).[11] In Mark 8:34–37 the disciple is given a lesson:

> If any man would come after me, let him deny himself and take up his cross and follow me. For whoever would save his life will lose it; and whoever loses his life for my sake and the gospel's will save it.

This is what it means to follow Jesus. It has to do with how existence is grounded, not with how one is to behave. And the discipleship teaching in 8:34–37 lacks definite ethical content. Following Jesus here is a stance whose description lacks the express ethical tendency of the teaching on discipleship in the two following chapters. In the latter the disciple is to be a servant of all (9:35), is to receive children (9:37), is not to cause believers to stumble (9:42–50). In 10:42–44 the disciple is to serve and not "lord it over" others. The discipleship teaching in Mark 9 and 10 draws out the ethical implications of the existential (faith) posture defined in Mark 8. The distinctiveness of faith is also seen in the two different ways in which Mark understands sin. On the one hand, sin (*skandalizō*) is moral fault—causing injury to a fellow believer (9:42–48). On the other hand, it is represented as blindness or failure to understand or to see the real meaning of Jesus' presence (3:28–30; 6:52; 8:17). And salvation is the gaining of the missing insight (8:22–26; 10:46–52). This insight enables one to make the correct christological confession, as the Roman centurion does (15:39). As we shall see in the subsequent exegesis, becoming like a child (10:13–16) is a category that stands on the boundary line between faith and ethics.

Since the Gospel does mark the distinction between faith and ethics, one does not overinterpret 10:17–27 by distinguishing there a faith disposition (freedom from oneself or from self-interest) from the act of abandoning, or not abandoning, one's wealth. While this text does presuppose that distinction, it also discloses the organic inseparability of the two factors. Language about salvation and language about ethical action are intertwined: having wealth prevents entering the kingdom (10:23); giving to the poor confers treasure in heaven (10:21). But however closely they are connected, their non-identity is clear in the Gospel. Mark makes paying homage to Jesus per se a claim which takes precedence over helping the poor. Or, closer to Mark's own dramatic terms: without diminishing the continuing obligation to do good to the poor there is a point at which it is more important to anoint Jesus' body for burial (14:6–8).

In the context of Mark 10:26–27 it is the interweaving of faith and ethical action that God's saving initiative enables. The latter generates both faith and conduct. But Mark is not so systematic as to say that the kingdom's action in Jesus enables faith, and faith in turn generates right character and behavior. Yet the logic of Mark's thought requires such an articulation as we shall see.

God: The Source of the Ethical Norm
(Love to the Neighbor)

Not only is God the enabler of the required conduct, God is also the source of the norms. The fundamental principle—love to the neighbor—has been given by God in Scripture (Mark 12:28–34). The Markan version of the double commandment, to love God with one's whole being and the neighbor as oneself, is the longest; and in comparison with Matthew and Luke, Mark extends the topic in two ways. (1) Only in Mark does Jesus cite the Shema (Deut. 6:4) with its reference to the oneness of God. (2) Only in Mark does the scribe who questions Jesus affirm his answer, thus repeating the theme of God's oneness.[12] The scribe asked Jesus about one commandment—which is the first of all—but Jesus mentioned two, saying in effect that no one commandment could be marked as first, but these two together comprise the essence of human responsibility. The second is not second in importance.[13] The fact that Jesus gives a double answer, including both faith and ethics, to a single question reveals the non-autonomy of ethics for Mark. It also reveals the inconceivability of a non-ethical faith. The responsibility of the disciple cannot be stated exclusively in either religious or ethical terms. The two belong together.

Love to the neighbor for Mark has a programmatic and encompassing significance because it is an inseparable part of the *first* commandment. Yet its content is not expounded upon in this pericope but must be discerned from the totality of Mark's view of ethical obligation, and from the model of Jesus. Because of the global significance of love, all other rules and principles may be regarded as expressions of it and all forbidden and immoral acts and attitudes, as violations of it.[14] In addition, the scope of neighborhood has to be defined from the larger context of the Gospel. Jesus' contact with children (9:35-42), his contact with people from Gentile areas (3:7-12; 5:1—20), and his healing of the Syro-Phoenician woman's daughter (7:24-30) show that the scope of neighborhood includes people both inside and outside the Christian community.

Victor P. Furnish has stated that Mark's teaching focuses neither on the meaning of love nor on the neighbor nor on the relation between love for God and love for neighbor. Rather, the interest is in the necessary connection between belief in the *one* God (*contra* polytheism) and obedience to the moral (as contrasted with cultic) law.[15] But it seems to me that Mark's stress on the oneness of God (absent from Matthew and Luke in this pericope) probably does bear on the relationship between love for God and love for the neighbor. Only if one is devoted to the one personal Power who is sovereign over all of reality can one love the neighbor as required. Money (11:15-16), political power (12:13—17), and the dead past (12:24—27) are potential gods which can claim the loyalty and restrict the freedom of the disciple. Only if the disciple loves with the whole being the one God over all, who can subordinate such powers and their claims, can the disciple be enabled to have the freedom to love without reserve.[16] From the other side, only a love for the neighbor without reservation can fittingly correspond to the reality of a God whose sovereignty is unlimited.

Is there a rationalistic strain in Mark's pericope on the twin commandments?[17] It is true that Mark uses more words for understanding in this passage than do Matthew and Luke. But all three Gospels have *dianoia*. Marks adds *synesis* and *nounechōs* ("wisely"), the latter to describe the answer of the scribe. Mark in fact redefines *dianoia* (12:30) as *synesis* (12:33), and he connects *synesis* with the heart (*kardia*), both in this passage and in 8:17. Thus, clearly for Mark love involves the whole self even if the stress is on the understanding.

Several related topics will aid us in understanding what Mark means by love for the neighbor. *Prayer* is related to ethics in that it is understood as a channel of power (9:29; 11:23-24). It is the means by which faith appropriates the power of God to change things in the world.[18] Mark's contextualizing suggests that one of the things which prayer enables is the forgiveness of the neighbor who has offended (11:25). This surely has reference to personal forgiveness extended by one individual to another (11:25). But it may also be that Mark understood the community as the instrument of God's eschatological forgiveness (2:5)[19]

To love the neighbor is to be last of all and servant of all, and Mark makes that stance concrete in the command to receive a child (9:35–42). This passage is an illuminating example of tensive language. There is tension between meanings of the child image, a literal child (9:36) and child as a symbol for the believer (9:42),[20] a tension that is enhanced by three parallel sentences in the passage. Each of these sentences contains four elements that are parallel to corresponding elements in the other sentences: (1) a subject (the ethical agent) which is expressed by an indefinite relative pronoun; (2) a verb of ethical action in the aorist subjunctive; (3) the naming of the recipient of the action (ethical other); and (4) a statement of the consequence for the agent.

> (1) whoever (2) receives in my name (3) one such child (in my name) (4) receives me . . . and . . . him who sent me (9:37).

> (1) whoever (2) gives a cup of cold water to drink because you are Christ's (3) to you (4) will not lose his reward (9:41).

> (1) whoever (2) causes to stumble (3) one of these little ones who believe in me (4) it would be better if a great millstone were hung around his neck and he were thrown into the sea (9:42).

In the two latter sentences the object or recipient of the action is a Christian—is Christ's (9:41) or is a believer (9:42). Thus the object in 9:37, the child, on the basis of the parallelism should also be considered a Christian. That is, "in my name" should be taken as modifying "one such child." But because 9:36–37 follows 9:35 the child should not be interpreted as a Christian, and "in my name" should be taken as qualifying the action of the agent. The agent is, then, seen as a Christian, as one motivated by the name of Jesus. The second interpretation is suggested by the fact that if a disciple is to be last of all and servant of all (9:35), this principle is better supported if the child to be received is a nonbeliever rather than a believer. We have seen that for Mark the scope of neighborhood extends beyond the Christian community. The tensiveness is created by the context which makes the child of 9:36–37 both a nonbeliever and a believer, which concretely universalizes the sphere of the disciple's service. It must be acknowledged, however, that in strictly poetic terms, given the strength of the parallelism in 9:37, 41, 42, the child is drawn more strongly toward being represented as a Christian than toward being represented as a nonbeliever. Yet on the basis of the parallelism between "in (*epi*) my name" in 9:37 and "in (*en*) your (Jesus') name" in 9:38, "in my name" in 9:37 should be taken as modifying the verb "receives," so the object of the action would not be a Christian.

When Mark says that to receive the child is to receive Christ and God (9:37), he is affirming that the resurrected Christ is somehow encountered in the act of serving love.[21] This is the principle that is expanded into an apocalyptic ethical parable in Matt. 25:31–46: as you did it to one of the least of my brothers you did it to me.[22] But Mark has probably brought this theme more explicitly within the sphere of salvation history than has Matthew. The ethical subject in Matthew's story, one of the sheep, does not know until the eschatological judgment that he is to inherit the kingdom and is surprised to learn that he has cared for the Son of man. In fact, he resists the idea. This means that he did not have intentions generated by a desire for his own salvation, nor was he motivated by faithfulness to Jesus when he showed love for the poor and helpless. The reader of the Gospel of Matthew will not be able to be so innocent, of course. The left hand will, to some extent, know what the right hand is doing (Matt. 6:3). Not only the reader of Mark but also the subject in the ethical sayings in 9:37, 41 is more calculating than the Matthean counterpart. It is the one who gives a cup of water *because* the recipient belongs to Christ who is assured that he or she receives Christ and will not lose his or her reward. By itself Matt. 25:31–46 might be taken as suggesting that serving love to the other is a general human (ontological) possibility which is also always actually realizable apart from the promptings of salvation history.[23] But the Gospel of Matthew makes this possibility of love a possibility in principle, which is actually realizable only as a result of the eschatological intervention of God.[24] Mark has made the point, not just throughout the Gospel but also specifically in 9:35–42, that serving love occurs as a knowing response to Christ (and God), who meets the disciple in the child who needs a cup of water. Actually, the ethical agent in 9:41, in view of 9:38–40, seems to be an outsider of some kind who is, nevertheless, favorably disposed toward Jesus and the church.

Consequences for the Subject:
Cultic and Moral Purity

The ethical agent or subject can gain or lose his or her eschatological reward, depending on the quality of his or her ethical life (Mark 9:41, 42).

The loss of the self in hell would be the last stage in the progressive deformation of character (being) by wrong conduct (9:43–48). We saw in chapter 1 that while Mark regards character as finally having more power than conduct (*you* can change your actions, you can cut off a hand or a foot), he also assumes that conduct molds character (your hand or eye can cause *you* to sin).[25] Of course, for Mark the whole dialectical process is undergirded by the eschatological grace of God implicit in 9:37 and explicit in 10:27.

This distortion of the character/self by conduct which we have just reviewed (your hand causes *you* to sin) Mark can also speak of in terms of defilement. The person is defiled by the evil (thoughts, murder, adultery, covetousness, deceit, etc.) which proceeds from the heart (7:20–23). Defiling is a cultic term. Mark has emphatically opposed faith and moral obedience to cultic obedience (2:15–17, 18–20; 3:1–6; 7:5–19; 12:28–34). Paul, according to Ernst Käsemann,[26] replaces the distinction between clean and unclean with one between following and not following conscience. Mark does not develop the latter point but replaces the distinction between cultic cleanness and uncleanness with one between a heart from which comes moral evil (7:21–23) and a heart from which comes love (12:28–34), while maintaining that immoral acts and dispositions have the same consequence that cult violations were traditionally thought to have: they defile (7:20, 23). If that is the case, then we should take a good look at the concept of cultic defilement.

Mark 7 uses both the adjective *koinos* ("defiled" or "unclean") (7:2, 5) and the verb *koinoō* ("defile") (7:15, 18, 20, 23). In Judaism, *koinos* could mean common, as held in common; profane or given to general use as opposed to holy; and ritually or cultically unclean.[27] In the sense of cultically unclean, *koinos* was virtually synonymous with *akathartos* ("impure," "unclean").[28] The cultically unclean was felt to be positively indwelt by an autonomous defiling power,[29] and a person was made unclean by contact with such as certain animals and foods, corpses, pagan rites, and sexual processes. According to Jacob Neusner, in the Old Testament Priestly code purity or cleanness was primarily a cultic matter. All sources of impurity had the one practical result that one could not enter the temple, and all rites of purity aimed at the goal of permitting participation in the cult. But food and other purity laws in places in Scripture outside the Priestly code, especially in Deuteronomy, cannot be supposed to be intended only for priests or people about to make sacrifice. In later times some food taboos were observed by people who had no expectation of entering the temple and who were not Pharisees or Essenes. Therefore,

in Judaism as a whole, cleanness was not just a cultic matter.[30] Yet
Neusner seems to suggest that the Pharisees prior to A.D. 70 turned
ordinary meals into a rite. Their dominant trait was a concern for certain
matters of rite, in particular the rite of eating one's meals in a state of
ritual purity as if one were a temple priest. The Pharisees, like the
Essenes, believed that one must keep purity laws outside the temple,
while other Jews, following the plain sense of Leviticus, supposed that the
purity laws were to be kept only in the temple. For the Pharisees, outside
the temple, in one's own home, a person had to follow the laws of purity
in the only circumstances in which they might apply, at the table. One
must eat the ordinary secular meals in a state of purity as if one were a
priest.[31]

In the New Testament as in Judaism, *koinos* can mean held in common
(Acts 2:44; Titus 1:4), profane (Heb. 10:29) and cultically unclean, which
is the meaning that it has in Mark 7. This chapter also displays the
connection between the terms *koinos* and *akathartos*. With the verb
katharizō (7:19), Mark states that Jesus cleansed the foods which the
Jewish food laws regarded as *koinos*. The verb *koinoō* in Mark 7 also
employs the third meaning of the root: to defile, to make or declare
unclean. But, as we have seen, Mark 7:15, 18, 20, 23 deny that physical
objects, such as food eaten with unclean hands, can defile a person as the
Pharisees claim (7:2, 5). Defilement from whatever source has two closely
related aspects. It is a negative condition of the *person* which injures his
or her relationship with *God*.[32] The woman with the hemorrhage (Mark
5:24–34) was considered unclean (Lev. 15:25–30), which brought about
a rupture in her relationship with God, the cult, the community, and
herself.[33] If immoral acts and attitudes produce the same condition or
consequence that cultic violations were once thought to produce, we may
gain some insight into this condition, and into the relationship between
the cultic and the moral, by pursuing the nature of cultic uncleanness.

What is the unclean in uncleanness? What constitutes the uncleanness
of the unclean object, bodily process or physical act? Friedrich Hauck[34]
suggests that association with a foreign deity or cult produced uncleanness, according to the Israelite understanding. The pig, for example, an
emphatically forbidden animal, was an ancient Canaanite, Babylonian,
and Syrian sacred animal. But foreignness or association with a pagan
god would not explain why, for example, leprosy (Lev. 13:44–46), men-
struation (Lev. 15:19), seminal emissions (Lev. 15:16), sexual intercourse
(Lev. 15:18), and childbearing (Lev. 12:1–5) made a person unclean in the
Old Testament. And while certain foreign elements *were* regarded as

unclean in Israel, others were assimilated (Hos. 2:5–9).[35] There must have
been some criterion for selection, some principle that constituted uncleanness.

Neusner declares that purity and impurity in Judaism were not hygien-
ic categories and did not refer to observable cleanliness or dirtiness.
Impurity refers to a status derived from contact with a source of impurity
and purity to a status which results from acts of purification.[36] Neusner
recognizes that at the level of popular religion, people believed in unclean
spirits and probably thought that uncleanness was a material force and
that the purification rites drove off the demon of impurity or its effects.
But Neusner is skeptical about theories, ancient or modern, that try to
explain uncleanness in physical, demonic, social, or cultic terms. He
argues that purity was not a cultic metaphor alone but was a term for
a basic, probably unanalyzable, religious experience. The sources, like the
Scriptures, are reticent about the "reality" perceived to inhere in uncleanness. We do not know what conceptions lay *behind* the idea of
impurity.[37]

I am quite prepared to agree that the experience of uncleanness or of
purification transcends reflective analysis. But at the same time I think
it possible to find at least a clue, or clues, to the meaning of the experience, some sense of wherein and why certain things are felt to be unclean.
E. R. Dodds's comments about the experience of uncleanness in ancient
Greece are useful for understanding the phenomenon as such. His approach is psychological. In archaic Greece, uncleanness was understood
as being contracted from infectious objects or inherited from the offense
of an ancestor. It comes as the automatic consequence of an action and
thus belongs to the world of external events and objects. It is indifferent
to motive or intention. In Dodds's view, ritual uncleanness served the
ancients as an explanation of guilt feelings generated by repressed desires. An archaic Greek who suffered such feelings was able to give them
concrete form by telling himself that he must have been in contact with
a source of impurity or had inherited the burden from the offense of an
ancestor.[38]

It seems to me probable that the sense of being cultically unclean is
in part the result of projecting the evil of repressed desires onto the
external world. But this explanation of uncleanness as deriving from
unconscious projection needs to be modified and supplemented by the
recognition that cultic prohibitions and commands are also the manifestation of conscious values; otherwise, why is guilt projected as uncleanness onto some phenomena and not onto others? At the same time I

would think it unlikely that a culture would be very consciously aware
of any precise relationship between its communal values and the details
of its cultic requirements. And I will argue that for Mark at least the
cultic system gives to certain phenomena an objective reality and power
which they do not really have.

According to Mary Douglas, we must forget hygiene, aesthetics, morals, and instinctive revulsion in trying to understand the Israelite view
of cleanness and uncleanness. Neither are the purity rules to be taken as
arbitrary means of discipline whose content has no significance nor as
allegories of vices and virtues. The intention of the rules is to give the
prescriptions for actualizing in human affairs the holiness of God.[39] Douglas points out that the root meaning of holiness in the Old Testament is
separation but that the connotations of wholeness and completion also
emerged early. Purity requires that this wholeness and completeness be
achieved in the cultic, social, and physical spheres. The human body, for
example, is seen as a perfect container.[40] That would explain why sexual
emissions (Lev. 15:16–30) and other bodily discharges (Lev. 15:1–12)
make a person unclean. They are a breach in the body as a perfect
container. It is also required by holiness that individuals conform to the
class to which they belong.[41] Blemishes or deformations are unclean.
Therefore a priest who was blind or lame or a dwarf or a hunchback would
profane the sanctuary (Lev. 21:16–24). Unclean animals are apparently
those that do not conform perfectly to their class. Sea creatures that do
not have fins and scales are unclean (Lev. 11:9–12). They are somehow
like fish (living in the water), but they lack defining characteristics. A
further extension of this principle is that classes and the categories of
creation are to be kept distinct and not confused. This requires correct
definition, discrimination, and order.[42] Cattle are not to be bred to a
different kind; fields are not to be sown with different kinds of seed;
garments made of two kinds of stuff are not to be worn (Lev. 19:19).
Human beings are not to have sexual relations with animals (Lev. 18:23–
24).

The analysis of this concern for order and the preservation of clear,
unconfounded forms and classes has been carried further by Fernando
Belo. Things cannot be mixed if they are not compatible or alike. Nor can
they be mixed if they are not different. It would seem, then, that the
principle of order, the principle that governs proper relationships, is that
elements related should manifest the right balance of likeness and dis-
similarity. This can be illustrated with sexual relationships. Relations
with animals are condemned (Lev. 18:23) because the two partners are

too different. At the other end of the spectrum, homosexual relations are condemned (Lev. 18:22; 20:13) because the two partners are too much alike (same sex), and incest is condemned for the same reason (same flesh or family). On the other hand, exogamous marriage is affirmed. The partners are sufficiently alike (more alike than a human being and an animal) and sufficiently different (more different than two members of the same sex or the same family).[43]

According to Douglas, of course, we ought to forget morals in trying to understand cultic cleanness and uncleanness, but her own discussion shows that there is a connection. She observes that moral goodness, as well as cultic purity, may illustrate holiness and form part of it,[44] as, for example, Isa. 1:4 and 5:16 make abundantly clear. More to the point, she observes that in Leviticus 19, which specifically calls on Israel to reflect the holiness of God (Lev. 19:2), we find both cultic and moral commands. We have already noted the prohibition against mixing different kinds (Lev. 19:19). But there are also prohibitions against such as stealing, lying (Lev. 19:11–12), hating your brother in your heart (Lev. 19:17), and cheating in the marketplace (Lev. 19:35–36). These acts involve a contradiction between what seems and what is. Thus she has shown that in Leviticus both cultic and moral rules have the purpose of establishing wholeness, unity, order, and integrity. Uncleanness is the confusion, confounding, disordering, and fragmenting of reality, while the purpose of purity rules and rituals is to reestablish order and wholeness.[45]

In sum, the unclean in uncleanness is disorder, confusion, the mixing of what cannot be mixed—a lack of wholeness, unity, and integrity which contradicts what makes God God (his holiness) and thereby makes one estranged from God. If the experience of uncleanness is in part derived from within, from the unconscious projection of repressed guilt onto the external world, then we can understand why this sense of disorder and estrangement achieved such an inescapable hold on people as to be attributed to an objective, demonic force. It is this disorder-confusion-fragmentation which, according to Mark, is the defilement visited upon human beings by the *moral* evil that comes from the heart (Mark 7:20–23).

The prophetic spirit has historically opposed ritual, if we may take Amos as a fair representative (Amos 5:21–24):

> I hate, I despise your feasts,
> and I take no delight in your
> solemn assemblies.
> Even though you offer me your

> burnt offerings and cereal
>   offerings,
> I will not accept them,
> and the peace offerings of your fatted
>   beasts
> I will not look upon.
> . . . .
> But let justice roll down like waters,
>   and righteousness like an ever-flowing
>   stream.

It should be observed that the burnt and cereal offerings mentioned here were part of the means for effecting purification from cultic uncleanness (Lev. 12:6; 14:10, 13, 21). But for Amos this is not the kind of purity that the holiness of God demands (Amos 4:1-2). Rather, it requires moral purity—justice and righteousness. Mark similarly rejects the whole cultic system and denies that certain material phenomena, as defined by tradition, have any defiling effect at all on the personal inner core of a human being or disturb the person's relationship with God. This also implies that rites of purification are useless. But if cultic purity and moral righteousness both have the same purpose in Israel—to create order conformable to God's holiness—why does Mark oppose the former and affirm the latter?

What Mark, and the prophetic spirit generally, objects to in the cultic system of purity is the belief that certain physical acts and phenomena *always* in themselves effect order and others always violate it. As Douglas has pointed out, for the cultic purity ethos there is no question of intention or of balancing duties and rights. The only question, unequivocally, is whether the forbidden contact has taken place.[46] Mark would find this approach unacceptable in principle even if an act of cultic purification genuinely expressed an inward intention. That is, the prophetic spirit would disagree that the rite automatically has within itself the power to effect the intention or that certain other acts and objects have within themselves the power to defile. The same kind of outlook is what inclines the prophetic spirit also to oppose ethical legalism. The latter says that certain moral acts always express the right and that certain others cannot. Neither codified ritual nor codified moral obligation allows the principle of order to be manifested in unanticipated ways.

Douglas is critical of the kind of religious outlook that rejects all ritual, liturgy, forms, and rules. On the one hand, ritual forms need not be empty. On the other hand, the nature of human beings is such that inward states require cultic practices and rules; they need external forms as the condition of their existence. Moreover, human beings are social animals who cannot have social relationships without symbolic acts. Ritual provides an ordering of time and space, including what is valuable and excluding the intrusive. Ritual suppressed in one place crops up in another.[47]

Has Mark taken the prophetic spirit to the point of denying the validity of all cultic forms and moral rules? That *only moral* fault defiles (7:18–23) means for Mark that only lovelessness, only the corruption of the heart in its various manifestations, produces the disorder, incompleteness, and imbalance in the individual and in society which were formerly thought to inhere also in cultic uncleanness. What emerges from Mark is that order and disorder are not objectively identified with particular acts—cultic or moral. Mark denies that certain physical acts, such as eating with unwashed hands, always produce chaos (7:15). In fact, they never do. Nor is it that certain moral acts, such as keeping the Decalogue (10:20–21), always produce order. Rather, the implication is that *whatever* engenders the order of humanity which the kingdom of God intends is good: such dispositions and acts as create the order modeled on Jesus' story are what loving the neighbor is.

Yet Mark is aware of the need for external order both in the cult and in ethical life. He narrates the institution of the Lord's Supper (14:22–25) which connects the meal with the saving intention of the Son of man (10:45) and with the establishment of covenant. And he affirms the validity of the Decalogue (7:10; 10:19). But given what we have seen of Mark's position, he could not have thought that the *elements* of the meal *made* the covenant a reality, although he may well have believed that the *enactment* of the meal *might* actualize it. And the Decalogue does not state definitively the content of the disciple's moral responsibility to God. Still Mark does not abandon his affirmation of the Decalogue,[48] although the narrative gives its role a distinct interpretation. And, of course, the double love commandment comes from the Old Testament as well.

Now we need to follow a certain chain of motifs in the Gospel. In Mark 7:9–13 Jesus notes that the tradition allows a person to declare something *Corban* (dedicated to God and so withdrawn from ordinary use) that might have been used to help the person's parents. This dedication to God might have been made intentionally or unintentionally as an oath uttered in a moment of emotion.[49] The import of Mark's treatment of this issue is that the cultic obedience required by the *Corban* declaration is to be subordinated to the word of God in the moral command to honor one's father and mother. It should be observed that the rabbis were on the side of Jesus and Mark on this matter.[50] The command to honor one's parents is then repeated in 10:19 along with other members of the Decalogue, which are cited as requisite for inheriting eternal life.

But obedience to the Decalogue is not enough, for the requirements of the Decalogue are relativized by the command to follow Jesus by giving up everything for the poor (10:21–22). (This same point is made in another way when Mark sets the will of God against the Scripture that allows divorce (10:4–9).) Then the command to give to the poor is relativized by the call to pay homage to Jesus' death (14:6–9). As we have seen and will see again, in Mark it is difficult for the disciples to grasp what the death and resurrection of the Son of man entails *for them* (Mark 8—10). The pursuit of the question of the ethical content of the disciple's responsibility has brought us full circle to the theme of revelation, faith, and salvation. And if we pursue the relationship of salvation to ethical obedience, we note again that human obedience cannot gain salvation, because only God can give the obedience that salvation requires: the freedom from self-interest (10:27) which would rid the human heart of evil thoughts, murder, adultery, deceit, and so forth, which defile (7:21—23), that is, which disorder the self in the human world.

Faith and Obedience:
Grace and Legalism

With human beings, salvation is impossible: they cannot do what is required to gain it (Mark 10:27a). But all things are possible with God (10:27b): *panta gar dynata para tō theō.* Notice the close parallelism with 9:23: *panta dynata tō pisteuonti,* all things are possible to the believer. Everything may be impossible for human beings as such, but all of the possibilities that belong with God may be effective in the believer. The parallelism connects 9:23 and 10:17–27. Faith (believing) is, in the light of the latter passage, the freedom from self-interest which is eternal life and which enables radical obedience from the heart and the giving up of all security for the other—the poor. Ethics grows out of faith. One needs the freedom from self given by God in order to act for the other. Faith is the possibility of ethical achievement.

We can use some categories of Jacques Derrida to express the difference between Mark's ethic and a legalistic one. A legalistic theological ethic will say that certain rules express what is unexceptionably the will of God: God's will is *present* in the *rule* without qualification. But if God's will can be set against specific scriptural laws, and if the eschatological situation relativizes ethical rules, then God's will is not present in the rule in an unqualified way. Rather, the rule is a *trace* of God's will. A trace is not the thing itself, but it is marked by it. The meaning of a trace (ethical rule) is not fully present in it but is *deferred* beyond. And I suggest that in Mark both the Old Testament laws and Mark's own rules, as on divorce, should be seen as traces. However, for Mark the ethical rule is not a trace in Derrida's sense. In the Gospel there *is* such a thing as the will of God (3:35), and God has brought it to expression as the principle of love (12:28–31). The commandments, then, are traces with an origin—the will of God, not traces of traces that have no origin, as is the case with Derrida.[51] Within this frame of reference, it may be suggested, Mark would also have approved of cultic forms—rites of purification. If uncleanness is seen as a trace of the human tendency to disorder, and if cleansing rites are understood as traces, not the effective presence, of the divine intention to restore order, Mark would have no reason to reject these categories.

Finally, we have seen that Mark does not have a legalistic ethic, an ethic of unexceptionable rules that can define in advance what must always be will of God. But Mark does have a subtle tendency to theological legalism or salvation by works, salvation by performance, even if what must be performed is faith itself and acts of love from the heart, derived from faith. Human beings cannot do what God requires for salvation. God enables their faith and action, so that living in love is grounded on grace. But in the end, people are saved or not saved by what they do (8:38; 9:37, 41, 42–48; 10:21–26; 11:25), even though God enables it.

This slight tendency to *theological* legalism is countered in Mark in three ways. First is his break with *ethical* legalism, his seeing ethical rules and acts as *traces* of the will of God. Even though there are explicit statements that ethical acts earn a reward (Mark 9:41; 11:25), if the will of God always transcends specific rules and acts, it could not be calculated whether in fact one had done enough good to earn one's reward or enough evil to lose it. Second, the faith and ethical life which God's salvation enables are not just conditions for entering eternal life or the kingdom but already are a relationship with God and entrance into his kingdom (9:37; 10:15). This is logically, but not theologically, akin to the Aristotelian view that the well-being which is the goal of virtue is already resident in virtue. The end is present already in the means. So in Mark the presence of God which is the goal of faith and love is already there in the act of love. Third, alongside the theme of grace as enablement is the affirmation that salvation is by the forgiveness of God. The cross of

Jesus does something for people that they cannot do for themselves (10:45; 14:24), and one of the things that Jesus does is to bring forgiveness (2:1–5). But neither the legalistic strain nor the forgiveness theme is as sharp in Mark as it is in Matthew,[52] so that the tension does not stand out so clearly.

NOTES

1. See Hauerwas, *A Community of Character,* 130; J. L. Houlden, *Ethics and the New Testament* (Harmondsworth: Penguin Books, 1973), 6–7.

2. Houlden comes close to saying that Mark lacks an ethic. The paucity of ethical material which Mark presents he does out of nonethical interests, namely theological ones: Christology and the kingdom of God. Mark was not interested in settling everyday moral problems (Houlden, *Ethics and the New Testament,* 42–45). But does the evidence that Houlden cites for his judgment not simply show that Mark did in fact have an ethic that was theological and nonautonomous? Houlden recognizes that the New Testament generally does not contain autonomous ethics (ibid., 5–7). Therefore it is not clear why he seems to be puzzled by the lack of ethical autonomy in Mark and he appears to oscillate between suggesting that Mark has no ethic and recognizing that he has a nonautonomous one (ibid., 46). Sometimes Houlden implies that an ethic which is not autonomous is not really an ethic, but at other times he clearly acknowledges nonautonomous ethics (ibid., 7, 123–25).

3. Wolfgang Schrage is quite aware that in Mark the criterion for discipleship is the way of Jesus. Christology is the key to conduct. But Schrage correctly speaks of Mark's teaching about the conduct of disciples as an ethic. See Schrage, *Ethik des Neuen Testaments* (Göttingen: Vandenhoeck & Ruprecht, 1982), 9, 132.

4. On rules and principles, see Gene H. Outka, "Character, Conduct, and the Love Commandment," in *Norm and Context in Christian Ethics,* ed. Gene H. Outka and Paul Ramsey (New York: Charles Scribner's Sons, 1968), 40–41.

5. On intentions and motives, see Gustafson, *Theology and Christian Ethics,* 127.

6. On circumstances and consequences, see Gustafson, *Theology and Christian Ethics,* 127–28.

7. On the difficulty of making clear distinctions between result and purpose clauses, see C. F. D. Moule, *An Idiom Book of New Testament Greek* (Cambridge: Cambridge Univ. Press, 1953), 138.

8. See William F. Arndt and F. Wilbur Gingrich, *A Greek-English Lexicon of the New Testament* (Chicago: Univ. of Chicago Press, 1957), 288.

9. For *en onomati hoti* as meaning "on the ground that" see C. E. B. Cranfield, *The Gospel According to Saint Mark* (Cambridge: Cambridge Univ. Press, 1959), 312.

10. Ibid., 309.

11. On the centrality of the death and resurrection of the Son of man for Mark's understanding of faith and ethics, see Schrage, *Ethik des Neuen Testaments,* 131–32.

12. See Victor Paul Furnish, *The Love Commandment in the New Testament* (Nashville: Abingdon Press, 1972), 25.

13. Ibid., 27.

14. Outka states that love to the neighbor is an unqualifiedly general ethical principle: (1) it is applicable to everyone; (2) it is applicable on every occasion; (3) it serves as a basis for subsidiary rules and principles (Outka, "Character, Conduct, and the Love Commandment," 40–41). I think that Mark would agree with this but would add that given the radical way in which he understands it, it is *possible* only for the believer.

15. Furnish, *The Love Commandment*, 30.

16. See Belo, *A Materialist Reading of the Gospel of Mark*, 190.

17. As claimed by Furnish, *The Love Commandment*, 29.

18. Kee, *Community of the New Age*, 161–62.

19. As suggested by Kee, *Community of the New Age*, 157–58.

20. See Best, *Following Jesus*, 85.

21. See Werner H . Kelber, "Mark and Oral Tradition," *Semeia* 16 (1979): 44.

22. See Schrage, *Ethik des Neuen Testaments*, 133.

23. Russell Pregeant interprets the underlying tendency of the whole of Matthew along this line. See Pregeant, *Christology Beyond Dogma: Matthew's Christ in Process Hermeneutic* (Philadelphia: Fortress Press; Chico, Calif.: Scholars Press, 1978), 30, 36–37, 48, 57–60, 81–82, 89–90, 122–23, 127, 130, 145, 156–58.

24. See Via, "Structure, Christology and Ethics in Matthew," 212–13.

25. Carl E. Braaten seems to hold that in eschatological ethics the movement is all in one direction. A new state of being is the source for a new stream of acts. See Braaten, *Eschatology and Ethics,* 121. But Mark rather seems to support the view that character and action affect each other reciprocally. See Outka, "Character, Conduct, and the Love Commandment," 51; Frederick S. Carney, "Deciding in the Situation: What Is Required?" in *Norm and Context in Christian Ethics,* ed. Outka and Ramsey, 14–16.

26. Ernst Käsemann, *Commentary on Romans,* Eng. trans. G. Bromiley (Grand Rapids: Wm. B. Eerdmans, 1980), 375.

27. See Friedrich Hauck, "Koinos," *Theological Dictionary of the New Testament,* ed. G. Kittel, Eng. trans. G. Bromiley (Grand Rapids: Wm. B. Eerdmans, 1965), 3:790–97. *Koinos* was used by Greek-speaking Jews as the equivalent of *ḥōl* (free for general use as opposed to the holy, *ḳāḏōš*). But from this it was extended to mean *ṭāmē'* (ritually unclean) since the two pairs of opposites— *ḳāḏōš* and *ḥōl* (holy and free for general use) and *ṭāhôr* and *ṭāmē* (ritually clean and ritually unclean)—were closely related though distinguished. See Cranfield, *The Gospel According to Saint Mark,* 232.

28. Friedrich Hauck, "Katharos," *Theological Dictionary of the New Testament,* 3:427.

29. Ibid., 416–17.

30. Jacob Neusner, *The Idea of Purity in Ancient Judaism* (Leiden: E. J. Brill, 1973), 118.

31. Ibid., 65.

32. See Hauck, "Koinos," 3:809.

33. See Marla Jean Selvidge Schierling, "Woman, Cult, and Miracle Recital: Mark 5:24–34" (Saint Louis University: dissertation, 1980), 78, 155–56.

34. Hauck, "Katharos," 3:416.

35. See Mary Douglas, *Purity and Danger: An Analysis of Concepts of Pollution and Taboo* (London: Routledge and Kegan Paul, 1979), 48–49.

36. Neusner, *The Idea of Purity in Ancient Judaism,* 1.

37. Ibid., 115–16, 128.

38. E. R. Dodds, *The Greeks and the Irrational* (Berkeley and Los Angeles: Univ. of California Press, 1968), 34–37, 44, 48.

39. Douglas, *Purity and Danger,* 43, 49.

40. Ibid., 51–52.

41. Ibid., 53.

42. Ibid.

43. See Belo, *A Materialist Reading of the Gospel of Mark,* 38–41. A slightly different way of explaining the prohibition of bestiality, homosexuality, and incest is that all of these behaviors require each of the partners to assume two roles or to belong to two classes at the same time. This is not to be done because to abolish distinctions is to subvert the order of the world. Disorder is uncleanness. A living being cannot be both human and animal (bestiality); a person cannot be both male and female (homosexuality); a woman cannot be both mother (or sister) and wife. See the illuminating article by Jean Soler, "The Dietary Prohibitions of the Hebrews," *The New York Review of Books* 36/10 (14 June 1979), 29–30.

44. Douglas, *Purity and Danger,* 51.

45. Ibid., 2–4, 53–54.

46. Ibid., 130.

47. Ibid., 61–63.

48. Schrage (*Ethik des Neuen Testaments,* 136) states that Mark cites it "without reserve."

49. See Vincent Taylor, *The Gospel According to Saint Mark* (London: Macmillan & Co., 1963), 340–42; Cranfield, *The Gospel According to Saint Mark,* 237–38; Hugh Anderson, *The Gospel of Mark,* New Century Bible (Grand Rapids: Wm. B. Eerdmans, 1976), 185–86.

50. See Vincent Taylor, *The Gospel According to Saint Mark,* 237; Anderson, *The Gospel of Mark,* 186.

51. See Jacques Derrida, *Of Grammatology,* Eng. trans. G. C. Spivak (Baltimore: Johns Hopkins Univ. Press, 1980), 61–62, 73. And see my discussion of deconstruction in Appendix II.

52. On this tension in Matthew, See Dan O. Via, "Narrative World and Ethical Response," 140–42.

7

Marriage and Divorce
Mark 10:1–12

Narrative Analysis

Since movement characteristically begins a sequence,[1] we have such a beginning in Mark 10:1, where the narrative functions of departure and arrival come to manifest expression. Jesus has *departed* from Capernaum, where he has apparently been since 9:33, and *arrived* in the area described vaguely as the region of Judea and beyond the Jordan. Thus the turn southward from Galilee has now been clearly made and Jesus is on his way to Jerusalem (10:32). But these are not the only functions implied or manifested in 10:1. We also have conjunction, with the crowds who gather to him. And Jesus teaches them, continuing his acceptance of the mandate that had been given to him earlier in the narrative (1:38).

There follows then a confrontation between Jesus and the Pharisees precipitated by their testing him on the question of the legality of divorce. Jesus answers the Pharisees in what had to be a surprising and unexpected way, and Mark apparently wants to say that Jesus dominated them, overcame their appeal to the law, by using Scripture against Scripture. The intention of God expressed in Gen. 1:27 and 2:24 forbids divorce in Jesus' view, while the divorce law in Deut. 24:1–4 allows it, and in so doing, the latter text expresses hardness of heart; Mark's Jesus sets God's primordial-eschatological will (Gen. 1:27; 2:24; Mark 10:6–9) against a particular commandment of Moses and thus clearly questions the authority of a certain portion of Scripture.[2] This has important implications for the nature of ethical norms. Mark's use of the Old Testament for both theological (as 8:31; 14:21) and ethical (as 10:19; 12:29–31) purposes clearly shows that he regarded it as authoritative, but its authority is not a priori or formal, as we have seen. That which in Scripture is will of God must be discerned.

The implications of this teaching of Jesus are then extended in a private teaching to his disciples. Undoubtedly what interests Mark in this section is the teaching, but the teaching is not given except in a narrative structure that entails movement in time and space and dramatic confrontation. The narrative consequence of Jesus' momentary domination of the Pharisees in one sense is postponed until the ending of the plot. It is the global consequence which resulted from all of the conflicts (3:6; 11:18): they provoked the Jewish leaders to kill him. But that ironically is the means for his redemptive victory (8:35; 10:45) expressed in resurrection. The ethical consequence of his defeating the Pharisees in debate—a new teaching on divorce for the new community (10:29–30)—is articulated in this immediate context (10:9–12), obviously before the passion narrative. Therefore we must deal with the theological-ethical consequences of the narrative functions of confrontation and domination. New understanding does not emerge in the abstract but emerges as a result of—in and through—conflict.

Indissoluble Marriage:
Irrational Divorce

Mark's teaching on marriage and divorce and its theological grounding need to be viewed in the context of what has already been said about this text. The conflict is introduced as a question about divorce, but Mark's teaching has to do more basically with marriage than with divorce, since divorce is condemned and forbidden, not because it violates a law, but because it violates the nature of marriage itself.

What, then, is the nature of marriage? Two primary qualifications are suggested. Marriage is a union between a man and a woman which takes precedence over other relationships, and it joins the two as one flesh. In the Old Testament, which Mark is quoting here, flesh sometimes represents the weakness of humankind in contrast with God. But it also has positive meanings. It can mean either a part of the human body or the whole body. It then moves in the direction of the personal pronoun, and, like *nephesh*, can mean humankind per se, but in the bodily aspect. Flesh binds people together and implies relationship. The one flesh in Gen. 2:24 suggests a common body, and whether or not the Old Testament writer drew the conclusion that this meant fellowship for life,[3] that is the meaning which Mark saw in it. Observe that Mark does not base the indissolubility of marriage on a oneness of heart or spirit but bases it on the oneness of the flesh. This term may well have the connotation of the whole person on its perimeter, but its focal center is physical. God has so created the union of the flesh that it is unbreakable. In a similar way, Paul implies that the sexual relationship, whether with a marital or a nonmarital partner, marks a person indelibly as nothing else does (1 Cor.

6:16–18). In Eph. 5:23–27 (non-Pauline) the mutuality of marriage, however much it may lack in equality, is grounded on its analogy to the relationship of love between Christ and the church. But this writer also acknowledges that a man in loving his wife loves his own body and flesh (Eph. 5:28–29).

Further, this union expresses what the divine intention has been since the beginning of creation; therefore human beings are not to sever it, they are not to undo what God has done. Since the divorce law came for hardness of heart (Mark 10:5), the adversative *de* ("but") in 10:6 suggests that the beginning, when God established the unbreakable one flesh union, was prior to hardness of heart. Because Mark's Jesus requires the unbreakable one flesh union in his own time, he assumes that in his time hardness of heart no longer prevails. As we have seen, eschatology recovers the original vitality of the first time; therefore the various occurrences of anticipated eschatology in the Markan narrative mean that the time inaugurated by Jesus is the new creation. It is the time of primordial vitality and spontaneity occurring in the midst of alienation and fatigue. On the basis of this new *archē,* marriage can be permanent, because it will not become habitual, repetitious, or old. The *kairos* of new beginning continues in the time of the kingdom's extension; it qualifies the world time, the chronological times of the believer. For those living in this kind of time the breaking of the one flesh union is not a rational possibility.

In Mark 2:22, using the imagery of wine and wineskins, Mark does not say that the new eschatological power of God in history works without forms but says that it can find forms appropriate to itself. Joanna Dewey has suggested that the point of Mark 2:21–22 is stronger than that the old and new do not mix. Rather, the position is that the new is an active threat to the existence of the old and may itself be harmed in the destruction of the old. The new is to be established, not the old preserved.[4] Since marriage is regarded as permanent by Mark, it is evidently seen as an appropriate wineskin, an appropriate form, amenable to indeterminate renewal. If the kingdom is a threat to an old marriage, it is similar to the threat experienced by the demoniac who did not want to be brought by Jesus out of his severely constricted security into the openness of the future (5:1–20). And if the eschatologically new, symbolized here by the presence of the bridegroom (2:19), cannot be actualized except in new forms, then a given marriage, a form renewed by the kingdom of God, must be different from what it was before and different from marriages not so touched. The skins in which the new wine can be contained are to be *kainos,* not just "new" in the sense of recent, but fresh in quality.[5]

Indissoluble Marriage
as Eschatological Possibility:
Marriage and Miracle Story

Gerd Theissen has connected the more radical early Christian ethical attitude of abandonment of property, home, family, and apparently marriage with the wandering charismatic bearers of tradition. This kind of behavior could be practiced only by those who had been released from everyday ties to the world by the expectation of the end of the world and who could expect support from the local communities of the Jesus movement.[6] The more conservative attitude, which took a positive attitude toward preserving marriage and the family (cf. Mark 10:2–12, 13–16), Theissen connects with the local communities, who felt that they could compromise with the world, since their charismatic leaders by way of compensation made such a clear distinction between themselves and the world.[7]

Theissen has assigned these two attitudes to two different components in the sociological situation of first-century Christianity. But once the reader is beyond this point of ostensive reference, he or she needs to ask what is the existential-ethical project that is the nonostensive referent of Mark's text. And we have to recognize that Mark as a unified whole story has, by means of his dual realized and futuristic eschatology, fused the eschatological attitude with an intensified concern about the quality of the believer's personal family and communal life in the world. Mark has thus established one paradoxical position which is the norm for all disciples. Let us say (with Theissen) hypothetically that in the pre-Markan tradition the belief in the near end promotes the abandonment of marriage (at least in principle), while world concern promotes the permanence of marriage. Mark then, by making *realized* eschatology the ground for revitalized life in the historical world, has reversed the way in which the tradition dealt with the issue of the permanence of marriage. No longer does the expectation of the end call for the abandonment of marriage. Rather, the actualized anticipation of the eschatological new creation is the basis for its indissolubility, as is the tacit continuation of primordial unfallenness. And world concern or compromise with the world is not the ground for the permanence of marriage but is rather an expression of the hardness of heart that undermines marriage. But Mark has also retained the position that has been transcended. Why should marriage be sustained if historical existence in the world may not have a positive value and dimension? And the eschatological per se, in its wholly futuristic aspect, *will* spell the end of marriage: there will be no marriage in the resurrection (12:25). We see again that the permanence of marriage presupposes an ongoing history which is eschatologically revitalized.

Indissoluble marriage is in Mark an eschatological possibility, a possibility resting on the anticipatory actualization of the kingdom of God and the new creation. It is as possible as is the narrative in which God's eschatological kingdom is manifested. It is, then, a possibility for anyone who can read himself or herself to be read into the story.

At first sight, one portion of the narrative does not seem particularly pertinent to the present theme but turns out, I think, to be relevant and illuminating. It is a miracle story section, which includes the episodes of the stilling of the storm, the Gerasene demoniac, the raising of Jairus' daughter, and the woman with the hemorrhage (4:35—5:43). Here we have a nature miracle, an exorcism, a raising from the dead, and a healing.

Following Antoinette Wire, I suggest that the structure which makes a miracle story whole and unified and which is more basic and general than the various types of miracle stories is a pattern that connects a struggle against a closed system of oppressive forces (confrontation) with a victorious breaking through these restrictions (success or domination) upon life.[8] To this it may be added that miracle stories typically end with a demonstration of the cure (Mark 1:31c) or an acclamation on the part of the audience: "They were all amazed and glorified God, saying, 'We never saw anything like this!' " (Mark 2:12b).

Theissen has argued that the very purpose of miracle stories is the acclamation. To account then for the fact that Mark's miracle stories do not always end in acclamations and never in acclaiming Jesus by title, he employs the argument that Mark deliberately intended to postpone titular acclamation until the climax of his Gospel: the Roman centurion in the presence of the rending of the temple curtain (Mark 15:38) confesses that Jesus is truly the Son of God (15:39). Mark's genre is thus a creative adaptation of the smaller genre miracle story. The arch which is inherent in all miracle stories, between the miracle and the intended reaction of the audience, Mark extends to the whole Gospel.[9] Paul J. Achtemeier has several criticisms of Theissen: (1) The centurion's confession is not any kind of climax in Mark 15. (2) Nor is the confession related to miracle, as Theissen would like. As the presence of "he breathed his last" in both 15:37 and 15:39 shows, the centurion's acclamation is in response to Jesus' death, not to the rending of the curtain. (3) Suffering is the key to Mark but has no role (presumably in connection with the miracle worker) in miracle stories.[10]

In response to Achtemeier I note the following: (1) I think that it is not the case that the centurion's confession is not any kind of climax. It is clearly not the very end of the story. But it is a climax because it is near the end and it is the one place in the narrative where someone from the world of the story, where Jesus' true identity is not known to human beings, confesses Jesus in a way that agrees explicitly with the theological discourse of the narrator: Jesus is the Son of God. Moreover, in terms of deep structure the centurion's confession is climactic. Jesus has already been accorded divine aid (1:10–11, 13c: qualifying test) and has secured the missing value, suffering obedience (8:31; 10:45; 14:24, 36: main test). Now his true identity is recognized (glorifying test). The climax of the Gospel is the dialectic between the clear confession of the centurion and the confession of the disciples, which is absent from the plot and only allusively pushed into the future of the narrative world. (2) Achtemeier is right that the centurion's confession is in response to Jesus' death. But in Mark, Jesus' death is the "miracle," the act of healing. And for Theissen the rending of the temple curtain may be more the dispelling of the secret than miracle as such. (3) Suffering can be understood as the extension of an element with which Mark characteristically expands the simplest healing story form, as Lane C. McGaughy has analyzed that development. I turn now to his discussion.

The simplest healing story of the Greco-Roman era had a tripartite form: (1) description of the illness; (2) act of healing; (3) audience response and/or demonstration of the cure (Mark 1:30–31). About half of the stories from the period add a further (fourth) element which typically comes just before the act of healing: an expression of doubt or an emphasis on the seriousness of the illness, which makes the cure questionable and thus enhances the marvel of it when it is actually performed (5:25–34). According to McGaughy, Mark's own contribution to the miracle story form, which is seen in the remainder of his healing stories (1:40–45; 2:3–12; 3:1–6; 7:32–37; 8:22–26; 10:46–52), is that he develops the fourth element, that of doubt or questionableness, by inserting something like another miracle story, a controversy, or a dialogue. This element in Mark's developed form presents a contrast with *faith* which heightens the latter. It introduces a challenge or impediment to faith, rather than a heightening contrast with the *act of healing.* Thus the characteristically Markan healing story has the following form: (1) description of the illness; (2) an episode that raises the issue of faith by challenging it; (3) the cure; and (4) the response of faith. This can be seen in the restoration of sight to blind Bartimaeus (10:46–52): (1) He is identified as a blind beggar. (2) His believing effort to obtain the healing mercy of Jesus is impeded by the crowd which wishes to silence him. (3) Jesus pronounces him well. (4) He follows Jesus in the way, expressing faith.[11]

The Gospel of Mark may be understood as an augmentation of this form, with the suffering of the Son of man manifesting and extending the element of impediment to faith. In reaction to McGaughy, I would say that in Mark, as well as in some of his healing stories, the response of faith is at least as closely connected to the act of healing as it is to the challenge to faith. In the light of the foregoing discussion, Mark's story may be structured as follows:

1. Description of the illness: sickness is a metaphor for the sin which needs a physician (1:4–8; 2:5, 15–17; 3:28–30).
2. Impediment to faith: the disciples cannot understand the meaning of the suffering Son of man, and they manifest hardness of heart (Mark 8—10).
3. Act of healing: Jesus' death has the power to ransom and to give insight (10:45, 46–52; 15:24–38).
4. The response of faith: the centurion acclaims the one on the cross as the Son of God (15:39).[12]

This structure of Mark accounts for the issues I have just raised and is not inconsistent with my earlier discussion of the Markan form. If the Gospel and some of its component miracle stories are related to each other as macrocosm to microcosm, then these two magnitudes mutually interpret each other, and each helps the reader to get into the other. Now I return to the four stories with which I am concerned in their relationship to marriage and divorce.

The marriage section attracts the story of the stilling of the storm, because permanent marriage rests on the proleptic actualization of the eschatological new creation and the stilling of the storm is a symbolic creation story. In the Old Testament the sea symbolizes the chaos monster which Yahweh had to subdue in order to bring an orderly cosmos out of chaos:

> Thou dost rule the raging of the sea;
> . . . .
> Thou didst crush Rahab (the sea monster)
>   like a carcass
>
> . . . .
> The heavens are thine, the earth also is thine;
>   the world and all that is in it, thou hast

founded them.
> (Ps. 89:9-11; see also Pss. 74:13-14;
> 104:5-9; Job 38:8-11; Jer. 5:22; 31:35;
> *The Prayer of Manasseh* 2-4)

In Mark 4:35-41, then, Jesus assumes the role of the Creator, and his struggle is with cosmic chaos. His victory over the stormy waves is a new creation, a new order, in which permanent marriage is possible; and it is a victory over the trials of historical existence as well, of which the sea is also a symbol (Pss. 69:1-2, 14-15; 46:2; 65:7; Isa. 43:2).[13]

The three stories that follow give added concreteness to the new situation, and the suggestion of restored sexuality in the stories of the demoniac, the woman with the hemorrhage, and Jairus' daughter takes on added positive significance when these three are contrasted with their negative counterparts in the story of the beheading of John the Baptist in the next chapter (Mark 6:16-29). Herod has married his brother's wife, Herodias, and despite his ambivalent regard for John and his remorse upon being enticed into a foolish and extravagant oath, he indulges himself in a kind of incest. That would be true whether or not the girl who dances so seductively is his own daughter or his stepdaughter. Herodias is vindictive, and in asking for the head of John the Baptist, she demands a symbolic castration. The daughter is a relatively passive participant but is, nevertheless, implicated in the castration. She is apparently quite ready to exploit her charms publicly, and if she is here represented as pre-pubescent,[14] there is something incongruous in the highly sexual nature of her dancing.

In the story of the Gerasene demoniac (Mark 5:1-20) Jesus' struggle is with a legion of demons, and his victory over them delivers the possessed man from a living death in the tombs which has alienated him from his society. It also delivers him from his inclination to self-injury (he bruised himself with stones) and from the self-alienation manifested in his tendency to speak as if he were the demons. Prior to the exorcism the man is possessed of a supernatural strength which leads to nothing but acts of futility and a crying out to the silent tombs and mountains. Afterward he is calm and in his right mind. The man wants to go with Jesus, but Jesus directs him to stay and tell his friends about the mercy which God has shown him. Why is the man instructed to proclaim rather than to be silent as is typically the case in miracle material in Mark (1:25, 44; 3:12; 5:43; 7:36; 8:26)?

It is often said that the man is told to relate the news because the setting is Gentile and therefore false messianic hopes were not likely to be aroused.[15] But I doubt that the idea of obviating false messianic beliefs is what finally motivates the messianic secret in Mark. The secret does, however, manifest the oppositional theme revealed/concealed. The conclusion to the demoniac's story emphasizes the revealed side of the opposition. Something must be revealed in order to be concealed. I will argue, in fact, that this is a proleptic resurrection story. It dramatizes the existential effect of the resurrection in one life and suggests that such an occurrence leads to the proclamation of the resurrection. On what grounds could this be called a resurrection story?

First of all, the resurrection is to inaugurate the revelation of Jesus' glory, the proclamation of who he really is (Mark 9:9), and the redeemed demoniac is to tell what has been done for him. And the word in 5:19 for "to tell" (*apaggellō*) in Jesus' instructions to him is used elsewhere of the announcement of the church's missionary message (Acts 17:30; 26:20; 1 Cor. 14:25; Matt. 11:4). Moreover, the word in 5:20 for his proclamation (*Kērygma; kēryssō*) is the usual New Testament word for preaching the gospel.[16] It is the angel at the tomb of Jesus in 16:1–8 who says that Jesus is risen, and in certain ways the freed demoniac is his counterpart. The demoniac is sitting clothed (*kathēmenon himatismenon*, 5:15), and so is the young man at the tomb (*kathēmenon . . . peribeblēmenon*, 16:5). Both the healed demoniac and the young man evoke fear (*ephobēthēsan*, 5:15; *ephobounto*, 16:8) and amazement (*ethaumazon*, 5:20; *exethambēthēsan*, 16:5). Both of the figures are associated with the tomb and victory over the tomb (*mnēma*, 5:3; *mnēmeion*, 16:2, 3, 5, 8). In view of the close parallelism between Mark 5:1–20 and 16:1–8 the reference to mercy in 5:19 interprets the resurrection as the occurrence of the mercy of God, and 16:1–8 interprets the mercy of God as the happening of the resurrection. And the parallelism between 5:19 and 5:20 interprets what God has done for the demoniac as what Jesus has done, and vice versa. The man is to tell how much *God* has done for him (5:19). But the narrator tells us that he proclaimed how much *Jesus* had done for him.

As we have seen, in Mark Jesus' resurrection is concealed revelation. The resurrected Jesus does not actually appear, and the women do not report that he has risen. But Mark does believe that Jesus is effectively risen and that this message is proclaimed. One of the places where that comes to expression is, unexpectedly, in the liberation of the Gerasene demoniac. In short, the liberated demoniac is to tell what has happened to him, because this is a resurrection story and the resurrection is to be proclaimed (9:9; 16:6–7). The motif of resurrection, generally speaking, offers the possibility of permanent renewal to marriage. But there is a more specific point of relevance in this story. It is male strength, which prior to the exorcism asserted itself without meaning or purpose, which is now clothed and in its right mind.[17] With reference to the story of Herod, no longer will male strength be asserted to take the wife of the brother, and no longer will it be subject to the wiles of a seductive (step) daughter.

The raising of Jairus' daughter is divided into two parts (5:21–24a and 35–43) by the intercalated healing of the woman with the hemorrhage (5:24b–34). Jairus struggles with the doubts of those from his house who do not think that Jesus can deal with death, a skepticism which must have aroused doubts in Jairus' own mind. But probably Jesus' struggle is more prominent in the story. Jesus also confronts the doubts of Jairus' people as well as the derision of the mourners and death itself. His victory frees the daughter from death at the age of twelve. Twelve was the age at which marriage became possible for a girl, so resurrection is associated with the beginning of marriage.[18]

The woman with the hemorrhage struggles with the aggravated seriousness of her illness, her own fear, and perhaps the thronging crowds. But she manages to touch Jesus and find healing. Jesus hardly struggles at all, except briefly with the disciples: the power simply flows out of him to the woman. It is largely her struggle which leads to success, but then she has been brought to Jesus in the first place by the power of his story. The woman has been made unclean by her malady (Lev. 16:25–27). But her touching Jesus heals her rather than making him unclean, thus reversing the Jewish cultic system.[19] This reversal suggests the nature of his power. Since her illness was a deformation of her female being, the healing and blessing are a restoration of her sexuality.

These two stories mutually interpret each other,[20] since one is intercalated in the other. Moreover, the woman's twelve years of suffering connect her with the twelve-year-old girl just restored.[21] Marriage can be lasting because female sexuality has been renewed, returned to its beginning by resurrection (new creation). Twelve years of suffering and of social and cultic alienation have been transformed into the resurrection of a twelve-year-old girl. Dead sexuality is turned into a sexuality restored to its original newness, the time of the first time for sex. This is the effect of the story of the young woman on the story of the older woman. But the story of the older woman suggests a healthy maturity.[22] The meaning, between the two stories, of renewed female sexuality is that with maturity the vitality of the first time is not lost. With reference to the story of Herodias and her daughter, no longer will female sexuality manipulate male libido for the sheer joy of exercising power, nor will it practice castration in the interest of revenge.

In chapter 1, I argued that symbols can be clarified by drawing out their conceptual implications. But the reverse is also a part of the whole hermeneutical endeavor. Pursuing an ethical concept—indissoluble marriage, irrational divorce—back to one possible symbolic grounding may both illuminate the idea and enable its enactment.[23] To appropriate symbols is to have a new world. Thus this discussion has been an interpretation of miracle story as ethical enablement. The sequence that I have discussed has a cosmic scope and thematic unity in that it brings us from creation, the subduing of the chaos waters, through conflicts of various kinds to apocalypse, the resurrection of the twelve-year-old. Each story displays its own drama of renewal. But the sequence as a whole is a redemptive narrative which transcends the parts. To have one's self-understanding transformed by the power of the narrative is to be enabled to live an indissoluble marriage.

The Double Prohibition of Divorce:
Divorce as Conceivable

But in the very fact that divorce is forbidden it is acknowledged that it will occur. As a matter of fact, it is forbidden in two different forms: an apodictic form in Mark 10:9 and a casuistic one in 10:11–12. The classification of the two sayings having been made, the claim must now be defended. A brief characterization of apodictic and casuistic laws is here needed to illumine the distinction, as I have applied it to these sayings.[24] I do not mean to suggest that Mark's ethic is conceptually legalistic in any thoroughgoing way but that legal forms sometimes influence the way his ethical teachings are stated.

The casuistic form begins with a conditional clause—If (or when) men quarrel and one strikes another . . . (Exod. 21:18–19)—and all of the people concerned with the case are spoken of in the third person. After the case has been described and the conditions defining it in its specificity have been fully set out, the penalty is then stated. Degrees of subjective guilt are carefully weighed (Exod. 21:13, 14), and the penalty depends on the seriousness of the offense.

The apodictic form states an absolute, unconditional, categorical command (more often a prohibition) in the imperative style (Exod. 20:3–17; 23:1–3): You shall not. . . . Typically the second person is used but not always (Exod. 21:15–17; Deut. 27:15–26). The style is much more compressed than is the case with casuistic laws, and no account is taken of subjective guilt or degrees of guilt. A penalty is usually not stated, because it is self-evident that the deity will step in to punish the offender. Another type of apodictic form opens with a participial subject; it strongly and bluntly states a penalty, usually death (Exod. 21:12, 15–17): Whoever steals a man . . . shall be put to death. Or the penalty can be the pronouncement of a curse, at the beginning: Cursed be he who misleads a blind man on the road . . . (Deut. 27:15–26). The participial type can be confused with the casuistic because the participial subject is often translated by a relative clause (Whoever strikes his father . . .), and a relative clause can be used in casuistic laws as the equivalent of a conditional clause to define a particular case. But in such examples as Exod. 21:15–17 the relative clause represents the participle. Yet Albrecht Alt recognizes that casuistic and apodictic forms are often mixed in various ways, one way being the replacement of the participle by the relative in the Hebrew forms.[25]

Mark 10:9 I take to be apodictic because it is a categorical, absolute prohibition without conditions or degrees of guilt. It is in the third rather than the second person, but it is in the imperative mood (not "let not man separate" but "man is not to separate"), and no penalty is stated. Mark 10:11–12 is more mixed, but, I think, is closer to the casuistic type than to the apodictic. We actually have two casuistic expressions here in parallel. Mark 10:11 states the case of the man and 10:12 that of the woman. The first sentence (man) uses a relative clause with the subjunctive, which might be taken as representing the apodictic participial expression, but it is much more likely to be the equivalent of a casuistic conditional clause, since it is paralleled by the conditional clause in 10:12. In 10:12 the subject is modified by a participle: and if she *divorcing* her husband marries another . . . , which again might be taken as reflecting the participial apodictic. But this is obviously a conditional clause, which is the strongest feature of the casuistic form. No penalty is stated, but there is a substitute for it: the person involved is pronounced guilty of adultery. The third person is used throughout, and there are degrees of guilt.

Mark 10:11 goes beyond Jewish practice of the time in maintaining that a man can be guilty of adultery against his wife. And 10:12 presupposes a Greco-Roman cultural attitude (probably in Syria or Galilee) in assuming that a wife can initiate divorce.

In Mark 10:9 divorce is inevitably wrong. In 10:11–12, however, before this passage was included in Mark, divorce is apparently not necessarily wrong, but the remarriage of a divorced person is.[26] Yet in 10:11–12 divorce is the occasion for culpable remarriage and thus probably does not altogether escape guilt. And certainly in the finished Markan context divorce is sinful in 10:11–12 because it has already been established as sinful in 10:9. Nevertheless there is an apparent tension between the *nature* of sin in the two passages (10:9 and 10:11–12). And there is a real tension in Mark between two views of the *source* or cause of evil more broadly. It is my judgment that in part this latter tension belongs to the fundamental paradox in the New Testament's understanding of historical existence in faith and is not resolvable. Consider for a moment, however, how the juxtaposition of 10:9 and 10:11–12 appears to resolve the question of how sinful divorce is. In 10:9 it is absolutely wrong without qualification. In 10:11–12 it may not be wrong at all, but if it is, it is not as wrong as divorce and remarriage. In 10:11–12 there are, then, degrees of guilt. When the two are put together, divorce is always wrong (the effect of 10:9 on 10:11–12), but not as wrong as divorce and remarriage (the effect of 10:11–12 on 10:9).

The foregoing discussion has suggested that since the casuistic form comes last, as a private explanation of the apodictic to the disciples, the casuistic appears to dominate. The apodictic is interpreted *as* casuistic. Matthew, of course, is often regarded[27] as turning Mark's absolute prohibition of divorce into a practicable community rule in that he allows one justification for divorce (Matt. 19:9). Mark, of course, allows no justification, but he has taken a step in the direction which Matthew extends in that he (Mark) turns an action that is (relatively) inconceivable (one is *not* to divorce, an imperative) into one that is conceivable, but wrong (whoever *may* [if anyone should] divorce and remarry, a subjunctive, commits adultery). What is the nature of sin (wrong), and why is it conceivable?

In Mark 10:9 divorce is absolutely forbidden, and if we ask why this is the case in Mark, it must be because it is contrary to the nature of things: contrary to history vis-à-vis the kingdom, contrary to the renewed time, that is, the new creation. The nature of sin, here sin as divorce, is that it contradicts the conditions that God has established for men and women for their good, conditions that he has given them the resources to fulfill. God did this in the original creation, and God has done it again in the new creation. In this light there is no reason for divorce; it is both unnecessary and contrary to human good; therefore it is irrational. But if Mark's theological position(s) makes divorce irrational, the very existence of the prohibition shows that it is conceivable. A person has the freedom to do the irrational.

In Mark 10:11–12 the nature of sin, as divorce, seems to be formal, not material. Divorce is forbidden, not because it violates the new creation, but because it will probably lead to remarriage and thereby make a person guilty of another moral fault, adultery, which is wrong a priori according to law, a formal authority. And in 10:19 Mark does cite the Decalogue's prohibition against adultery. But that is not the whole picture in Mark. Adultery is not wrong simply because it has been forbidden by law. It is also one of the evils that originates in the heart (7:21–23) of a person. Therefore it is a manifestation of hardness of heart and is just as fundamental a sin as divorce. Divorce springs from hardness of heart and leads to more hardness of heart (adultery). Once again character (being) and conduct interrelate. Mark fundamentally does not see sin as violating a law, but that view is still there on the perimeter.

The conceivability of divorce which is implicit in 10:9 is made more explicit in 10:11–12: whoever may . . . if anyone does. This is the subjunctive condition; it is undetermined whether or not it will be fulfilled. It may be that this kind of conditional clause denotes what is expected,[28] but the element of the hypothetical,[29] the uncertain, is still there. If it is undetermined whether one will get a divorce, then one need not, and if one does, one acts in freedom. That is reinforced by the implications of 10:9. Divorce is totally unnecessary. Thus to do it is to make a free choice which is yet irrational because it is against the goodness which God has newly created for men and women in marriage.

Once again I will connect the moral and the cultic. It has been suggested that in the Old Testament phenomena that violate class criteria and distinctions are unclean because they are unthinkable.[30] I would suggest "irrational" in place of "unthinkable." Unclean phenomena are actually not unthinkable, because they can be thought. But they cannot be rationally conceived; that is, they cannot be fitted into the categories that give order and structure to life and make it livable. We have also seen in Mark that divorce, and by implication other acts in violation of love, is irrational in that it violates the order inaugurated by the eschatological new creation. So the cultic and the moral are akin in that both cultic uncleanness and the immoral are expressions of the irrationality of causing disorder.

And I suggest that it is the confrontation with the irrational that is the existential basis for the apodictic legal form: such and such is not to be done. There are no degrees of guilt for the contemplated act and no stated punishment if it is committed, because the act itself is not rationally conceivable. I have observed that the very existence of the prohibition shows that the forbidden act is in fact at least thinkable if not conceivable. But the two legal forms that I have dealt with reveal differing degrees of conceivability. The casuistic form with its conditions, degrees of guilt, and graded punishments regards the contemplated act as highly conceivable. The apodictic form, on the other hand, is (more) paradoxical. That it exists as a requirement at all expresses the conceivability of the act, but its *particular form* denies the act's rationality. The apodictic form whenever it appears expresses, at least in an attenuated way, the paradoxical overlapping of the eschatological presence of God (or the continuance of the unfallen moment of creation) and fallen human history. So the violation of God's order of well-being is both irrational and conceivable: irrational because it makes no sense to violate the primordial or eschatological order yet conceivable for the reasons yet to be noted. But the casuistic form with its fuller acceptance of the conceivability of the act manifests a greater adjustment to the reign of hardness of heart in human life. The irrational violation of order has become *quite* conceivable. But it still ought not to be; thus order has not been lost sight of, a different degree of the paradox. That the irrational has become so thoroughly conceivable is rooted in the deformation of the inner core of understanding and action: hardness of heart.

Indissoluble marriage is a possibility enabled by the miracle of the eschatological new creation. But people are free to reject that possibility and choose divorce, however irrational that choice against the good may be. Yet at the same time, divorce is not simply chosen. The hardness of heart with which divorce is connected is not only a free misdirection of the will which refuses to respond to the presence of the kingdom of God. The fragility of even Christian marriage is a problem with roots deeper than personal individual failure. That is, divorce is also a conceivable possibility, hearts are also hardened, because of a certain qualification of history: time is *un*renewed because the kingdom is still future; hardness of heart is determined. In Mark, divorce, and other moral faults, flow out of hardness of heart, which involves *both* the freely chosen misdirection of the individual's will *and* the fate of unrenewed time. Since that is the case in the Gospel as a whole, should we question the suggestion in 10:1-12 that indissoluble marriage is an unqualified possibility and that divorce and remarriage, therefore, are unqualified moral faults which are freely chosen and which are completely in conflict with the Christian view of existence?

Hardness of Heart

We have observed that divorce in our text is an expression of hardness of heart. Whether the *pros* ("for") in *pros tēn sklērokardian* (10:5, "for your hardness of heart") means "against" (as a curb upon), or "in view of,"[31] or "in accordance with" (as an expression of), the point is still that there would be no divorce apart from hardness of heart; and this term may be Mark's characterization of the fundamental fallenness of the human condition. The distinctiveness of Mark's use of the expression and concept may be seen from the following evidence. There are four references to "hardness of heart" in Mark: 3:5; 6:52; 8:17; 10:5. Luke omits three of the Markan pericopes that contain the references and omits the reference to hardness of heart in the one pericope that he retains (Luke 6:6–11). Matthew reproduces all four of the Markan pericopes but retains the reference to hardness of heart only in the divorce pericope (Matt. 19:1–12). The concept has roots in the Old Testament.

Heart is the most important and the commonest word in the vocabulary of Old Testament anthropology. It stands for the inaccessible, hidden core of a person which is concealed from other people but visible to God (1 Sam. 16:7; Prov. 15:11; 24:12; Ps. 44:21). The heart is sometimes the seat of certain feelings (Ps. 104:15; Isa. 7:2), but it is primarily intellectual activity, understanding and thinking (Deut. 29:4; Isa. 6:10; 42:25; Job 12:3; Hos. 7:11), which is ascribed to the heart. And since the Israelite mind made no facile distinction between perceiving and choosing, the heart is the place of decision, intention, and the impulse of the will (2 Sam. 7:3, 27–28; Prov. 4:23; 1 Sam. 14:6–7; Isa. 10:7; Exod. 35:32; 36:2). And the heart, like other anthropological concepts, can be a term for the whole person (Ps. 22:26; Jer. 23:16).[32] From this quick overview we might surmise that hardness of heart will be a deformation and impairment of the very wellsprings (Prov. 4:23) of understanding, including the understanding of God or faith, and of decisive action.

One classical Old Testament portrayal of this theme is Isa. 6:9–10, which is not only quoted in Mark 4:12 but in other New Testament writers as well (Matt. 13:14–15; John 12:40; Acts 28:26–27; allusions perhaps in Rom. 11:8; 2 Cor. 3:14; 4:4). Isaiah saw or came to see that his proclamation produced a hearing without understanding and a seeing without perception. This failure of understanding is represented as a fat heart.

Our specific term, hardness of heart, receives its most prominent treatment in the exodus story. The pertinent material comes from both the Yahwist (J) and Priestly (P) sources (or traditions), and there are differences of tone and emphasis,[33] but my interest here is in the finished narrative as it came from the hand of the redactor-narrator. The source of Pharaoh's hardness of heart is spoken of in three ways: (1) Pharaoh hardens his own heart (Exod. 8:15, 32; 9:34), (2) God hardens his heart (Exod. 4:21; 7:3–4; 9:12; 10:1; 11:10), and (3) Pharaoh's heart is spoken of in the passive as being hardened without the agent's being specified (Exod. 7:13–14, 22; 8:19; 9:7). While the passive probably implies divine agency in these passages, the passive in Exod. 9:35 clearly has in mind Pharaoh's own agency, since that is stated in 9:34.

Hardness of heart, then, is both Pharaoh's doing and a fate created by God. It is concretely in this text a stubborn refusal (Exod. 13:15) to see the "finger of God" in the events leading up to the exodus or a refusal to listen (Exod. 7:4; 8:19), and it is a refusal to do what God wills, that is, to allow Israel to go (Exod. 4:21; 8:32). As such, it is a manifestation of self-exaltation (Exod. 9:17).

The depiction of hardness as due both to the human subject and to God's action has often been interpreted as meaning that the willful human refusal to understand is punished by the fact that the choice not to understand becomes an inability to understand which the human will cannot then reverse. Both Brevard S. Childs and Gerhard von Rad reject this approach as "psychological" and foreign to the concerns of the biblical writers. For Childs,[34] hardness is not a psychological state, not a state of mind, but a specific negative reaction to signs from God. Nor are the writers trying with this concept to develop a theology of divine causality. Both the J and the P sources are simply concerned with interpreting the signs. In J hardness of heart prevents the signs from revealing God, while in P it results in a multiplication of the signs.

Von Rad rejects the psychological approach because he wants to affirm that in a sense the biblical text (e.g., Isaiah) *does* assert divine causality. The Old Testament holds that hardening is an act of God and not a law of human nature. Human acts so foolish as to bring about ruin and self-destruction must come from the inscrutable working of God and not arise simply from the human level. Isaiah's prophetic word effects judgment in the recesses of the human heart by inciting the refusal of the offer of salvation. The hardening of Israel's heart is a particular mode of Yahweh's dealing with Israel (Isa. 29:9–14).[35]

One should note, however, that the imperatives in Isa. 29:9–10 suggest that Israel also has responsibility. Israel blinds and stupefies itself as well as having this condition visited upon it by Yahweh.

It may be that the biblical writers were not very interested in the polarity between hardness as a human decision and hardness as an act of God,[36] but the tension between the two is nevertheless there in the texts. It certainly prompts us to suggest that the acts of God and the human being somehow coalesce, and to the extent that hardening is a human act it can be and needs to be understood psychologically. Let us recall Hans-Georg Gadamer's[37] inescapable reminder that the only access we have to texts of the past is the lens formed by our own horizon. And why is it any more nonbiblical to suppose that God works *through* psychological processes in a hidden way than it is to affirm that he so works through historical processes? Isaiah already knew that the intentions and action of God in international historical confrontations might be quite unknown to the actors in those events (Isa. 10:5–11). That establishes the theological principle: God acts through human structures without destroying the limited autonomy of the latter. If Isaiah had been in a position to know anything about psychological dynamisms, there is no reason to think that he would not have applied his principle. In fact, he and the Pentateuchal redactor do apply it implicitly in the very fact that they juxtapose in tension the two hardening motifs. Walter Wink has made the useful suggestion that the irreducible, essential elements of *every* level of reality are a manifestation, though not an exhaustive manifestation, of the divine.[38] One cannot sharply separate the biblical hardening motif from the later theological and psychological interpretations of it, because the later questions would not have been raised were the issues not at least implicitly present in the Bible. The meaning of a text is its effect in the history of interpretation.[39] Both the content of the Old Testament texts and the hermeneutical points raised in connection with them are pertinent for our further interpretation of Mark.

What I have been calling "hardness of heart" occurs in the Greek text of Mark in three forms. In Mark 6:52 and 8:17 we have a noun and a perfect passive participle: the heart (*kardia*) is hardened (*pepōrōmenē*). In 3:5 two nouns appear, one cognate with *pōroō*: hardness (*pōrōsis*) of heart (*kardias*). Mark 10:5 presents us with one compound noun: hardness of heart (*sklērokardia*). Mark 3:5 attributes it to Jesus' opponents; 6:52 and 8:17, to the disciples; and 10:5, apparently to Israel generally throughout the centuries and, by implication, to all people. Hardness of heart is a culpable failure to understand the kingdom occurring in Jesus (6:52; 8:17) so far as it pertains to the disciples, and with regard to Jesus' opponents it is a hostility to him which puts ritual correctness above doing good and saving life (3:1–6). The fact that it is predicated of both groups may suggest that the disciples are in effect no less hostile than the opponents to the real meaning of Jesus' mission. In 10:5–9 hardness of heart is the ground for conduct inappropriate to God's dealing with the world. It is the opposite of faith and is illuminated by the meaning of faith in Mark. Heart in Mark, as in the Old Testament, is the hidden inner core of the human being, and hardness of heart is its religious and moral deformation. That the heart is the inner core is made clear in 7:14–23, where the heart (7:19, 21) is explicitly the inside (esōthen, 7:21, 23), as contrasted with the outside (exōthen, 7:15, 18). Mark implies the complete interpenetration of the external and internal self. It is the unison of external selves, one flesh, that makes marriage indissoluble. But it is the deformation of the inner self, hardness of heart, that threatens the indissolubility. This way of understanding shows how far Mark has departed from objective ritualism. In the sphere of interpersonal moral relationships and divine-human relationships (4:10–12; 8:17; 10:23–27) heart and flesh interpenetrate each other radically. But in the sphere of ritual it is denied that what affects the external self has any bearing at all on the internal (7:14–19).

In Appendix II, I will discuss Maurice Merleau-Ponty's concept of the relationship between inner and outer in the human body, which in part parallels Mark. There is an interesting "eschatological" element in Merleau-Ponty's thought. The complete interpenetration of subject and object, seeing and visible, touching and touched, is always an "imminent" possibility and never fully realized in fact.[40] Similarly in Mark prior to the imminent end of the age heart and flesh can be against each other. They interpenetrate in principle, because each is an aspect of the whole self. But these two aspects which should undergird each other—a one flesh union in which the inner core (heart) of each flesh is vitally given to the other—may be in conflict.

Merleau-Ponty states that this hiatus between subject and object is not an ontological void but is spanned by the total being of the body and the world.[41] One could claim that Paul says very much the same thing with his concept of the body. Mark does not have the developed anthropological vocabulary that Paul has, but with his image of the way, as well as with his eschatology and Christology, he does suggest the progressive cohering of the self of the disciple.

Regarding the source of hardness, the texts themselves do not say whether God or the people concerned hardened the hearts (similar to the third usage in Exodus), so the context will have to decide it. In Mark 8:14–21 the disciples seem to be held responsible and culpable for their hardness (8:17), so perhaps here the emphasis is on the human refusal to understand. The other passages have to be interpreted in the light of Mark's overall view of why human beings reject God's word and will.

In Mark 4:12, as in Isa. 6:9–10 which is being quoted, the proclaimed word which is intended to save has the opposite effect. Jesus' parabolic word, like the prophet's word, God's word, produces non-understanding, which is hardness of heart (6:52; 8:17). Although it would fit, Mark does not quote the reference to heart in Isa. 6:9–10: "Make the heart of this people fat." Not only does Jesus' own parabolic word produce hardness, that is in fact its *purpose (hina),* but also Jesus is rejected and killed because it has been decreed in Scripture (8:31; 14:21); therefore, those who plot his death are fated to do so.

On the other hand, Jesus speaks openly to his disciples and explains his actions; thus the disciples are responsible and blameworthy for not understanding (6:52; 7:14–18; 8:17–21, 32a; 9:10, 32; 10:26–27). And those who reject Jesus and kill him act on their own volition (3:6; 12:12; 14:1–2; 15:1). Since, then, the refusal of Jesus by human beings is regarded as both determined by God and chosen, hardness of heart is a matter both of fate and of recalcitrance, as it was in the Old Testament. Hardness of heart and temporality are related in Mark in that the fated element in hardness is that in this age revelation is concealed when it is given. Its full effectiveness awaits the future. Hardness of heart is the fundamental defect at the inner core of human being. It is both willfully chosen and fated. Therefore divorce, or any other expression of hardness of heart, is conceivable both because people freely, if irrationally, choose it and are fated to choose it.

Recall that Childs and Von Rad argue that hardness in the Old Testament is a specific response and not a state of mind. In Mark the three passages other than 10:2–9 might be understood as referring to a direct and specific negative response to Jesus' action and preaching. But in 10:2–9 it is more a continuing condition which is being depicted. This is suggested by the overall content of the passage. Hardness of heart is something that has generally obtained from a time before the giving of the law by Moses until now. Also the nominal term *sklērokardia* is more abstract than the noun and verb together in 6:52 and 8:17. Mark must have thought that specific acts of rejection produce a general condition, a habit of mind.

We have seen that Mark attributes both the failure to understand the manifestation of the kingdom in Jesus, or lack of faith, and moral fault to hardness of heart. Since both of these negative phenomena proceed from a distortion of the hidden inner center of human beings, they have an organic and impenetrable interrelationship. We would therefore expect their positive opposites, faith (9:23) and love (12:31), to be just as intimately related in those who have been renewed by entering the kingdom (10:15); we have seen this to be the case (chapter 6).

Content Criticism: Unexceptionable Rule and Qualifying Factors

For Mark the kingdom of God occurring in Jesus as love has brought forgiveness of sins (2:5, 15-17) and deliverance from demonic constriction (1:21-28, 34; 3:11-12; 5:1-20). In response the disciple is to love the neighbor (12:31). We have also observed that the hardness of heart from which divorce and remarriage proceed is both freely chosen and divinely determined, so that the forbidden acts, which manifest a failure to live in the ever-new love that belongs to the beginning of the world, are also both chosen and fated. In the light of these two principles we must practice content criticism (*Sachkritik*) on Mark. Does the specific teaching on divorce accord with the Gospel as a whole? In view of the meaning of the narrative as love and in view of the partial concealment of revelation and fatedness of sin, should divorce and remarriage be unqualifiedly condemned as adultery and absolutely forbidden as an unexceptionable rule?[42] Mark has suggested that the anticipation of the end in the present has brought the beginning of creation again into the middle of time, and that means the possible re-creation of marriages broken down in this middle. But Mark has also proclaimed that the kingdom is coming, which means that in some sense it has not come.

Eschatology and Ethics

Jack Sanders may be right that imminent eschatology has a certain prominence in Mark.[43] Since he believes that Jesus too had an imminent eschatology,[44] what he says about the relationship between eschatology and ethics in Jesus he ought to say in principle about Mark as well. It is Sanders's view that Jesus' radical love commandment is possible only if the kingdom of God is imminent or is believed to be imminent.[45] Once the pressure of imminence is released, the command must be relaxed.[46] The realizability of the ethic depends on the imminence of eschatology. But Sanders marginally implies another position which points to what I think is actually the case in Mark: the kingdom is so near that one might live as if it were present.[47] In fact, the kingdom *is* present for Mark, and it is because it *is* present or actualized that the ethic is possible, and it is because the kingdom is not yet present that the ethic is not possible.

In the light of Mark's eschatology the narrative text as a whole does not understand indissoluble marriage as simply possible *or* impossible but as dialectically possible *and* impossible. The ethical considerations depend radically upon the character of the time.

The eschatological new creation has both come and not come, so everything is not thoroughly redeemed. The realistic interpreter is compelled by Mark's own eschatology to grant that. Thus it may be that even when a serious and responsible effort has been made, some marriages cannot be saved. They cannot be saved, because the time in which even the believer lives is not totally renewed and not just because there has been an insufficient act of will. Or there has been insufficient will because the very temporal structure of existence does not permit any more than there is. The divine resources are not there yet, because the age to come does not sufficiently penetrate this age. There is still "hardness of heart," because the revelation that would redeem completely is as yet postponed until the future. This is the almost tragic element in the Markan understanding of temporal existence. But the redemptive element is also prominently there.

The very existence of the prohibition against divorce shows that the divine resources (eschatological revelation) for indissoluble marriage are not unequivocally there. According to Jer. 31:33–34, for instance, in the time of the eschatological new covenant there will be no place for an ethical imperative, for knowledge of God—including his ethical will—will be implanted in the heart, inscribed on the inner core. Obedience will be innate and spontaneous. Augustine, speaking from the standpoint of an imperative delivered by the self to itself, knows that disobedience occurs because the will does not wholly order itself to will the good. But if the will were whole and entire in its power and not divided, it would be unnecessary for it to give itself an order in the first place.[48] The self's imperative to itself is a sign that it is divided and fallen. We may say then, from the vantage point of Jeremiah and Augustine, that the consciousness of ethical demand is itself a sign of fallenness, a sign of an inclination to disobedience. Thus in the Yahwistic creation story (Genesis 2) Adam is fallen from the beginning, fallen before he disobeys, because he is from the beginning aware of the prohibition (Gen. 2:16–17). This is one reason why the Eden story (Genesis 3) should not be taken as teaching that there was a *time* before the fall, before hardness of heart. The story rather represents the fundamental human situation in fallen time. But there is also something significant in the story's suggestion that Adam falls (awareness of prohibition, Gen. 2:16–17) before he falls (disobedience, Gen. 3:6–7). It means that there is no unfallen time or situation in human history. But it is also implied that there was a time when Adam was not fallen (he has not yet disobeyed, not until 3:6–7). This means that despite the fall there is in the human self a vital potentiality for existence in the world before God, however much it may have been distorted by the conditions of existence. Mark's appeal to the creation as the time of indissoluble marriage is, then, an appeal to the unfallen side of the fallen/unfallen paradox.

Mark's understanding of the relationship between the actualization of divine revelation and the ethical demand is similar to that in the Garden of Eden story but different from that presupposed by the Deuteronomic divorce law. The Genesis story represents the overlapping of the unfallen moment of creation with the history (time) of fallen humanity. Mark portrays a similar overlapping. In Mark 10:1–12 there is overlapping between unfallen creation time and the historical time of hardness of heart. Globally, in Mark, there is the overlapping between historical time and eschatological time, which recovers the lost creation. That Mark actually does have in mind this overlapping, and not the unmoderated eschatological time, is clear from the fact that in the time of the resurrection there will be no marriage (12:24–25). Hence the question of divorce cannot even arise. *That* there is a prohibition against divorce, a call for indissoluble marriage, signifies the fallen time of world history, hardness of heart. But the *what,* the content, of the demand presupposes the unfallen time of creation and eschaton. The ethical demand presupposes at one and the same time the presence of the fallen time which is and that of the unfallen time which is no longer and is not yet. This is the Markan paradox: If the coming of the kingdom of God had completely realized the new creation, marriage could be perfect and indissoluble. But if the eschaton were in fact fully realized, there would be no awareness of a demand and no marriage. The Deuteronomic divorce law, on the other hand, while it presupposes a responsible attitude toward life in this time, does not assume the inescapable tension of the fusion of two different kinds of time.

John Dominic Crossan has argued that paradox about ethical matters or the relativizing of ethical principles turns us toward silence[49] or, at best, toward the silent darkness where ethics is forged in risk and danger.[50] Risk and danger, yes! And a residue of mystery will always remain. But our task is to reflect as far as we can on the ethical implications of the New Testament's paradoxical view of existence.

Mark suggests that since time is not fully renewed, there may be cases in which a marriage is like an old wineskin into which no new wine will be poured. In a time that is both fallen and renewed not all marriages (wineskins) will be able to be forms for the expression of eschatological newness (wine), and no marriages will be able to be this completely. On the other hand, a divorce and remarriage may be the opportune moment for the gospel, for the good news introduces a new beginning into the broken-down middle of time, including the time after irreparably broken marriages. Thus the remarriage of a divorced person may be the beginning of a new story shaped by the gospel as well as an act of adultery. Divorce and remarriage *are* an offense—adultery; and they express hardness of heart. The latter is an offense because on one of its sides it is a refusal to understand how God is working in the world with people and a refusal to continue love to the most intimate neighbor, the relationship with whom is to take precedence over all others. Hardness of heart is an offense in that it is the choice to violate the new order of temporal reality, the reintroduction of the time of creation with its vitality and spontaneity into the wearied middle of time. However, to the extent that the kingdom is still to come, these forbidden acts are not just an offense but also a near-tragic inevitability. And whether they are chosen, fated, or both, they are an occasion for the gospel to shape lives anew, for Mark's narrative takes its new beginning in the worn-out time when Israel was sinful and without the Spirit, and it offers itself to individuals in whatever circumstances they find themselves. Those who divorce and remarry obviously need this new beginning. Those who marry and do not divorce also need it, for in the middle of time no marriages remain at the beginning; none fail to decline from the eschatological first time, the time of the first time for love.

NOTES

1. Patte, *What is Structural Exegesis?* 45.

2. *Contra* Vincent Taylor, *The Gospel According to Saint Mark,* 415; Cranfield, *The Gospel According to Saint Mark,* 319; Hugh Anderson, *The Gospel of Mark,* 241.

3. See Hans Walter Wolff, *Anthropology of the Old Testament,* Eng. trans. M. Kohl (Philadelphia: Fortress Press, 1974), 27–30, esp. 29. W. D. Davies has argued that in Mark 10:1ff. Jesus saw the purpose of God in creation as indissoluble marriage. See Davies, *The Setting of the Sermon on the Mount* (Cambridge: At the University Press, 1964), 430.

4. Dewey, *Markan Public Debate,* 93.

5. See Vincent Taylor, *The Gospel According to Saint Mark,* 213.

6. Gerd Theissen, *Sociology of Early Palestinian Christianity*, Eng. trans. J. Bowden (Philadelphia: Fortress Press, 1978), 8, 10–15, 19, 22–23.

7. Ibid., 17–19, 22–23.

8. Antoinette Wire, "The Structure of the Gospel Miracle Stories and Their Tellers," *Semeia* 11 (1978): 87, 91, 92, 109, 110.

9. Theissen, *The Miracle Stories of the Early Christian Tradition*, 211–15. See also Paul J. Achtemeier, "An Imperfect Union: Reflections on Gerd Theissen, *Urchristliche Wundergeschichten*," *Semeia* 11 (1978): 61, 62, 64.

10. Achtemeier, ibid., 62, 63.

11. Lane C. McGaughy, "Mark 10:32–52: An Analysis in Terms of Surface Structure," a paper presented in the SBL Seminar on Mark, 1979.

12. For a different point of view on the question of genre, see the recent splendid book of Werner H. Kelber, *The Oral and the Written Gospel* (Philadelphia: Fortress Press, 1983). Kelber has identified Mark generically as an augmented parable (pp. 13, 216–20). In his judgment a parable is not constituted by a specific narrative or compositional form (p. 58), but it has other defining features, which are manifested in Mark's Gospel.

(1) One of these is metaphoricity: there is a double meaning effect which suspends meaning and delays comprehension. The whole narrative is both the revelation of mystery and an impenetrable riddle so that the whole points beyond itself to the kingdom of God. This metaphorical functioning of the narrative creates a division between the outsiders who do not understand and the insiders who do (pp. 123–24).

(2) The second one is extravagance. Mark has installed the disciples as insiders and Jesus' family and opponents as outsiders. But this parabolic scheme is no sooner introduced than it begins to be inverted. The disciples progressively become outsiders, and certain people from the outside become believers, so that the structure of expectations is reversed. And this reversal occurs in the Gospel in many connections (pp. 124–29, 215–16).

According to Kelber, the Markan narrative rejects the disciples from three different perspectives. In linguistic terms the disciples are among the bearers of oral tradition who are demoted. Parabolically speaking, we have the reversal of the insider role. And from the standpoint of the history of religions, at the very end of the story (16:1–8) they do not receive the life-giving message from the women. Therefore, says Kelber, the disciples are irrevocably negated, and their rehabilitation is positively excluded. Yet Kelber speaks of the ending as an open and inconclusive parabolic ending (pp. 129, 186).

In response to Kelber's position: First, I would make a closer connection between metaphoricity and extravagance than Kelber does, although he implies it. Mark as parable is a metaphor *in that* it manifests extravagance, the semantic extravagance of predicating outsider characteristics of insiders, and vice versa.

Second, if the ending is open and inconclusive, then the disciples cannot be irrevocably rejected. And Kelber's own view of the insider-outsider dialectic requires that the disciples not be regarded as irretrievably lost. If insiders become outsiders and outsiders become insiders, then the disciples (insiders), having become outsiders, *may* become insiders again. The plot itself leaves it open, but 10:39 and 13:5–11 strongly suggest that at least some of the disciples were brought to faith beyond the end of the plot.

This may suggest that other generic possibilities should be considered. The parabolic model illuminates some of Mark's themes and the metaphorical interrelationships of his diction. But the miracle story model may take us closer to the plot structure (for which parable does not prescribe) and to the rationale for the unambiguous salvation of some characters: Jesus has the power to overcome the constrictions of life. If the disciples are negated from three different perspectives, linguistic, parabolic, and history of religions, that makes their redemption all the more remarkable. The overcoming of seemingly impossible obstacles is characteristic of the miracle story genre.

Kelber does not find miracle story to be the clue to Mark's genre (p. 117) and has argued for an opposition between miracle story and parable. Miracle story functions to support structure and culture, the wresting of order from chaos. It is difficult to see how anyone could be unsettled or alienated by its message. Parable, on the other hand, inclines toward culture-subversion, the inversion of priorities, and the amplification of paradox. Mark's oral legacy contained ordering and disordering forms which were straining against each other (pp. 74–77).

There are differences between the two forms, but do they oppose each other so sharply? The order which miracle stories restore is not the cultural order but the eschatological new creation. To be delivered from the restrictions of illness and self-alienation is not in principle different from deliverance from the restrictions of law and religion (parables). There is good reason to see Mark as a parabolic miracle story.

13. See Eduard Schweizer, *The Good News According to Mark,* Eng. trans. D. Madvig (Atlanta: John Knox Press, 1970), 109; Hugh Anderson, *The Gospel of Mark,* 145. On Christ as the bringer of a new creation or new beginning in Mark and Paul, see W. D. Davies, *Paul and Rabbinic Judaism* (London: S.P.C.K., 1948), 40–43, 151–52, 304.

14. As suggested by Kermode. On this story, see Kermode, *The Genesis of Secrecy,* 130.

15. See Vincent Taylor, *The Gospel According to Saint Mark,* 285; Bilezikian, *The Liberated Gospel,* 71; Belo, *A Materialist Reading of the Gospel of Mark,* 130.

16. See Hugh Anderson, *The Gospel of Mark,* 150.

17. See Kermode, *The Genesis of Secrecy,* 135.

18. See Belo, *A Materialist Reading of the Gospel of Mark,* 132.

19. Ibid.

20. See John R. Donahue, *Are You the Christ?* (Missoula, Mont.: Scholars Press, 1973), 42, 58–63.

21. Belo, *A Materialist Reading of the Gospel of Mark,* 132.

22. See Kermode, *The Genesis of Secrecy,* 132.

23. David L. Miller suggests that a remythologizing of doctrine might bring hidden possibilities of meaning to light. His mode of theologizing is not faith seeking understanding but theology's many understandings seeking life-sense in myth. See *Christs,* xvi–xviii.

24. For discussions, see Albrecht Alt, *Essays on Old Testament History and Religion,* Eng. trans. R. Wilson (Garden City, N.Y.: Doubleday & Co., Anchor Books, 1968), 113–15, 135–37, 140–41, 146, 151–53; Martin Noth, *The Laws in*

the Pentateuch and Other Studies, Eng. trans. D. Ap-Thomas (Philadelphia: Fortress Press, 1967; London: SCM Press, 1984), 7; Brevard S. Childs, *The Book of Exodus* (Philadelphia: Westminster Press, 1974), 389; W. J. Harrelson, s.v. "Law in the OT," *The Interpreter's Dictionary of the Bible;* S. Greengus, s.v., "Law in the OT," *The Interpreter's Dictionary of the Bible,* Supplementary Volume; Erhard Gerstenberger, "Covenant and Command," *Journal of Biblical Literature* 84 (1965): 49–50.

25. Alt, *Essays on Old Testament History and Religion,* 134–35, 145.

26. See Schweizer, *The Good News According to Mark,* 201.

27. For example, Georg Strecker, *Der Weg der Gerechtigkeit* (Göttingen: Vandenhoeck & Ruprecht, 1971), 130–32.

28. See F. Blass and A. Debrunner, *A Greek Grammar of the New Testament,* Eng. trans. R. Funk (Chicago: Univ. of Chicago Press, 1961), 188.

29. See Moule, *Idiom Book,* 148–49.

30. Soler, "The Dietary Prohibitions of the Hebrews," 29.

31. Moule, *Idiom Book,* 53.

32. See Wolff, *Anthropology,* 40, 43, 46–50, 51–54.

33. Childs, *The Book of Exodus,* 171–74.

34. Ibid., 171–72, 174.

35. Von Rad, *Old Testament Theology,* 2:151–55.

36. As Childs (*The Book of Exodus,* 174) claims.

37. Gadamer, *Truth and Method,* 350, 358, 429.

38. Walter Wink, "The Elements of the Universe in Biblical and Scientific Perspective," *Zygon* 13/3 (1978): 233–36, 240–41.

39. Gadamer, *Truth and Method,* xix, 351.

40. Merleau-Ponty, *The Visible and the Invisible,* 146–48.

41. Ibid., 148.

42. Outka suggests that rules which are derived from the love commandment, which would be the case in Mark given the presiding role of love, are subject to reconsideration and revision in the light of that commandment. See Outka, "Character, Conduct, and the Love Commandment," 48–49.

43. Jack Sanders, *Ethics in the New Testament* (Philadelphia: Fortress Press, 1975), 33.

44. Ibid., 9, 17, 29.

45. Ibid., 9, 16–17, 28.

46. Ibid., 17.

47. Ibid., 9.

48. Augustine, *Confessions* VIII.9

49. Crossan, *Raid on the Articulate,* 68.

50. Ibid., 112–14.

8

Becoming Like a Child
Mark 10:13–16

Narrative Analysis

This passage has more directly to do with faith than with ethics. That is to say, it puts in the foreground the question of how one is to receive the kingdom of God rather than the issue of how a disciple is to live out this relationship with God in various kinds of connections with other people. But the integral relationship between faith and conduct is exemplified in that this passage comes between two others that have a very specifically ethical interest. Moreover, the two framing sections (Mark 10:1–12 and 10:17–22) have their own internal theological concerns, while 10:13–16 itself has a certain ethical import.

The act of bringing the children to be touched by Jesus is an act of obedience, the acceptance of a mandate. The latter is not manifested in this pericope itself but is evident in Mark's narrative world generally. The meaning of Jesus' whole mission is the imperative to repent and believe in the good news (1:15). And this call continues to be effective in the circulating story about Jesus which brings people to him (1:45; 5:27; 10:47). The disciples immediately rebuke the efforts of these people to get the children into Jesus' presence (10:13b), which constitutes a confrontation. But Jesus indignantly notices this rebuke and calls for the children to be brought to him (10:14). He thereby accepts, as he characteristically does, his own mandate to be the redeeming Son of God/Son of man (1:11; 2:17; 8:31; 10:45). Jesus' acceptance of his mandate enables those bringing the children to dominate the disciples who have confronted them. The dual consequence of the domination is the teaching about receiving the kingdom like a child and the blessing of the children (10:15–16). Ernest Best has observed that 10:14c–15(Jesus' sayings connecting children and the kingdom) probably did not belong to the earliest version of the story. This addition has shifted attention from concern about actual children to the need to be like a child in order to enter the kingdom.[1] It should also be noted that the addition is what enables a segment of story about Jesus, bringing children to him, to have a consequence that speaks to any situation, childlikeness as an image of discipleship.

What Is the Meaning of Childlikeness?

What is the meaning of the child image here? When Jesus says that whoever does not receive the kingdom of God like a child shall not enter it, what childlike quality is it that for Mark defines the proper receiving of the kingdom?[2] Perhaps the first thing to observe is that the kingdom itself is something given and received, not something merited.[3] One can find many different opinions as to what it is about a child that qualifies appropriate receiving. Is it any or all of the following: humble and receptive, simple and natural;[4] no subjective qualities, but objective littleness and helplessness which allows itself to be given a gift;[5] passive, defenseless, and without achievement;[6] obscure, trivial, and unimportant;[7] unromanticized trusting;[8] neither knowing nor creating status;[9] the practice of play and pleasure with some aggressiveness but no relations of dominance?[10]

The multiplicity of the meanings that have been suggested for the child image underscores the fact that Mark does not say what childlike quality he has in mind, if any, and it also points to the subjectivity of the answers that have been given. Let us then take another approach and look at the logic of telling an adult that he must receive the kingdom like a child. To do so obviously involves a change, from adult to child. Thus the adult is being told to *become* like a child, which is what is actually said in Matthew's version of the saying (Matt. 18:3). Matthew has given a satisfactory interpretation. And since the Markan context does not give us the *particular* meaning of childlikeness, let us ask about the *most formal* meaning of the image, one from which all particular meanings must derive. This is to inquire into archetypal meaning, since the archetype of any given experience (childhood), thought, action, relationship, and so forth, is the formal possibility or structural grounding for that phenomenon, which resides in the collective unconscious.[11] It is the class name.

An Archetypal Interpretation

Without making a total commitment to Jung's system of thought, I take it that there is something to his theory of archetypes. If that is the case, then we should not only expect the archetypal symbols to manifest themselves in myths, fairy tales, dreams, and the phenomena of clinical practice[12] but also in the experience, texts, and specific symbols of early

Christianity. That is, archetypes are universal but undergo particular cultural modifications. Gerd Theissen expresses the judgment that biblical symbols represent and give form to psychodynamic processes and do not simply obscure them.[13] And recall David L. Miller's similar statement but from a slightly different vantage point, that one way to conceive of theology is as understanding seeking life-sense in its archetypal underpinnings.[14] If action, thought, and archetypal symbol form a living continuum, as James Hillman[15] has suggested, then one could start with any one of the three foci and move toward the others. What we have in our Markan pericope is that the name of the archetype appears on the surface of the text. Our task is to see what meaning emerges as the Markan narrative and discourse give particularity and definition to the universal archetypal image.

According to Jung, one of the essential features of the child archetype is its futurity. By that Jung means that the child is potential future. The appearance of this image is the anticipation of future developments even though at first sight it may seem like a retrospective configuration.[16] The future is anticipated because the child is evolving toward independence. It cannot do this without detaching itself from its origins; therefore abandonment is a necessary condition for the child to go through. Jung himself observes that when the Gospel calls upon people to become like a child, this refers to a development and transaction that is difficult and dangerous.[17]

In the archetype itself the child as potential for the future moves through the abandonment of a secure origin, through risk and danger toward adulthood. In the Gospel of Mark the adult is called on tacitly to become a child. If the adult does so, he or she must retrace the steps that the child takes in becoming an adult. That is, the adult must take risks and abandon security in order to move back to childhood. Of course, the inescapable implication of Mark's theology is that the adult has not really taken the dangerous way. He or she has, rather, held on to false securities (4:19) and has become fixed, hardened in a dependence on something that cannot really sustain life (8:36–37). The adult has become hardened in heart, so that the inner center of life is not open to a different future. Thus if one is to have life, one must make the move that one had not made before. One must move back to childhood and begin again. This entails renouncing the shape of one's present existence in order to recover an abandoned potential. Life must be lost in order to be found (8:34–35). The very terminology of the loss of life expresses the radicalness of this move. But the pain and terror of it are more dramatically portrayed, as we have seen, in the story of the Gerasene demoniac. Imprisoned and constricted as this man is in alienation, death, and meaningless self-destruction, he experiences the possibility of release into an open future—Jesus' intention to deliver him—as a tormenting threat to his false security, empty as it is (5:6–8).

In Mark 10:15 the kingdom of God is a gift: it can only be received. The rule of God is his power for which all is possible (10:27). It thus can bring about in a person the fitting kind of receiving; that is, it makes one a child, and this, as we have seen, involves passing through death. When that passage is accomplished, when that receiving takes place, one enters the kingdom, the power of God for a new narrative existence. To receive the kingdom like a child is to be brought by God's kingly power along the passage through death to a new potential for the future, to childhood. Both receiving and entering the kingdom are presented as a present possibility; the two acts are simultaneous. This interpretation is based on the fact that both verbs are in the same tense and mood (aorist subjunctive).

But the kingdom of God for Mark is also future (9:1; 13:32–36). Therefore to enter the kingdom is to be placed in a new story which moves toward a redemptive future. It is to be walking on a way, the way to Jerusalem (10:32). It is only after Bartimaeus has received the new insight (10:52) that makes him a child again that he can *begin* to follow Jesus in his way. In summary, then, the move from hardened adulthood to restored childhood is one that requires the passage through death. And achieving childhood is a new beginning that puts one on the way *toward* the cross. Becoming a child is the potentiality for living the new life which constantly requires death to self-interest in dealing with the life realities of marriage (10:1–12), wealth (10:17–22), and the interrelationships in the new community (10:29–30)—the new life which is now (1:15; 9:37; 10:15) and will be (1:15; 9:42–48; 10:30; 13:27) eternal life. In order to enter the kingdom which is ultimately the fulfilled future, one must go back to the beginning. One must move from fixedness back to a restored potentiality which looks anew into the future. The description of this double movement in Mark interprets and is interpreted by the child image.

According to Paul Ricoeur, the same symbol can point backward toward infancy, and support the Freudian hermeneutic of the unconscious, and forward toward adulthood, and support the Hegelian hermeneutic of the Spirit. For Freud, meaning proceeds from the past, from the unconscious. And for Hegel, it proceeds from the future, from Spirit. One of the tasks of hermeneutics is to disclose a symbol's, or a symbolic configuration's, multiple levels of meaning.[18] The child image in Mark in its capacity to focalize both the movement back to a new beginning and the movement forward to an open future discloses in an essential way this polyvalent character of symbols. Being a child is both the end and the beginning of the process of salvation.

Childhood and a Pre-Ethical Ethic

Ricoeur, again, speaks of a certain ethical moment as an ethic of desire or of the effort to be in the awareness of lack of being. This is a kind of pre-ethical ethic, a hearkening to a word that reveals a mode of being that is prior to doing, a desire that seeks to reappropriate the power to exist.[19] The meaning that collects around the child archetype in Mark seems close to this "pre-ethical ethic." We have seen that Mark's statement, "Whoever does not receive the kingdom of God like a child shall not enter it," contains an implicit imperative. For an adult to become a child does require a decision, an effort, which is a response to a word—the story of Jesus with its power to transform. The effort called for is the effort to reappropriate childhood, a new beginning, the power to exist which is prior to the achievement of being through doing.

Finally let us note the inner connections between this passage on becoming a child and the marriage and divorce pericope that precedes (10:1–12) and the story of the rich man that follows (10:17–22). We have observed that the call for insoluble marriage and no divorce rests on the reawakening and continuance of the beginning of creation. And 10:13–16 is an exhortation to make the turn and grasp the beginning again, become a child, obviously using different imagery. Mark 10:13–16 also points forward to the story of the rich man to which it is related as potentiality to actuality, as pre-ethic to ethic. Becoming like a child discloses the kind of faith stance that is necessary in order to engage in the kind of ethical action called for in the rich man pericope. And the latter shows what is required of the one with the new self-understanding of the child. Here we may note the same paradoxical relationship between eschatological renewal and ethical demand which we observed in connection with marriage. Such radical action and risk can be *called for* because existence itself has been transformed through the eschatological renewal. And the radicalness of the demand (sell all) presupposes the complete realization of the eschatological new creation. But if the latter were fully realized, there would be no more poverty and no awareness of an imperative (sell and give). Mark's ethic is not in a really proper sense the ethic of the kingdom of God. It is the ethic for that highly paradoxical overlapping of the eschatological kingdom and fallen human history. The demand in its absoluteness seems to reflect the finality of God's eschatological kingdom. But the enablement reflects the paradox of the overlapping: it is final and less than final.

Here I have focused only on the meaning of the exhortation to receive the kingdom like a child. It should not be lost sight of that the pericope also reveals Jesus' love for children.

NOTES

1. See Best, *Following Jesus,* 107.
2. It should be noted that the sentence can be read not only as "whoever does not receive the kingdom in a childlike way shall not enter it" but also as "whoever does not receive the kingdom as he receives a child shall not enter it." See Hugh Anderson, *The Gospel of Mark,* 246.
3. See Taylor, *The Gospel According to Saint Mark,* 423-24.
4. Taylor, *The Gospel According to Saint Mark,* 423.
5. Cranfield, *The Gospel According to Saint Mark,* 324.
6. Schweizer, *The Good News According to Mark,* 206.
7. Hugh Anderson, *The Gospel of Mark,* 246.
8. Best, *Following Jesus,* 107-8.
9. Gager, *Kingdom and Community,* 34.
10. Belo, *A Materialist Reading of the Gospel of Mark,* 170-71.
11. See C. G. Jung, "The Psychology of the Child Archetype," trans. R. F. Hull in *Psyche and Symbol: A Selection from the Writings of C. G. Jung,* ed. V. S. de Laszlo (Garden City, N.Y.: Doubleday Anchor Books, 1958), 117. See further *Psyche and Symbol,* xvi, 19, 61, 118-19, 123; C. G. Jung, *The Archetypes and the Collective Unconscious,* trans. R. F. Hull (New York: Pantheon Books, 1959), 38, 48, 57, 66.
12. See Jung, "Child Archetype," p. 115.
13. Theissen, *Sociology of Early Palestinian Christianity,* 124.
14. Miller, *Christs,* xvi-xvii, xviii, xx.
15. Hillman, *Re-Visioning Psychology,* xiii, 44, 115-17, 120, 122-23, 127, 130, 132, 142, 145, 156.
16. Jung, "Child Archetype," 127.
17. Jung, "The Special Phenomenology of the Child Archetype," in *Psyche and Symbol,* 133-34.
18. Paul Ricoeur, "The Hermeneutics of Symbols and Philosophical Reflection: II," Eng. trans. C. Freilich, in *The Conflict of Interpretations,* ed. D. Ihde (Evanston, Ill.: Northwestern University Press, 1974), 325-26; *De l'interprétation* (Paris: Éditions du Seuil, 1965), 446, 476-79, 495-99.
19. Paul Ricoeur, "The Demythization of Accusation," Eng. trans. P. McCormick; "Religion, Atheism, and Faith," Eng. trans. C. Freilich, both in *The Conflict of Interpretations,* 340-42, 449-52.

9

Selling Property and
Giving to the Poor
Mark 10:17–22

Narrative Analysis

What is expected of one who has become a child? Again the mandate is only implied, but the man who comes to Jesus has heard something that makes him think that Jesus is good and may know the way to eternal life (Mark 10:17), something that summons him. His running to Jesus is the acceptance of this implied mandate (10:17) and simultaneously a mandate to Jesus to tell him the way to eternal life. In a brief and undeveloped confrontation Jesus rejects the qualification of good (10:18). Then he accepts his mandate to tell the man the way to eternal life which is at the same time a mandate to the man to follow the familiar commandments of Moses (10:19). Thereupon the man claims that he has been doing these things since his youth (10:20). Jesus replies that he lacks one thing and issues the additional imperative that the man sell all that he has and give to the poor, and come follow him (10:21). These commands suggest how much the law really requires and in so doing render ironical the "one thing." The one thing that is lacking is really everything. The man rejects the mandate to remedy this lack, showing that he is not prepared to obey the commandments and serve God radically (10:22).

Retaining Security as the Problem

The development of the story shows that the real concern of the man is to make himself secure (10:22): he will not abandon his possessions (*hosa echeis*). Howard Clark Kee states that the man's verbalized reliance on obedience to the commandments (10:19) is belied by his unacknowledged confidence in what he has (10:22).[1] But I would argue that his confidence in his wealth is the clue to the character of his obedience to the law. They are shown to be of one piece. The uncovering of his basic disposition of dependence on wealth shows that his obedience to the law is similar: he accumulates possessions and he accumulates obedience in order to make himself secure. Thus his observance of the commandments is not the kind that Jesus wants. The similarity of the two dependences is also seen in that they are both subject to the same kind of criticism. It is implied that his possessions keep him from acquiring eternal life: sell *whatever you have* and *you will have* treasure in heaven. And it is stated that his obedience is lacking. Given his dual dependence, he would be equally threatened by these two criticisms. Yet in some sense he already knew that obedience to the moral law and his wealth would not give foundation to his existence. When he came to Jesus he knew already that he was moral and that he was rich, but the very fact that he came inquiring shows that he sensed that these could not confer eternal life. One act would solve both problems. If he sold all he had and gave to the poor and followed Jesus, he would remove the impediment to the acquiring of treasure in heaven and also liquidate the lack of his obedience. These are two aspects of the same problem.

Love as Radical Obedience

The kind of obedience that, in Mark's view, the law really requires is interpreted by the command to sell all one has for the sake of the poor and to follow Jesus. The Jesus who is to be followed has already ignored the distinction that the law establishes between the cultically clean and unclean (2:15–17) and has in fact denied the validity of the cultic system (7:15). In the ethical realm he has set the will of God over against the law (10:3–9), and this relativizing of the ethical law is carried further in 10:17–22. A disciple does not have the security of knowing in advance exactly what he or she is to do, except to love (12:28–34). Love is particularized in the present passage. Jesus commands the one who would have eternal life to show total concern for the other/neighbor and to abandon his or her own security. This is more than the law requires as traditionally understood. The laws, then, are traces of God's will; they are marked by it, but they cannot be relied on in particular circumstances necessarily to be the exact manifestation of the will of God. Yet since the law is cited and not abandoned, since it *is* a trace of God's will, it is a clue to what the latter requires and points one in the right direction. Laws and rules reveal the kind of concrete issues the will of God is concerned about and in a provisional way show one how one ought to address oneself to these issues. But what the will of God finally requires cannot be derived from the laws. The list of the man's moral accomplishments apparently is intended to suggest that his obedience to the law is complete: he has not killed, committed adultery, stolen, borne false witness, or defrauded; and he has honored his father and mother. Jesus believed him and loved him. But this obedience to the sum of the moral law does not offer sufficient acknowledgment of the demand of God's will. What the will of God requires cannot be derived from the law. This is seen in the fact that the man's comprehensive obedience is said to lack one thing—everything: total giving to the other and total relinquishment of security. It is also seen in that another command is given: sell all and follow. This is not one more command but the meaning and aim of all the commands. In view of this it is not quite the case that Mark in 10:19 cites the Decalogue without reserve.[2]

Giving to the Poor for the Sake of One's Own Salvation

As we have observed before, the poor figure in the statement of the ethical norm: *whatever you have* sell and give to the poor. But it is tacit in this passage and clear in the next one that Mark has more interest in the consequences of possessions for the ethical agent who might give than he has in the consequences for the other/neighbor/poor to whom the money might be given. His question is: can the *rich* man enter the kingdom of God. Giving to the poor, as Mark implicitly interprets it by means of this story about the rich man, is intentioned by self-interest. The reason for acting is to inherit eternal life or enter the kingdom of God: "What must I do to inherit eternal life?" "Give to the poor, and *you will have* treasure in heaven." But the self-interest which is served by gaining eternal life is a paradoxical one, for eternal life here as interpreted by the story, is the freedom from the self, from self-interest, which enables one to give all for the poor.

The pattern of radical concern for the poor intentioned by the desire to gain eternal life for oneself may have a christological parallel and basis in Mark. The Son of man gives his life as a ransom for the many (10:45). But his reason for acting is that he wants to be obedient to the necessity (8:31) which has been written for him in Scripture (14:21) and grounded in the will of God (14:36). He wants to be faithful to his destiny; he wants to be who he is. And so he acts in obedience; he suffers. And what is the consequence of that in the tragicomic world into which Mark offers us entrance: "My God, my God, why hast thou forsaken me?" (15:34). And shortly thereafter comes the resurrection. Mark wants to give to those who decide to follow Jesus some idea of what to expect.[3]

Is Abandoning All Property a Demand Made of All Disciples?

Gerd Theissen has attributed the abandonment of wealth and family in the Gospel to a pre-Markan stage of the tradition and connected it with the wandering charismatic leaders.[4] To some degree, Mark does make the question of possessions or wealth a symbol of the problem of faith (10:23–24); wealth is *whatever* gets in the way of one's entering the kingdom. And this move in some degree moderates the sharpness of the ethical side of Mark's treatment of the subject: sell *whatever you have* and give. But Mark continues to be concerned about the *material* side of the Christian community (10:29–30) and the plight of the poor (14:7). And even if the abandonment of possessions was a pattern of behavior for the wandering charismatic, and not for the community at large, in the pre-Markan tradition, Mark has placed the imperative to abandon one's goods in an arresting way in the middle of his primary ethical discourse and has made giving one's all to the poor a part of the ethical norm for all disciples.

But does that mean that all disciples are literally under the imperative to give up all of their possessions for the poor? The text of Mark seems to suggest two different answers to that question. On the one hand, it is not to be taken literally, which is supported by two motifs in the Gospel. First, not every disciple is asked to give up what he or she has (5:19–20). Second, material wealth symbolizes whatever inordinate attachment a person may have which must be given up in order to follow Jesus (10:23–24),[5] so only in particular cases may all property have to be given up. This is also supported by Mark's own overall tendency to relativize the authority of specific ethical rules. On the other hand, a literal interpretation seems to be favored by Mark's declaration that the Christian community is to be composed of people who have actually left their families, homes, and lands in order to form this new community. This is what the Christian community ought to be. But since those who have relinquished all sustain one another in both personal and material ways, we must be careful about the sense in which we could speak of Mark as having an ethic of poverty.[6] Perhaps the two approaches to the command to give up whatever one has for the other can be synthesized. There is to be a community of disciples, and those who are members must give whatever is necessary to sustain the community materially. And they must give up whatever else stands in the way of total commitment to following Jesus and love for the community. But in view of the full context of the Gospel it is probably too much to say with reference to 10:28–30 that the abandonment of everything is an absolute and universal demand laid upon every disciple.[7]

This episode (Mark 10:17–22) dramatizes the theme stated earlier in 4:19 that the deceitfulness of riches or possessions chokes the word of the gospel. Here the desire to retain his wealth has deflected this man from his pursuit of eternal life. According to Fernando Belo, the man "who has" is unfruitful because he lives in a class society, a society in which desires are bewitched by the dominant codes, in this case the desire for material wealth.[8] One may doubt that it is only or peculiarly in a class society, a non-Marxist society, that material wealth is a spiritual problem in which one's desires are bewitched. Surely Mark understands himself to be dealing with a fundamentally human problem, the problem of how human beings deal with, and are dealt with by, material wealth in the middle of time where hardness of heart is endemic. Deceit is an element—perhaps both weapon and symptom—of hardness of heart. Riches and possessions deceive in the precise sense that they seduce one into believing that life can in fact be found in them (8:36) rather than in following Jesus. And yet one *knows* that he is letting himself be deceived, otherwise why would the man have gone away sorrowful?

NOTES

1. Kee, *Community of the New Age,* 154.

2. As claimed by Schrage, *Ethik des Neuen Testaments,* 136.

3. For a fuller discussion of Mark 15:34 in relation to Psalm 22 and in relation to the rest of the Markan narrative, see Via, *Kerygma and Comedy,* 146–47.

4. Theissen, *Sociology of Early Palestinian Christianity,* 10–14.

5. For the view that the total renunciation of possessions is not a demand placed upon every disciple but that it represents whatever must be given up in order to follow Jesus, see Schweizer, *The Good News According to Mark,* 212; Cranfield, *The Gospel According to Saint Mark,* 330.

6. Gager (*Kingdom and Community,* 24) holds that such passages as Mark 10:25; Luke 6:20; Matt. 5:3; James 5:1–3 point to a clearly formulated ethic of poverty.

7. As claimed by Best, *Following Jesus,* 113.

8. Belo, *A Materialist Reading of the Gospel of Mark,* 172.

10

Salvation and the Christian Community
Mark 10:23–31

Narrative Analysis

This passage is connected to Mark 10:17–22 in at least two ways. The problem of the relationship of possessions to the possibility of salvation is taken up in an explicit way and universalized. And the practical consequences in actual historical existence of renouncing property or possessions are addressed by the projection of what the Christian community ought to be. This pericope, then, has two themes: the possibility of salvation and the communal nature of salvation. But it is a narrative whole, for all of the functions of the test sequence, (see chapter 3, excursus) as well as others, are manifested here.

Jesus' words about the difficulty of entering the kingdom (with riches) are in context a mandate to the disciples to renounce wealth (10:23–25). They in effect reject this as an impossible demand (10:26). Jesus then assures them that although salvation is impossible with human beings, all is possible with God (10:27). This is a promise which fuses the consequence or attribution function of both a qualifying and a main test. Divine help is promised and also the value (salvation) that God's help confers. Note that this consequence logically follows a confrontation and victory, but in this immediate context nothing is said about a struggle and difficult victory. The disciples are astonished at the stringency of the demand and then are simply promised salvation, since it comes from God, for whom all is possible. But we will see that the confrontation has not been omitted.

Now that he has been addressed by this promise, Peter, having just been a part of the group that objected to the requirement to renounce all wealth, now claims that they have in fact given up everything and followed him (Mark 10:28). Peter's threefold denial of Jesus (14:66–72) and the flight of all the disciples (14:50) when Jesus was arrested turn Peter's claim here into a manifestation of the narrative function which Vladimir Propp called unfounded claims by a false hero.[1] Jesus' counter-

139

statement that no one had left anything without receiving a hundredfold (10:29–30) is the promise of the attribution of salvation and the exposure of the false hero.[2] The one who forsakes wealth and security will receive far more than he or she gives up. This statement renders paradoxical Jesus' demand that everything be renounced: to renounce all is to be given all. The all that is received is brothers and sisters, houses and lands. The placing of a person in a new community is as organically contained in that person's renouncing family and property for Jesus' sake and the gospel's as the saving of life is organically contained in a person's losing his or her life for Jesus' sake and the gospel's (8:35b). The individual faith-existential principle is exactly paralleled by the communal moral principle. And Jesus' statement also reveals a defect in Peter's claim to have given up everything. Had he really abandoned it all, he would have had a sense of fullness rather than of relinquishment. Thus Jesus here suggests that Peter's claim is false, and his later behavior demonstrates it (14:32–42, 50, 66–72).[3]

Salvation in these verses is presented as a promise or hope and not as actualized, because the disciples have not yet successfully passed through confrontation or conflict to victory. They have shown resistance to finding life by losing it. But this sequence does not omit the conflictive element, the confrontation with death as the way to life. This function, too, appears at the end of the sequence (10:31), but as teaching or discourse rather than as action. The first will be last and the last first. This is another way of saying that one comes to life (becomes first) by passing through death (becoming last). Salvation is possible with God, but he accomplishes it by bringing people along this way. What that means for an ethic of property and community is what 10:17–31 is concerned about.

The Possibility of Salvation

Why are the disciples astounded (*ethambounto,* 10:24a) at the statement that the rich will find it hard to enter the kingdom? One view is that this passage refers to a later time in the life of the church, and the disciples symbolize the rich who by that time had actually joined the church.[4] Thus they are astonished because of the threat to themselves. On the other hand, it could be argued that they are astounded, not because of a threat to themselves since they are not rich, but because it is an assumption of theirs that wealth is a blessing from God and a sign of righteousness.[5] Perhaps the second is the more natural interpretation. But then in 10:26 their reaction is mentioned again, and the astonishment has been heightened to exceeding amazement (*perissōs exeplēssonto*).

Why is that? The motif that it is hard for the rich to enter the kingdom of God in 10:23 is enforced in 10:25 by the metaphorical statement that it is easier for a camel to go through the eye of a needle. But in the statement about the difficulty of entering the kingdom in 10:24b the reference to riches is omitted, which makes the assertion of difficulty/ impossibility apply generally to anyone.[6] This ties in with the hint in 10:17–22 that holding on to security in the world (8:36), any security, is the real problem. The recognition that everyone has something to hold on to produces the shocked question, "Then who can be saved?" With human beings it is impossible, but not with God, comes the answer. Yet there are the specific references to the rich in 10:23, 25. Perhaps Mark's paradoxical position is that salvation is impossible for all, but more impossible for the rich.

According to Fernando Belo, the omission of the reference to the rich in 10:24b, which generalizes the difficulty of salvation, has the function of showing that wealth is what determines all of the codes of the social formation. That is, wealth determines not just economic matters but political and ideological ones as well. The generalizing omission also shows that the level of wealth is the focal concern of the Gospel. In the framework of this social system, one based on wealth, it is impossible to be saved.[7] I would argue, however, that given Mark's belief that evil proceeds from the heart (7:21–23) rather than from wealth, it is not so much that wealth determines all factors in the social situation as it is that the heart, hardened, can turn to wealth in any amount, or to anything else in the social order equally well, as an object of inordinate devotion. It could be argued, of course, that while Mark may have rooted evil in the heart, it really arises from material factors. But that contention, if true, would still not be an interpretation of the Markan text. Or it could be argued that Mark *unconsciously* grasped the material or economic root of evil, whatever he might have said explicitly. But we do not know what Mark thought, unconsciously or consciously, other than what is written in the text. Then it could be argued that the *text* presupposes the material basis of evil. But unless there is some indication of tension in the text on this subject, then it cannot be maintained that the text presupposes something that is directly contrary to what it says. There is no indication in Mark that evil arises fundamentally from wealth! But the text does clearly say that *pleonexia* (the grasping desire for advantage) comes forth from within, from the heart (7:21–22); and *pleonexia* attaches itself to possessions (10:22).

How does God save? Salvation comes, as we have seen, through Jesus' death (10:45) and through his giving sight/insight (10:46–52) to the blind/hard of heart (8:17–18). The cross saves by giving insight. But obviously this is not a matter of information. Understanding/sight/ insight (4:10–12) is resident in the heart (6:52; 8:17–18), the hidden inner core of a person. Therefore a change of understanding is a change in the *person.* This change effects the ability to understand the revelation of the dying-rising Son of man as a possibility for *oneself.* The *mis*-understanding of the death and resurrection of the Son of man on the part of the disciples (9:32) was an inability to grasp suffering as the pattern for their own lives. That is seen from the fact that all three suffering Son of man passages are followed by suffering discipleship passages (Mark 8—10). Since understanding and decision making are intertwined in the heart (see chapter 7), a change of self-understanding is also a renewal of the well-springs of moral activity. Moreover, a new *self-understanding* in relation to the suffering Son of man is the same as faith (believing) in the Gospel (1:15), whose content is the Son of God/Son of man.

Salvation is impossible for human beings in that they do not have the resources to sell what they have and give. They cannot relinquish their attachment to whatever it is in the world that gives them security. God saves by giving faith's new self-understanding. And faith, which is freedom from the self and for the other (10:17–22), enables the character and action (9:43–48) which are requisite for eternal life (8:38; 9:42–48; 10:30; 13:27) and which now are eternal life (9:37; 10:15). The renewal of sight/ understanding, which is resident in the heart (8:17–18), enables the reversal of inappropriate conduct, which is rooted in hardness of heart (10:5). The divine activity which thus transforms life becomes effective through the power of the narrative (see chapter 4). Here I have tried to summarize what I think salvation is for Mark. The extent to which and the way in which it is realizable are defined by narrative factors which we have considered and still have to consider.

The Communal Character of Salvation

It has been denied that there is any direct connection between Mark 10:17–22 and 10:28–31,[8] but there is one. The existence of a community based on the renunciation of natural family and personal wealth (10:28– 29), or, more accurately, the affirmation that there should be such a community, is the social horizon which makes conceivable the imperative to sell all one has and give to the poor (10:17–22). Mark 10:17–22 needs 10:28–29 in order to make sense at the level of social-historical existence. There is a direct line (1) from the "rich" man's refusal to sell his property and give to the poor (2) to the discussion with the disciples about wealth and the kingdom (3) to Peter's claim to have forsaken all (4) to Jesus' assertion that no one has left family and property without receiving the same. Those who renounce property in 10:29 are contrasted with the "rich" man in 10:17-22. They do what he should have done, and their doing it leads to the new community. Therefore the poor to whom the "rich" man was commanded to give are, in part, the community, whose members are in a certain sense poor because all of them have given their personal wealth to the group as a whole. Each one who gives becomes a member of the brothers and sisters who share in the houses and lands given by all. That is why renouncing one's wealth is a conceivable act. The disciple is called on to abandon his possessions, but renunciation is neither for the sake of nor with the consequence of asceticism. Neither is this action intentioned just by the desire for eschatological reward,[9] for the very existence of communal life in this world is already an anticipation of eschatological salvation.

As I have observed before, the community of sharing is not an accident of salvation but is essential to it. The emergence of the community is as immanent in forsaking family and property as finding life is immanent in accepting death (8:35). Receiving a community comes from forsaking, and forsaking one's own goods for the other is inherent in the fundamental experience of faith. It enacts the freedom for the other which is the reverse side of freedom from oneself. Freedom from oneself has to be freedom for the other unless faith has to do wholly with God, but for Mark it does not. What is required of human beings cannot be described except as love for both God and the neighbor (12:28-34). Love is faith's "freedom for," for God and the neighbor. Wolfgang Schrage has pointed out that, in Mark, Jesus is surrounded by disciples from the beginning. It is perhaps no accident that the first call narrated is not to one disciple (2:13-14) but to four together (1:16-20). The call places one immediately in community and creates community.[10]

In view of the inherent relationship between salvation and communal life I am inclined not to agree with Ernest Best's contention that the reappearance in 10:30 of the list of goods and relations from 10:29 is clumsy and unnecessary.[11] It was at least necessary for Mark to say that those who forsake family and property (10:29) receive *something* (10:30), for his fundamental point is that forsaking leads to receiving. It is not relinquishing for its own sake. He might have said something relatively general such as, "They will receive whatever they gave up." But the repetition of the list makes it more concretely emphatic that eschatological salvation is a new arrangement of human relationships, houses, and lands. Moreover, a couple of additional points are made by means of the list. One is that the receiving is a "hundredfold." Another is a significant omission. In 10:29 fathers are among the relations forsaken. But in 10:30, while brothers, sisters, mothers, and children are received, fathers are not.

The Community as Eschatological

Carl E. Braaten has observed that the proleptic eschatological renewal of the world will require a fundamental change in the conditions of human existence. The church cannot be satisfied to treat poverty on an individual institutional basis but must seek to deal with the causes of poverty which lie in social connections.[12] Obviously Mark does not have any programs for dealing with these issues. But he does clearly maintain that the believer as believer is involved in a social project that is to deal with the causes of poverty because the bases of society have been rearranged.

The establishment of the new community precipitates a certain rupture in the bond of the natural family. Mark 10:29–30 picks up the issue of 3:19b–21, 31–35, which portrays Jesus as being in tension with his own mother and brothers, if not actually estranged from them. In 3:19b–21 the family thinks that he is beside himself, and in 3:31–35 Jesus states that his real mother and brothers are the disciples around him, those who do the will of God. These two pieces about the family frame a section in which the scribes maintain that Jesus has a demon, and they in turn are held guilty in their blindness of an eternal sin. That which is framed casts its light on the frame, in this case augmenting the distance between Jesus and his family. The scribes and the natural family are assimilated to each other. In 10:29–30 we see that disciples also are expected to leave their natural families, but those who do so will receive a new family, a new community of brothers, sisters, mothers, and children. There will also be a new space—houses and lands. An essential part of eschatological salvation is the restructuring of social relationships on a material basis. And in what kind of time?

The community exists explicitly now in *this* time (*nun en tō kairō toutō*), the time of suffering and persecution (10:30; 13:9–13), which is clearly distinguished from the age to come, which is the time of eternal life. How, then, can the community be called new or eschatological? It can be, because for Mark, as we have seen, the coming kingdom has already dawned in this age and overlaps it. And the imagery of this passage shows that the community in particular is qualified by the eschatological newness. The disciple will receive brothers and sisters, houses and lands, now a *hundredfold;* and hundredfoldness is the mark of eschatological fulfillment. This derives from its employment in the parable of the sower (4:8) and in the interpretation of that parable (4:20). Here we observe that the seed which is described at the *end* of the story produces thirtyfold, sixtyfold, and a hundredfold. Three declining processes of sowing which end in complete unfruitfulness are followed by a rising process which issues in extraordinary productivity. Therefore hundredfoldness signifies climactic success. Moreover, there is something surprising in the series thirty-sixty-hundred. We have some reason to expect thirty-sixty-ninety or thirty-sixty-one hundred and twenty, but there is a certain dissonance and asymmetry in thirty-sixty-hundred which suggests that the eschatological fulfillment is a new future which stands in some discontinuity with the historical process.[13] The eschatological significance of hundredfold is also supported by the immediate context in Mark 4. This extraordinary fruitfulness is paralleled by the harvest (4:29) in the parable of the seed growing secretly and by the greatest of all shrubs (4:32) in the parable of the mustard seed.[14]

The paradoxical overlapping of this age and the age to come in the Christian community is given a particularly forceful expression in 10:30 because the term "hundredfold" (the eschatological sign) is juxtaposed immediately to "now in this age." The eternal life of the age to come, signified by hundredfold, is the quality of life in this time. And the dissonance and discontinuity associated with hundredfold mean that the Christian community will be different from and will stand in tension with the societies that simply belong to this time. It will be different in that those who follow Jesus are given freedom from self-interest (10:17–29) and so are free to relate to the other, not for the sake of the self, but for the sake of the other, although Mark does not specify the well-being of the other as an *intention* for love and service. Those who enact God's will (3:35) as love (12:31) do not exercise authority in the way the Gentiles do (10:42–43) but as servants.

I have stressed that those who have possessions, and all disciples, are summoned to give up everything for the poor and to abandon all security in the world. Is the element of risk involved in this posture then undercut by Mark's belief that those who abandon property and family will be received and sustained in a new community? In part, yes. The demand is not as stark and severe as it appears to be at first. If it were, it would not be in any way practicable in ongoing historical existence, and Mark does not mean to deny historical existence. But the risk element is far from erased. Yes, a community is to be established, *will* be established where faith is real, in which people can give up all their possessions and still be safe. But if some do not give all, take the risk, before there is a sustaining community, there can be no community at all. So one is to give knowing both that it is dangerous and that one might be upheld by the community. Moreover, if such a community did exist (remember that we are talking about Mark's existential-ethical project, not his description of his church in Galilee-Syria) as it might, it would still be a risk to give up one's possessions for it and to become a member of it. A new kind of love reigns in this community because the eschaton has dawned in it, the new creation. But the age to come and eternal life are still awaited and are thus not here. One's brothers, sisters, mothers, and children in the new community, in relation to whom the disciple dies to his or her own self-interest, are both renewed by having stepped into Jesus' story and are infected with the hardness of heart that belongs to the middle of time. In Mark it is dangerous to follow Jesus, because it is a matter of responding totally to the kingdom of God in a time and place in which the kingdom of God is not totally present.

The Community Without a Father

We have observed that while fathers are forsaken, they do not reappear in the new context. Other family relationships are changed in the new community: they can serve as symbolic terms for the relationships in this new situation. But the father relation is altogether displaced; there is no new father. What is the import of that? The patriarchal order of the Old Testament was still in force in first-century Judaism, and a man had great authority over his wife and children.[15] If there is no father in the Christian community, then patriarchal, autocratic authority has been removed. According to James M. Robinson, the omission of the father in 10:30 is intentional, as it is in 3:31–32, 33–35; and 6:3, because, for Mark, God is the father of Jesus absolutely (8:38; 14:36); and he is also the father of disciples (11:25). The gap in the spiritual family is filled by God. He is the only father in the Christian situation.[16] The fatherly presence of God suggests that the community is protected from human authoritarianism. But what if God himself is seen as oppressive?

Must God under the image of father be perceived as an oppressive and even destructive power? According to Freud's well-known theory, the primal horde killed its father and later on deified him as the monotheistic god. The Israelite experience recapitulated this with Moses' murder by the Israelites, which was repressed, being a reiteration of the murder of the primal father. Monotheism and its concomitant moral power are based on the memory of the aggrieved primal father, whose will is to be obeyed all the more because we have grieved him. The murdered father binds us to himself by guilt. For Freud, the primal horde construct is the collective expression of the individual Oedipus complex with its threatening father. If God is so understood, then a relationship with him must be seen as inimical to personal growth and maturity.[17] Mary Daly has recently maintained that the patriarchal God of the Bible epitomizes an authoritarianism which at best enforces structures that obstruct human becoming, structures of permanence, and at worst produces rape, genocide, and war.[18]

The Bible itself, however, does not understand God in a way that would justify reading such oppressive schemes into it. The pre-Mosaic ancestors of Israel may well have thought of their god, or gods, as their sexual progenitor to whom they were bound by nature. But the faith that emerged from the exodus replaced natural generation with the image of adoption (Exod. 6:6–8). The covenant between Yahweh and Israel is a matter of free choice on both sides (Exodus 19). Since there is no longer a bond of nature with God, there is a break in the collective Oedipal situation.[19] One way in which this break is developed in the Old Testament is that the father image is fused with other symbols of God. A father who is also the forgiving husband of an unfaithful wife (as, e.g., in Hosea) is no longer a begetter or a threat to his sons, but is rather quite the opposite (Hos. 11:1–9). If in the New Testament the death of Jesus is in some measure another reiteration of the death of the primal father, the Freudian construct has nevertheless been further metamorphosized. In the death of the righteous sufferer human aggressive impulses against the father are satisfied. But because Jesus takes the place of the father, and dies for others, the meaning of the death is reversed, and the paternal image is transformed in the direction of kindness and compassion.[20]

What is the case in Mark specifically? God as Jesus' father does will his death (14:36). If that is all we had to go on, we might have to grant a good deal to Freud. But Jesus is also God's beloved son (1:11; 9:7), and the death which God wills him to die is for the many (10:45). And in the end the son is glorified by the father (8:38), who is also forgiving toward the many for whom Jesus died (11:25). And recall that Mark rejects both objective ritualism and moral legalism, which leaves the individual considerable freedom to act creatively in the moral realm, discovering what love requires.

Even though post-exodus Israel rejected the idea of Yahweh as its natural progenitor, his faithfulness to Israel can be spoken of as working through the continuity of the generations (Exod. 3:15; Pss. 90:1; 100:5; Dan. 4:3). Matthew and Luke accord to this scheme a certain formal acknowledgment when they portray the salvation history leading up to Jesus as a succession from father to son.[21] Both of these Gospels also effect a material break with this scheme by means of the virgin birth image: the male line is broken; Jesus is not Joseph's real son (Matt. 1:16; Luke 3:23).[22] God's purpose is not bound to the Israelite father-son succession. Mark moves even farther from any suggestion that the natural father-son relation is the form through which salvation history operates by not having any genealogy at all. But Mark does have a historical continuity between old and new covenant by means of the language tradition (see chapter 4).

In sum, the inclusion of the disciple in a new community in which God, and no human being, is the only father, along with the break with the natural family, achieves liberation both from traditional authority and from natural fate.

The significance that Belo sees in the omission of the father from the new community takes on a more explicitly sociological and economic focus. Mark belongs to the tradition of the prophets and Deuteronomy, which opposed the class system that was brought in by the Davidic monarchy and which aimed at social equality and the avoidance of class: there are to be no poor in Israel (Deut. 15:4). In Mark the kingdom of God is for children, not fathers, and for the poor. Women and children are the possession of the father, who holds sway in the house. He is the focal point of relations of dominance, but the practice of children is play and pleasure without relations of dominance. To remove the father is to remove relations of dominance and to direct the church toward the satisfaction of the poor who break with society and follow Jesus.[23] The father is the symbol of a class society. The Messiah cannot be the Son of David (Mark 12:35–40), because a restored kingdom of David would be a reformed social formation but nonetheless one based on class exploitation. The proper eschatology is seen in Mark 13. The Son of man coming with power and glory (13:26) means that there is no more authority or wealth, since the sociological codes have collapsed. The elect are gathered from the ends of the earth to the ends of heaven (13:27). Earth and heaven are no longer opposed, for the two terms have exhausted their separateness. Heaven has collapsed upon earth (13:24–25). The difference that makes narrative possible has disappeared, so there can only be closure—the advent of the eschatological Son of man (13:26).[24]

For Belo there is a connection between what the earthly Jesus does as Son of man and the final advent of the Son of man signaling the achievement of a classless society. This continuity is seen, for example, in the seed parables of Mark 4. Harvest issues from sowing (4:26–29) and a great shrub from a mustard seed (4:30–32).[25] But in arguing that complete social redemption necessarily ends the story (history), Belo tacitly attributes to Mark the view that history is based in evil; there would be no chronological movement were it not for the conflict between good and evil, heaven and earth. That is one side of Mark's paradoxical view: hardness of heart does produce the conflicts that generate the story. But we have also seen (chapter 4) that for the Gospel, as for the Old Testament, time as chronological extension is the matrix of the divine activity. Mark seems to presuppose both that time is in principle good and that final redemption will end the time-space continuum as we know it (12:24–27; 13:24–27). But that is not a contradiction unless finitude is equated with evil.

Belo argues that the Markan community, understood as the place for sharing loaves as an alternative to subverted society, is the same alternative that is sought today in the revolutionary struggle to break with capitalist modes of production. The Jesus of Mark's Gospel did intend to eliminate power relations among the classes and hence classes. He sought to gather into the kingdom circle the poor, who are evidently no longer poor, without the rich, disciples without scribes, brothers without fathers. There are no relations of domination. This community is the space of the resurrection, the place of the rising of bodies. Jesus thus stood against the Zealots, whose messiah would be a king bent on political power.[26]

One would want to say that the political institutions of modern communist countries are diametrically opposed to the Markan community as Belo has defined it. But can it be denied that the new community that Mark projects (10:21, 29–30) is one in which personal wealth has been eliminated or minimized through the members' support of the community and in which all members share in the community resources without the directing dominance of a "father"?

The Christian Community
and Other Social Relationships

The Natural Family

Stanley Hauerwas has observed that the family becomes demonic if it is the only thing there is to protect people from death. Ironically the family is threatened today partly because there are no other institutions that have the moral status to stand over against it, to call into question its demonic tendencies.[27] We could say that an institution is demonic when it exerts destructive power over us because we have inflated it with more value than it can bear. Mark's understanding of the relationship between the new Christian community and the family speaks to this problem. Belonging to the new community places a constraint on the inflation of the family, and one who has passed through death to life will belong to the new community because communal existence is integral to the experience of salvation. And because of the experience of salvation, one will not expect the family to save one from death.

As we have seen, in Mark the new community of equal brothers and sisters sharing houses and lands in common is composed of people who have forsaken their natural families. On the other hand, Mark 7:9–13 takes the command to honor fathers and mothers as word of God, and 10:19 includes honoring parents as one of the requisites for eternal life. How is this tension to be interpreted? One possibility is to say that the natural family becomes a part of the new community and is related to in terms of the new eschatological order of equality without having any special claim at all. No more is owed to a natural mother than to a metaphorical mother.[28] Or one could say that the effect of the teaching on abandoning the natural family (3:20–21, 31–35; 10:29–30) is simply to turn father and mother in 7:9–13 and 10:19 into symbols for any member of the Christian community. The practical result of these two interpretations is the same: any special claim of the natural family is denied; one element of the tension is completely absorbed in the other. But that ought not to be done in this case, because Mark could easily have avoided the tension had he wanted to. He could have omitted the command to honor father and mother from the selective Decalogue in 10:19, because he felt free to substitute a prohibition against defrauding for the Decalogue's prohibition of coveting (but coveting is condemned in 7:22). And in 7:9–13 he could simply have found another example of a conflict between a moral and a cultic obligation. Or he could have used the *Corban* example to elevate the moral above the cultic without any suggestion of a special claim for the natural family; he could have said something like: Moses commanded you not to harden your heart or shut your hand against your poor brothers (Deut. 15:7). But you say, "If a man tells his brother (fellow Jew), 'What you would have gained from me is *Corban*,' " then you no longer permit him to do anything for his brother.

But Mark does not do that. He lets both elements in the tension stand, so that if we want to understand the text, we have to take account of both sides. Mark does not state a rule on the relationship of church to family but articulates two extremities of a spectrum. A disciple is to forsake his or her family for the sake of the new community; a disciple is to honor a special claim of his or her family.

A disciple has a responsibility to his or her natural family, including the father, which takes precedence over responsibility to his or her meta-phorical brothers, sisters, mothers, and children. But the claim of the family cannot be allowed to compromise the fact that the meanings and values of the disciple, including the responsibility to sustain the commu-nity materially, come from the story of following Jesus, not from the family's tradition. Nor can the family's claim be allowed to compromise the equality of all members of the new community or to introduce father-ly autocracy into it. If the family cannot be assimilated to this situation without falling apart, then it shows itself to be an old wineskin which has been burst by the new wine of the gospel, and it will have to be replaced by a new wineskin which the new wine can make use of without destroy-ing. The commandment to honor the natural family is a trace of the will of God which is always subject to relativization by the new eschatological situation. Just how a disciple is to place himself or herself in the spectrum of possibilities must be discovered in individual cases.

Marriage

What about marriage in the Markan new community, as distinguished from responsibility to natural father, mother, sister, or brother? Wives and husbands are not among the relations and objects abandoned in Mark 10:29; therefore they are not among the relations to be shared in 10:30. We have noted Mark's view of the indissolubility of marriage, and certainly for Mark marriage is an exclusive relationship. Let me pursue Mark's position on marriage and the community in the light of two things that Hauerwas, again, has to say about Christian marriage. First, the sexual exclusiveness tradition associated with the Christian understand-ing of marriage is but a form of the church's commitment to support exclusive relationships. Second, in the Christian community the sexual ethic is a part of the political ethic because the community's central convictions require it to take stands against societies built on no knowl-edge of the one true God. Christian marriage is not a natural institution but rather the creation of a people who marry for very definite purposes. It is the political purpose of the Christian community, the something beyond themselves and their love for which the Christian couple marry, that is able to make sense of the sexual exclusiveness and lifelong fidelity of Christian marriage.[29] This gives us an interesting position in relation to which we may sharpen our understanding of Mark's point of view.

Is the Markan community committed to support any exclusive relationships except marriage? It seems to me that it is not. The nature of the community is to break down exclusivity in other relationships. A man's relationship with his wife excludes other wives. But his relationship with his mother in the Christian community is less exclusive than it would be outside of it. His mother may have provisional first claim on him in the mother-son sphere, but his belonging to the community relativizes that because there he has mothers by the hundredfold.

Regarding Hauerwas's second point, it may be that the political purpose of the Christian community is an added bond for holding together exclusive marriage. The married couple would share in a political task because ways of ordering relationships and the management of common material resources would have to be worked out. But it is the position of Mark that indissoluble marriage is grounded in creation. Christian marriage, all marriage, is a natural institution, but nature is God's creation. For Mark, the eschatological new creation enables marriage as such to be what God intended it to be when he created nature a certain way. God has so created human beings that the one flesh union is indissoluble. The eschatological new creation both recovers the possibility of permanent marriage and reconstitutes the structures of the community. Both marriage and a concern for all of the brothers, sisters, children, and so forth, rest on faith as freedom for the other. This freedom-for will have to be enacted in political ways. But all of the members have this political responsibility for all other members without its creating exclusive relationships. Only marriage has an exclusive character, for only it rests on the one flesh union. So it is creation that confers on marriage a different quality from that which either it or the community confers on other relationships.

Secular Social-Political Order

Finally, how is the Christian eschatological community related to the secular social-political order? The members of the church are not to refuse to support the political order (12:13–17), but do they have a moral responsibility, explicit or implied, to seek to change the secular order so that it will take on the character that is expected of the Christian community? That the church has such a responsibility is not explicit in the Gospel, but certain lines of thought tacitly support this position.

For Mark, the church is clearly not identical with the general human community, the world. He is conscious of the distinction between insiders and outsiders (4:10–12), but we have seen that Mark makes this distinction ironical (chapters 3 and 4) and thus diminishes it. It is not as firm as it appears to be. However, the distinction is not erased, for the disciples have a mission to the world, which does not have what the disciples have to give. The believing community takes the pattern for its posture from the mission of the Son of man, who suffered for the many (10:45). The church also is to extend itself into the world, serving as the Son of man did (9:35). The believing community wants to be heard and received in order that others, repenting, might become a part of it (6:11–13). The church preaches, heals, and casts out demons. In enables people to be delivered from the demonic constrictions that prevent openness to others. The borders of the community are to be ever open to the world, and the latter is always invited to cross over. But can the secular order which remains unbelieving be expected to actualize the kind of social order which is to characterize the eschatological community itself? Is that a goal toward which Mark directs the church to work?

We have seen that according to Mark the communal life of believers is an integral part of salvation. The community rests on faith. The kind of communal order in which each person sees all others as brothers, sisters, mother, and children and in which each is sustained by the houses and lands of all—that communal order is grounded on the forsaking of personal wealth and the relativizing of the natural family's claims for the sake of Jesus and the gospel. This renunciation is an enactment of faith as freedom for (love) the other. And faith is the self-understanding that life comes through death, which is gained by the disciple's being given to follow in the way of the suffering Son of man. So the shape of the community rests in an essential way on faith and the actualization of the kingdom of God in the mission of Jesus. Therefore this kind of community cannot exist in the unbelieving secular order.

Yet the difference between church and world is not absolute. I have already indicated how the narrative texture ironically diminishes the distance between believers and nonbelievers. Moreover, in Mark's theology, since God is good (10:18), the structures in which he created the human world (10:6–9) can be counted on to be for the well-being of humankind. What God is now doing in the eschatological community is what God intended through creation. Thus there is continuity as well as discontinuity between church and world. In the eschatological community God is overcoming what hardness of heart did to God's original intention in creation. But hardness of heart is still present in the church (6:52; 8:17–18—do you *not yet* understand?), and God's creative intention is still present in the world. Faith emerges only when a person brings to the hearing of the word a measure of his or her own human understanding (Mark 4:24–25, 28). There is continuity. Thus it is plausible to argue that the world can approximate what God is achieving in the eschatological community. If it is the responsibility of the new Christian community to serve the world, then it must work toward that approximation.

NOTES

1. Vladimir Propp, *Morphology of the Folktale,* Eng. trans. L. Scott (Austin and London: Univ. of Texas Press, 1968), 60.

2. Ibid., 62.

3. Schrage (*Ethik des Neuen Testaments,* 135) takes Peter's claim in a straight-forward way and sees here a contrast with the rich man's unwillingness to follow. There is a *logical* relationship between the unfounded claim of the false hero and the exposure of him. But the way in which Mark manifests the two functions here involves a break in the realism of the narrative. That is, Peter's claim to have given up all is shown to be false by reference to the principle that to abandon family and property is to be given family and property in a new community. Such a situation did not exist in Peter's time. This break in the realism results from having the narrative about Jesus speak to the situation of the church in Mark's time. On the other hand, what is described in 10:30 was probably not an actuality in Mark's time either, or not in a complete way. It is a statement of what the church ought to be. So in the end it is not so much a tension between two actual situations (Peter's and Mark's) as between what believers tend to do and what in Mark's view they ought to do.

4. Schrage, *Ethik des Neuen Testaments,* 135.

5. See Belo, *A Materialist Reading of the Gospel of Mark,* 173; Cranfield, *The Gospel According to Saint Mark,* 331.

6. See Best, *Following Jesus,* 111; Schrage, *Ethik des Neuen Testaments,* 135.

7. Belo, *A Materialist Reading of the Gospel of Mark,* 7, 173. Belo quite self-consciously reads Mark with the help of Marx (3, 6).

8. Best, *Following Jesus,* 110.

9. See Schrage, *Ethik des Neuen Testaments,* 135.

10. Ibid., 132.

11. Best, *Following Jesus,* 114.

12. Braaten, *Eschatology and Ethics,* 22, 156–59.

13. For a much more elaborate development of this approach to the parable, see Theodore J. Weeden, "Recovering the Parabolic Intent in the Parable of the Sower," *Journal of the American Academy of Religion* 47/1 (1979): esp. 108, 116. Actually one of Weeden's general intents is to play down the role of discontinuity and reversal in the parables.

14. See Belo, *A Materialist Reading of the Gospel of Mark,* 122.

15. See Robert Hamerton-Kelly, *God the Father* (Philadelphia: Fortress Press, 1979), 55.

16. James M. Robinson, *The Problem of History in Mark* (London: SCM Press, 1957), 81. See also Best, *Following Jesus*, 114.

17. Sigmund Freud, *Moses and Monotheism*, Eng. trans. K. Jones (New York: Vintage Books, 1967), 85, 99–110, 140–41; see also Hamerton-Kelly, *God the Father*, 18.

18. Mary Daly, *Beyond God the Father* (Boston: Beacon Press, 1973), 95–97, 114–22.

19. Hamerton-Kelly, *God the Father*, 22, 30–32.

20. See Paul Ricoeur, "Fatherhood: From Phantasm to Symbol," Eng. trans. R. Sweeney, *The Conflict of Interpretations*, 486, 489, 491–93.

21. See James Muilenberg, "The Biblical View of Time," *Harvard Theological Review* 54/4 (1961): 239.

22. For an elaboration of this move in Matthew, see Via, "Structure, Christology and Ethics in Matthew," 210–11.

23. See Belo, *A Materialist Reading of the Gospel of Mark*, 38, 56, 170–71, 174.

24. Ibid., 192, 199–200.

25. Ibid., 287.

26. Ibid., 259–62. Étienne Trocmé has written a blistering critique of Belo's book, attacking it for its thick verbosity, its ignorance of scholarly exegesis balanced by attacks on the foolishness of scholars, its generally platitudinous interpretations, and its attribution of Mark to a Roman provenance while dealing with the economic background of Palestine rather than of Rome. I should say that the last matter is part of Belo's general tendency to confound the Markan Jesus and what he apparently takes to be the historical Jesus. Trocmé does praise Belo for his treatment, although undeveloped, of the opposition between the strategy of Jesus and that of the Zealots and for his discussion of the new community in materialist terms. See Étienne Trocmé, "Trois critiques au miroir de l'évangile selon Marc," *Revue d'Histoire et de Philosophie Religieuses* 2 (1975): 293–94.

27. Hauerwas, *A Community of Character*, 168.

28. Obviously I am letting the command to honor father and mother symbolize all claims of the natural family.

29. Hauerwas, *A Community of Character*, 189–93.

11

The Suffering Son of Man and the Ethics of Servanthood
Mark 10:32–52

First Narrative Analysis

This section of Mark ties into the refusal of the man with possessions to do the one thing lacking (10:21–22). It also connects with Peter's claim in Mark 10:28 that the disciples have left all and followed Jesus. The motif of "following" is resumed in 10:32. That this is a, if not the, central theme in 10:32–52 is seen from the way in which "following" frames the pericope (cf. 10:32 and 10:52c). This section discloses what is really entailed in following and thereby deepens, by contrast, the falsity of Peter's claim that the disciples have given up all and followed. Already, at the beginning of the section, they are following with fear.

Structural analysis is subject to the hermeneutical circle; it sees something as something and, thereby, involves an interpretive judgment. A stretch of text may be seen as manifesting more than one kind of deep structure, and I will try to show that this section has features that enable it to be seen as the manifestation of two different ways of grasping the deep structure of narrative functions. Mark 10:32–52 seems to fall into four parts: (1) 10:32–34; (2) 10:35–41; (3) 10:42–45; (4) 10:46–52. And it can also be seen as having three parts: (1) 10:32a; (2) 10:32b–52ab; (3) 10:52c. Each of these outlines registers the segmentation produced in the surface structure by a deep structure. And as in the previous chapters, the surface content, organized by the deep structure, will be the basis for interpretive reflection. I begin with the fourfold outline, and because the structure of 10:32–52 is more complex than that of the earlier parts of Mark 10, I will set it out in a schematic way before commenting on it.

Sequence of the Twelve (10:32–41)

1. *Mandate* to the Twelve to follow the Son of man in the way of suffering (10:32–34)
2. *Refusal* (in the persons of the two and the ten, 10:35–41)=
   Subsequence of the two (10:35–40)

Mandate of the two to Jesus to give them places of honor (10:35–37)

Refusal by Jesus (10:38–40) +

Subsequence of the ten (10:41)

Confrontation (the ten are indignant at the two)

Second Sequence of the Twelve (10:42–52)

3. *Mandate* of Jesus to the Twelve to serve and suffer (10:42–45)
4. *Acceptance* (10:46–52)=

Subsequence of Bartimaeus

Mandate (10:46–47a). Hearing of Jesus prompts Bartimaeus to action.

Acceptance (10:47b). He responds to the prompting by seeking mercy from Jesus.

Confrontation (10:48). The many oppose Bartimaeus' effort to get Jesus' attention.

Domination (10:49). But he has overcome the opposition and secured Jesus' attention.

Disjunction and *Conjunction* (10:50). Bartimaeus leaves his seat and comes to Jesus.

Domination (reprise) (10:51–52ab). Bartimaeus receives his sight from Jesus.

Attribution (10:52c). He follows Jesus in the way.

That the passion prediction (10:32–34) is an implied mandate is confirmed in 10:42–45 when the disciples are explicitly mandated to renounce authority and the seeking of first place in favor of servanthood and being last. And this mandate is grounded in the servanthood and self-giving of the Son of man (10:45), whose suffering is predicted in 10:33–34.

James and John represent the Twelve in their uncomprehending refusal of the mandate to suffer, for it is the disciples as a whole who fail to understand and who behave inappropriately after the passion prediction in Mark 9 (see 9:32–50). As a matter of fact, for Mark a number of characters resist suffering and thus represent each other—the two (10:35–40), the ten (10:41), the Twelve, Peter (8:32–33), and, by implication, the multitude (8:34).

The refusal of James and John is elaborated as an effort on their part to mandate Jesus to give them places of glory. Thus the subsequence of the two is introduced. Jesus refuses them and this subsequence aborts, but before returning to the Twelve there is manifested a part of another subsequence, that of the ten.

The confrontation, in which the ten are indignant because of the ambitions of the two, presupposes that the ten had mandated the two to walk the way of suffering or had themselves walked it. But the ten had no right to make such a claim, because they had earlier been involved in the discussion about who was the greatest (9:34), and in the end they too would fail Jesus (14:50). Thus the indignation of the ten manifests not only the function of confrontation but also the function which V. Propp called unfounded claims by a false hero.[1] This subsequence aborts because the claim implied in the indignation is pretentious and unjustified to begin with. The confrontation lacks the energy to continue or to generate additional actions because its moral basis is fraudulent. The subsequence of the two aborts, as we have seen, because Jesus refuses their mandate, and the sequence of the Twelve aborts because the mandate of the two (representing the Twelve) to Jesus is a refusal of Jesus' mandate to them to suffer. We here see the interaction between literary and ethical categories of interpretation. To identify the indignation of the ten *as* unfounded claims by a false hero (Propp's term for a narrative function) points up the pretense of self-deception in the ten's implied moral claim. And it was also undoubtedly the case that ethical considerations conditioned Propp's naming of the function in the first place.

Thus we are brought to a second sequence of the Twelve (10:42–52). Jesus mandates them to follow him as Son of man in the way of servanthood and suffering. As the preceding confrontation between the ten and the two was also an unfounded claim, so in relation to that latter function is this renewed mandate also an (implied) exposure of the false hero.[2] When Jesus tells the disciples that whoever would be great among them must be servant, he is suggesting that they have missed this paradoxical greatness and have rather chosen the greatness of the "Gentiles" (lording it over, *katakyrieuō*) as indeed they had (9:34). The verb *katakyrieuō* in the LXX usually is used of the rule of an alien and has the sense of using lordship for the disadvantage of the ruled and the advantage of the ruler.[3] The ten are exposed as no different from James and John.

The command to love the neighbor (12:31), to be open to the need of the other at risk to oneself (10:21), is reflected in the paradoxical statement that whoever would be great will be servant (*diakonos*), whoever would be first will be slave (*doulos*) of all. A *diakonos* is one who typically waits on tables, and a *doulos* does the work of a slave.[4] In these sayings, well-being (being great or first) is presented as the object of will and, by implication, as the intentional reason for human action. This intention is expressed in a relative clause which serves as the subject of the sentence: whoever wills to be first. The predicate of the sentence then states the means whereby one gains this well-being: will be slave of all. This formulation expresses the ethical actualization of the faith stance (8:35) that whoever loses one's life (by being servant of all) will find it (will be first). These ethical sayings (10:43-44) are connected to the service and death of the Son of man (10:45) by the causal *gar;* the disciple serves *because* the Son of man serves. He is the model for imitation (10:45a). But his death as a ransom for the many (10:45b) is also the ground that enables the disciples' imitation.[5]

That a second mandate has been issued to the Twelve makes more pressing the question whether they will accept or refuse it. The acceptance/refusal function so far as it pertains to the disciples is postponed; in fact, the disciples' acceptance is never manifested in the plot. In its place at this point we have the Bartimaeus story, which is an acceptance function expanded into a subsequence containing functions of its own.

The explicit change of place (10:46) in part signals a new sequence. The mandate to Bartimaeus is Jesus' coming (*erchontai*) to Jericho (10:46) which enables what Bartimaeus heard (10:47). These elements pick up Jesus' orginal coming (*ēlthen*) into Galilee (1:14) with the imperative to repent and believe in the gospel (1:15) and his coming (*exēlthon*) into the towns to preach (1:38). Bartimaeus' acceptance of the mandate to believe is also his mandate to Jesus to be what he (Jesus) has been mandated by God to be (redeeming Son of God/Son of man—1:11, 38; 2:17; 8:31; 10:45). Note that the "many" who oppose Bartimaeus' effort to get Jesus' attention are the "many" for whom the Son of man gives his life (10:45). Bartimaeus' domination of the opposition to his efforts to regain his sight is also Jesus' acceptance of Bartimaeus' mandate to him to have mercy. Jesus stops and has him called. We could penetrate the surface further by observing that Jesus' acceptance of Bartimaeus' mandate to have mercy is a mandate by Jesus to the blind man to persist in faith and be healed.[6] That which is finally attributed to Bartimaeus is following Jesus in the way. "Way" (*hodos*) is a frequent word in Mark. It is often Jesus' *way* (1:2, 3; 8:27; 9:33-34; 10:17, 32, 46, 52; 11:8), and in our text it is clearly the *way* (10:32) that leads to suffering in Jerusalem (10:33). Bartimaeus at the beginning of his story can only sit *beside* the way and beg (10:46), but by the end he has overcome obstacles and is following Jesus *on* the way (10:52). This is not the attribution of a helper, nor is it recognition, but it is a good or value, what has been lacking—the last that is first (10:44), the loss which is saving (8:35). As Ernest Best has said, to see is to go with Jesus to the cross.[7] Thus this is a main, not a qualifying or glorifying test.

The Image of the Way

It may be that Mark images Jesus' whole life as a journey along *the way* (1:2–3).[8] The figure has its background in one of Israel's most striking symbols for its experience. The way image essentially expresses the onward moving and changing character of time in the Old Testament, and it figures in the epochal moments of Israel's life: the way from Egypt, from Sinai, and from Babylon. With its pointing to beginning and end the figure of the way opposes cyclical views of time.[9] Recall, however, that Second Isaiah's metaphor (Isa. 51:9–11) tends to break up the chronological direction of the way image by predicating the way (space)-of-creation-time of other times as well (see chapter 2). Mark, on the other hand, with his distinct beginning and end and by his having the kingdom of God overlap a stretch of time (see chapters 2 and 4) straightens out the way. Yet the really interesting thing about the "way" symbol is its capacity to allow a synthesis of time and space.

A "road" (*hodos*) is a spatial phenomenon, but it is one that enables the expression of movement, process, and change and allows the differentiating of points that belong to time: before/beginning—now/middle—afterward/end. It takes time to walk down a road. Moreover, the spatiality of the way corresponds to the spatializing or staying of time by means of the correspondences, repetitions, and interpenetrations of the plot. In Mark, space and time form a unity within which incomplete redemption is on the way toward completion.[10] This final episode in Mark 10 connects with the earlier parts of the chapter which deal with specific ethical issues. The grasp of the human situation in 10:2–9 and 10:17–31 calls for the image of the way. The call for indissoluble marriage and for renouncing property and family for the new community presupposes the presence of the eschatological new creation in the ongoing, fallen middle of time. In this overlapping of the times, existence must be a dialectical movement between possibility and actuality. And if the realism of Mark's Gospel is taken seriously, this movement can only take place along a way which is extended in space, passage through which takes time. It is the way of the child, from deformed adulthood back to a new beginning and forward to a different adulthood.

Bartimaeus and the Fate of the Disciples

What light does the Bartimaeus story shed on Mark's view of the disciples? Werner Kelber sees Mark to be contrasting the disciples with Bartimaeus. The insiders who received instruction fail to see, while the outsider who received no instruction sees and follows in the way. In Kelber's view, the disciples abandon the way of discipleship totally, and because of the failure of the women at the tomb (16:1-8) their fate in separation from Jesus is sealed and they never return to Galilee.[11]

An argument can be made, however, on the basis of a number of elements in Mark that while the *plot* does not narrate the restoration of the disciples to faith and service, Mark's narrative *world* nevertheless assumes it.[12] Norman Petersen[13] has developed such an argument: Mark 9:9 suggests that the incomprehension of the disciples will end after the resurrection. This seems to be a necessary presupposition for Mark's view that the disciples will be related to Jesus (8:34—9:1) and will be his representatives until the parousia (13:5-8, 23, 31) and that they will be vehicles of the Holy Spirit (13:11). Mark 14:28 and 16:7 anticipate the reunion of the resurrected Christ with his disciples. Since the predictions made in the course of the story tend to be fulfilled, the reader is encouraged to think that this one will be too. The coming to pass of what Jesus intends does not depend on the reactions of the disciples, or of the women at the tomb.

I had also made a similar argument.[14] In Mark the authoritative (1:22), forgiving (2:5), life-giving (1:41; 5:41-42) word of Jesus never passes away (13:31). Moreover, the resurrection and the word that brings life out of death (8:34-37) are alternate ways of expressing the function of victory: they belong to the same paradigm or chain of associations. Since the life-giving word as resurrection can be present at any time, the disciples are not beyond the hope of salvation for Mark.

Now what does the Bartimaeus story in its context specifically contribute to Mark's hope for the disciples? Vincent Taylor sees almost no organic connection between this story and the rest of 10:32-52 and comes close to denying any justification for its presence.[15] But Bartimaeus' acceptance of the mandate to suffer occurs where we might have expected a response from the disciples; therefore, what occurs in the encounter between Jesus and the blind man is suggestive for what will ultimately be the response and destiny of the disciples. What should have occurred in their case (8:31—9:1; 9:30-37) does now occur with Bartimaeus. It still, then, may happen with the disciples, for the response of Bartimaeus (10:46-52) continues the sequence that begins again with the Twelve (10:42); it is the acceptance which the mandate (10:42-45) calls for. The Bartimaeus story continues the sequence of the Twelve by suggesting, but not stating, how they will finally respond.

The request of James and John to have privileged positions in Jesus' glory is equivalent to Peter's calling Jesus Messiah (8:29) and rejecting his suffering (8:31–32). But that the two brothers will in the future confess Jesus' true identity is suggested by his saying that they too will suffer (10:39). Since the cup and baptism of suffering (see 14:36 on the connection between cup and suffering) are mentioned in 10:38–39, it is probable that the death of James and John, which is suggested here, should be thought of more as sacramental than as literal. Mark refers to the sacramental or symbolic expression of their existential passing through death to life. This interpretation also would be consistent with the principle that the great or first must be slave of all (life through death, 10:43–44, is the pattern for continuing discipleship).[16] The mention of the cup also recalls that eating is a mark of discipleship.[17] The disciples share with Jesus a final loaf and cup which symbolizes his death for them (14:22–25), and they are also present when he eats with tax collectors and sinners (2:15),[18] for which he is attacked (2:16). The reference to the cup in 10:38–39 may suggest that in some sense the disciples share the fate visited on Jesus for eating with sinners.

Moreover, that the disciples will move from seeing themselves as followers of a king, or divine man, to seeing themselves as followers of the suffering Son of man is intimated by the Bartimaeus episode; he seems to pass through a similar transformation. The very movement of the story suggests that Mark tends to discredit[19] rather than affirm[20] the Son of David title. If Mark himself inserted the Son of David motif,[21] it must have been to criticize it. In the early acceptance of the mandate to believe and on into the confrontation with the crowd Bartimaeus calls Jesus Son of David: he is blind. After he has succeeded in getting Jesus' attention and has made the effort to move toward Jesus, he changes his address from Son of David to *rabbouni* (10:51), master, a term stronger than rabbi and one that implies a master-disciple relationship.[22] But for Mark this is still not a fully adequate title, and it is only after Jesus has restored his sight that Bartimaeus can follow *on the way*.

Second Narrative Analysis

This brings me to a briefer consideration of the threefold structural outline. Mark 10:32 may make a distinction between disciples in the broader sense and disciples in the narrow sense, the Twelve. If that is the case, probably those who were going up amazed are the larger group, while those who followed afraid are the Twelve. That is supported by the fact that it is the Twelve who have *followed* in 10:28.[23] One of the things that holds Mark 10:32–52 together as a unified sequence is that the beginning and ending contain the same significant Markan vocabulary. In 10:32a we have *en tē hodō . . . hoi de akolouthountes ephobounto* ("on the way . . . and those following were afraid"). And in 10:52c we have *kai ēkolouthei autō en tē hodō* ("and he followed him on the way"). What is present in the beginning but not in the ending is fear. Fear is a negative surplus, or a lack. The initial function, then, is a situation of lack, a lack of resolute following. And in the final function (10:52c), the goal or result function, the lack is liquidated.

Since a lack can always be liquidated, it *is* a possibility for amelioration, and that possibility begins to be actualized in the process which begins at 10:32b. Jesus' speaking to them does actually begin the process of amelioration, because in Mark Jesus' word is effective (1:22; 1:41; 2:5, 11; 5:8, 13, 41–42; 7:34; 9:25–26). And the process begun by the word of suffering and death is one of amelioration, because for Mark life in the fullest sense can come only through loss and death (8:34–37; 9:35; 10:43–45). Jesus, then, seeks to lead them into the way, the process, of life through death. That evokes a process of opposition when James and John seek places of glory and the ten manifest an unjustified indignation, a process that reaches no goal within the confines of our text. The process of amelioration resumes with Jesus' word about paradoxical greatness and continues in the response of Bartimaeus. The process reaches its goal in Bartimaeus' following Jesus on the way. This threefold structure can be schematized as follows:

1. Initial
   situation
   of lack

   10:32a

2. Process:

   amelioration   amelioration   amelioration
   ---   ---   ---
   10:32b–34   10:42–47   10:48b–52ab

                opposition   opposition
                ---   ---
                10:35–41   10:48a

3. Goal —
   lack liquidated

   10:52c

The Repeated Last
(Eschatological) Chance

A review of the fourfold structure of this section will aid us in dealing with the theological implications of the section. A mandate is (1) given and (2) refused. The mandate is (3) given again and (4) accepted: There is a *second* chance. This sequence in Mark's narrative moderates one aspect of the "extravagant," as Paul Ricoeur has identified it in the parables of Jesus. There is only *one* opportunity, which makes everything hinge on one momentous decision, and if that decision is not properly made, all is irretrievably lost (Matt. 5:25; 22:11-13; 25:1-12; Luke 16:1-8).[24] There is no second chance. Ricoeur[25] contrasts this paradoxical and hyperbolic vision with our actual experience in which we expect another chance.

One could say that Mark also should have presented the one-opportunity vision in view of his eschatological theology. Because the Son of man who suffers, dies, and rises is the eschatological Son of man who has authority to forgive sins (2:10) and dispense with the Sabbath (2:28) and who will come at the end as judge and savior (8:38; 13:26-27), his death and resurrection is the eschatological event, as is his word about it. Therefore, the choice to walk or not to walk in his way is a once-for-all decision. It would be just as possible to write a gospel-length, or novel-length, narrative portraying one opportunity that must be grasped or lost as it would be to tell a parable-length narrative with this vision. Mark does not do that, but neither does he abandon the eschatological for the ordinary. Rather, the paradox portrayed by his narrative is that the once-for-all opportunity/demand may recur repeatedly; what can occur only once, the last chance, occurs again. Thus the course of the narrative overcomes or moderates the hard saying of Jesus in 8:38: if a person is ashamed of Jesus, the Son of man will be ashamed of that person when he comes as final judge. Or at least it turns out that one act of denial will not necessarily seal one's final doom.

This interpretation of Mark is not, of course, dependent only on 10:32-52. The mandate is given twice in each of the earlier passion predictions (8:31, 34-37; 9:31, 35). Jesus' death and resurrection occur in various symbolic ways throughout the Gospel; transfiguration, resurrection, and parousia especially belong to the same paradigm.[26] A number of eschatological opportunities are plotted and they are projected into the indeterminate future beyond the plot.

We have had ample opportunity to observe that for Mark discipleship would be impossible without a divine miracle.[27] Apart from the latter there is no opening of the eyes (10:52); following Jesus is not a human possibility but must be enabled by God (10:21–22, 26–27). As I have argued above, the disciples have repeatedly had revelation experiences. More specifically, James and John, who in this very context do not see, have had their eyes opened by what they saw at the transfiguration and the ensuing interpretation: the glorified Son of God (9:1–3, 7) is the suffering Son of man (9:12–13). The revelation which they have received is no less God's real disclosure than is the opening of Bartimaeus' eyes and the resurrection before which they still stand. But they do not see. They typify the situation of the disciple in a history of revelation. They stand both before and after the resurrection. Revelation is both given and withheld—yet to be given.

As Wolfgang Schrage has pointed out, following in the way of the crucified one in Mark is not without hope, because the crucified Son of man is also the risen Son of man and the future judge of the world who returns in glory to gather the elect (13:26–27).[28] The revelation yet to be given is a hope pushed out finally beyond the plot into the narrative world. Both in Mark 13:26–27, 30, and 8:38—9:1, Mark's Jesus predicts the apocalyptic end of the world within the lifetime of his contemporaries. And in 14:62 he says to the high priest: "You [plural] will see the Son of man seated at the right hand of Power, and coming with the clouds of heaven." This could mean either that they will see him during their lifetime or that they will see him later on, and so is not strong evidence either for or against an imminent end. However, Mark 13:26–27, 30, and 8:38—9:1 taken *by themselves* probably do refer to a literal imminent end, and that belief *may* be Mark's actual position. But no case whatsoever can be made for the contention that this expectation puts into question Mark's ethic or undermines its motivation. The ethic is articulated in and grounded upon other terms and will have to be judged on those other terms.

If we approach the issue in traditional Bultmannian terms from our own modern standpoint *outside* the Gospel and assume for the moment that Mark believed in the near end, it may be declared that the real meaning of the imminent expectation of the end is to point up the decisive significance of the present. This enhances rather than negates the ethic, and the modern believer simply has to live with the tension between literal falsity and possible existential truth.

But certain factors *within* the Gospel make it questionable whether it actually gives voice to an imminent eschatology. *Some* of those standing with Jesus in Mark 9:1 will not die until they see the kingdom having come with power. Then after six days (9:2) Jesus takes *some* of them—Peter, James, and John—up onto the mountain, where he is transfigured. Thus Mark (but not his tradition) may have interpreted the transfiguration as the fulfillment of the prophecy about the imminent coming of the kingdom in 9:1.

Mark ends his apocalyptic discourse in chap. 13 with Jesus' disclaimer that the Son has exact knowledge about the time of the end and with the parable of the doorkeeper (13:32–37). Together these texts make the point, not that the end *will* be *soon,* but that it *may* be *anytime.* Both of these positions lend to the present a dimension of crisis, but the first is discredited at the literal level with the passage of time—and the failure of the end to come—while the other is not. Since Mark *ends* the apocalyptic discourse with the could-be-anytime theme, that may have the effect of reinterpreting everything that has been said about the imminent end in this light. However much the *author may* have believed in some corner of his mind that the end would occur within decades, the effect of the parable of the doorkeeper on the text is that the end is not so much near to the author's time as possibly near to any time. Thus while Mark has a futuristic eschatology, it is by no means unequivocally clear that he has an imminent eschatology. If that is the case, the Gospel's position is that the present moment of a person who reads himself into Jesus' story—follows in his way—always has an elastic relationship to the fulfilling eschatological event. In Mark's own terms: one does not know how far one is from the ultimate apocalyptic goal and consequence of one's own story. In demythologized terms: one does not know how far one is from a more revealing future which will draw out the import and consequences of one's own story. I say *more* revealing rather than *most* revealing because in demythologized apocalyptic the coming kingdom is a receding, but always possibly imminent, horizon of historical-event-and-meaning rather than a final cosmic event. It is not that the Son of man will come in the clouds but that all which is associated with the Son of man both enables and judges one's existence as a human being in community. Yet the horizon of meaning connected with the Son of man is not simply a theological theme abstracted from life. It encounters persons in the intervolvements of moral life in the stream of time, for whoever receives a child in Jesus' name receives him (9:37).

Whether or not Mark had an imminent eschatology, none of the ethical categories that come to concrete expression in Mark is shaped by the belief in the near end. Ethical norms are derived from the teaching and example of Jesus in his historical ministry. The radical content of and the enablement for these norms are grounded not in the imminent end but in the present realization of the eschatological new creation (1:1; 10:6). God alone gives the freedom (9:23; 10:27) which can rid the heart of evil (7:21–23) and permit love (10:21; 12:31). He does this by giving insight (10:46–52), and the means for this is the story of Jesus which creates faith (1:28; 3:7–12; 5:27, 34; 10:47, 52). Gaining life and forgiveness and avoiding damnation appear both as the future consequences of certain kinds of action (or being) and as forward-looking reasons for acting (8:38; 9:43–48; 11:25), but their content and import do not depend on the datable nearness of the end.

What is constitutive of Mark's ethic as far as temporality is concerned is that there is a future toward which one moves along a way, that there is movement from new possibility (new eschatological creation) through difficulty (the overlapping of hardness of heart and new wine) to some degree of actualization. And it is further constitutive of Mark's viewpoint that every present moment is critical (the Son of man could come *any* time) for the future outcome of one's life. One should watch out to do now what will prevent the future testing from being disastrous—whenever it might come (13:33–37). But Mark's ethic is not constituted by an integral relationship to the literal near end of the world and therefore is not undermined by the failure of that event to occur, even if the Gospel predicted it. I have observed that the demythologized imminent expectation supports the ethic (the cruciality of the present). And it may be that the *positive* meaning of the literal *failure* of the Son of man to return within the lifetime of Jesus' contemporaries is that this failure opens up a temporal space for the occurring of repeated eschatological events, a space for the continuing overlapping of eschatological and fallen time.

NOTES

1. Propp, *Morphology of the Folktale*, 60.
2. Ibid., 62.
3. See Cranfield, *The Gospel According to St. Mark*, 341.
4. Best, *Following Jesus*, 126–27.
5. On this dual function of the service and death of the Son of man, see ibid., 126–27.
6. We might note that structural analysis, by showing that a segment of text actualizes more than one formal possibility, explains why a passage intuitively felt to be powerful actually is so.
7. Best, *Following Jesus*, 143.
8. Kelber, *The Kingdom in Mark*, 67–68.

9. See Muilenberg, "The Biblical View of Time," 233–34.

10. On the way as both physical and theological, see Rhoads and Michie, *Mark as Story*, 64.

11. Kelber, *Mark's Story of Jesus*, 56, 75, 77, 84.

12. For the distinction between plot and world in Mark, see Petersen, *Literary Criticism for New Testament Critics*, 49–52.

13. Ibid., 64–65, 70–71, 76–78.

14. See Via, *Kerygma and Comedy*, 160–63.

15. Taylor, *The Gospel According to Saint Mark*, 100.

16. See Best, *Following Jesus*, 124–25.

17. Dewey, *Markan Public Debate*, 84–85.

18. Ibid., 84–85, 128–29.

19. See Paul J. Achtemeier, " 'And He Followed Him': Miracles and Discipleship in Mark 10:46–52," *Semeia* 11 (1978): 127, 130–31.

20. See Vernon K. Robbins, "The Healing of Blind Bartimaeus (10:46–52) in the Marcan Theology," *Journal of Biblical Literature* 92/2 (1973): 234–36, 239–40.

21. As Robbins (ibid., 235–36) argues.

22. See Cranfield, *The Gospel According to Saint Mark*, 346; Achtemeier, "And He Followed Him," 124.

23. See Schweizer, *The Good News According to Mark*, 217. Cranfield (*The Gospel According to Saint Mark*, 335), has the opposite view of the identity of the two groups.

24. Paul Ricoeur, "The Specificity of Language," *Semeia* 4 (1975): 116–17.

25. Ibid., 116.

26. Via, *Kerygma and Comedy*, 117–18, 121, 123, 140, 142.

27. On this, see Schweizer, *The Good News According to Mark*, 217.

28. See Schrage, *Ethik des Neuen Testaments*, 132.

CONCLUSION

12

The Messianic Secret, Faith, and Ethics

Narrative Form and Messianic Secret

Here we return to the structure of the Markan narrative as a whole. This requires a last look at the messianic secret, the fundamental thematic dimension of the plot. I will deal with the messianic secret summarily in order to relate it to some aspects of the Markan narrative. Then the secret must be treated so as to show more fully its relationship to faith and ethics.

The multiplicity of eschatological revelations in the Gospel raises the question of the relationship of Mark's narrative form to his theological interpretation of Jesus in the light of two recent treatments of this matter. According to John Dominic Crossan, Mark created the gospel form in order to counter the authority of Jesus' relatives and disciples, who confessed Jesus' abiding presence to intervene and save his own, with the authority of Jesus himself, who proposes that he will be absent. The Markan sequence is: (1) death of Jesus; (2) resurrection-as-departure; (3) absence from the community; (4) parousia-as-return. In Mark 16:6 the sequence is resurrection-absence, but in Matt. 28:6 and Luke 24:6 the sequence is absence-resurrection. Absence in Matthew and Luke is only from the tomb pending appearance, but in Mark it is from the earth pending parousia. Mark trapped the other Evangelists in his form with a content they could not accept: the others portray the resurrected Lord as present.[1]

But Mark could have accomplished the purpose that Crossan attributes to him just with individual stories and sayings presenting the absence motif. He did not need the gospel genre for this purpose. What Mark and the other Gospels have in common is the tragicomic plot developed in a realistic mode interlaced with the extraordinary. Absence has no unique or necessary relation to this but is just a theme that Mark inserted (if in fact it is a theme in Mark) which was omitted by the other Evangelists. Since it was readily omissible and could have been expressed in the first place apart from a whole Gospel, it can hardly have been the formal generative principle of Mark. If Mark, on the other hand, was generated by the kerygma of Jesus' death and resurrection activating the tragicomic genre,[2] any number of themes could have been inserted into the various performance texts that manifest the genre.

In Norman Petersen's view, the narrative form was necessitated by Mark's desire to undercut the authority that certain "errorists" claimed from some of the disciples by showing that the disciples themselves once held an erroneous view but later abandoned it.[3] But this intention does not *necessitate* a narrative form. It could simply have been stated propositionally that the view once held by the disciples and now maintained by the "errorists" has been proven wrong.

I return to the Markan affirmation that the last chance occurs more than once. Perhaps the interplay of narrative form and the theological sense of repeated eschatological opportunities is one reason why Mark wrote a narrative rather than simply affirming Jesus' death and resurrection as a once-for-all event. Writing a narrative is a way, if not the most natural way, of representing an experience that recurs. And if one aspect of the meaning of the narrative is that the death and resurrection of Jesus (salvation event) is offered repeatedly in the course of time, then the narrative has not been adequately accounted for if its chronology is reduced without remainder to a set of logical relations among abstract units.[4] Even if it were possible, which it is not completely, to rearrange chronological connections as logical ones, it may be an essential part of the meaning of particular stories that things take time, which is often the case in Mark.

William Wrede long ago argued forcefully that Mark presents Jesus as both the revealed and the concealed Messiah. According to Wrede, these two contrasting motifs generate a series of contradictions, but in Mark's mind they did not clash. Mark's objective is to present Jesus as the Son of God; therefore he must be revealed and not completely concealed. But it was necessary to portray Jesus as concealing his messiahship in order to reduce the tension between the non-messianic tradition about Jesus and the belief in his messiahship which arose after the resurrection.[5]

What Wrede calls contradiction I would call paradox: a logical tension that is yet believed to be necessary to account for reality as experienced. The phenomenon under discussion expresses itself in Mark as two related paradoxes. Revelation when given is still concealed: the disciple stands both before and after the resurrection. When revelation does occur, human beings resist the existential entailments of what they know intellectually.

These two paradoxes are intertwined in Mark: the full existential appropriation of what is known intellectually is prevented by the incompleteness of the revelation.

The revealed/concealed motif is illuminated by our immediate text (Mark 10:32–52) and has a bearing on the problem of Mark's use of the narrative form. That Jesus is revealed is seen in the facts that James and John know that he will enter into glory and Bartimaeus senses in him a wonder-working power which he then demonstrates. His true glory is concealed, however, in that it lies within and on the other side of suffering and death (10:33–34). The concealment is manifested in that James and John do not understand what Jesus' particular kind of glory entails for them (10:42–44), as is seen in their inappropriate request (10:36–37). Yet the disciples can at least understand intellectually what Jesus says about his coming fate, and they must have had some inkling of its implications for them. Otherwise why would they be afraid (10:32)?

Mark's use of the narrative mode is one factor that inclined him to give expression to the revealed/concealed motif. Paul, writing explicitly from a post-resurrection position and not narrating the earthly ministry of Jesus, can generalize the latter as an unmoderated humiliation. But a circumstantial narrative expressing a Christian interpretation of Jesus' ministry would need to *present* the revelation which is concealed. Moreover, if Jesus is now the Son of God and exalted Son of man (14:61–62), and if there is continuity in his existence, which Mark's narrative assumes, then Jesus must always have had that dignity. Mark's belief about who Jesus is and his sense of continuity required that Jesus be portrayed as revealed (not too different from Wrede's position). His understanding of revelation and its interrelationship with faith required that Jesus' identity be concealed (considerably different from Wrede's position). Because the revelation is never fully given in history, faith must be a seeing beneath the surface (3:28–30; 15:39). Although the "I believe; help my unbelief!" comes to explicit expression only once in the Gospel (9:24), it is quite congruent with Mark's overall view that faith is in need of being completed. It would be possible to reconcile Wrede's view of the secret and my view by saying that his pertains to the historical author, while mine pertains to the implied author (the author as he is in and for this work, the principle of coherence in the text as a semiautonomous *Gestalt*).

In sum, Mark's belief in repeated eschatological opportunities found appropriate expression in narrative, and narrative along with his view of revelation inclined him to portray Jesus' true glory as both revealed and concealed. But the vision of the recurring last chance does not necessitate narrative, for this position can be stated propositionally, and the vision of one and only one opportunity can be rendered narratively. I am inclined to acquiesce in the view that narrative does not say anything *conceptually* that cannot be said otherwise. What narrative does accomplish that cannot be otherwise accomplished, at least in the same degree, is to attract the attention and involvement of the reader by the informing of content and to create the sense of living the portrayed possibilities for existence in the course of time.[6]

First Messianic Secret Paradox:
Concealed Revelation

Jesus, the Son of God/Son of man and bringer of the kingdom of God, conceals his identity, conceals the meaning of his mission. In some Old Testament texts (see Deut. 29:29; 30:11, 14) there is a mysterious dimension of God that remains unrevealed, but what *is* revealed is clear and perceptible to human beings. Other Old Testament texts, however (see Isa. 6:9–10), relate the hidden and the revealed in a different way. The hidden does not remain in heaven with God while that which is revealed on earth is clear, but rather the concealed or hidden dimension extends into the world, veiling the revelation and making it problematical. Mark develops this second position.

Ernst Käsemann has suggested that Mark's messianic secret had its origin in the early Hellenistic Jewish christological formulas (perhaps with Palestinian influence, such as Rom. 1:3b–4; Acts 2:36; 13:33) according to which the earthly Jesus was not the divine Son (or preexistent). This dignity came with his exaltation and enthronement.[7] I suggest that if this motif was the source, or a source, for the Markan concept, Mark has developed it in a far-reaching way, beginning with the affirmation that Jesus *was* the divine Son during his earthly ministry but his identity was concealed. In sum, Jesus' identity in Mark is concealed in the following ways: (1) The demons are sometimes ordered to silence (Mark 1:25, 34; 3:12); (2) silence is ordered in the case of three miracles (1:40–45; 5:21–24, 35–43; 7:31–37); (3) outsiders are prevented from understanding Jesus' parabolic word (4:10–12); and (4) the disciples are not to tell anyone that Jesus is the Messiah (8:30).

These commands of silence are often interpreted as having a limited practical purpose within the Markan narrative world; they are intentioned by the need to avoid a particular difficulty. We may consider the following examples of this interpretation of the concealment motif:

(1) Jesus is harassed and pressed by the crowds and wants to escape them.[8] (2) He wants to prevent a premature misinterpretation of his mission which would see him primarily as a healer-exorcist rather than as a sufferer.[9] (3) Jesus' strategy toward the demons, his disciples, and the crowds is to avoid being conspicuously successful. He does not want the narrative of his practice to be short-circuited, or read prematurely, so as to lead to the conclusion that he is a zealot or political Messiah. He teaches in parables-riddles for the same reason.[10] (4) Jesus needs to avoid exciting the crowds and to protect himself from incriminating charges by the authorities until the right time.[11]

I here suggest that the concealed revelation theme is more than a tactic for avoiding specific difficulties. Later (179–82) I will argue that this theme is necessary for Mark's understanding of who and what Jesus is as the instrument of the kingdom of God, the bearer of revelation. The practical interpretation is cogent up to a point. In Mark the crowds do seem to be a problem for Jesus (1:37–38, 45; 3:9; 5:21; 7:24; 8:10). And Jesus either does not want his messiahship to be known at all or does not want a false view of messiahship to be spread around (8:29–30; 9:9). But the concealment of revelation paradox, the concealing of Jesus' identity, is more than a practical device for dealing with specific problems. Along with the second messianic secret paradox it is the governing theme of the whole narrative; and, as we saw (chapter 7), it interlocks with and closely parallels hardness of heart, also a characteristically Markan theme.

Frank Kermode[12] has stated that proper interpretation of a narrative requires identifying the work's "impression point," the moment or element that gives structure and sense to the total work, the part with a privileged relationship to the whole. He then goes on to suggest that the story of Peter's confession (8:27–30), viewed by many as central to Mark, may be seen as the Markan impression point, if it is recognized that it translates into narrative the schematic opposition proclamation/silence[13]— or revealed/concealed. I have been saying that this theme is dominant in Mark, and I should like to examine further Kermode's view of the matter. Peter's confession, "You are the Christ" (*proclamation*), comes shortly after Jesus' criticism of the disciples for their hardhearted *blindness* (8:17–18) and the delayed recovery of the *blind* man (8:22–26); and it is followed by Jesus' order of *silence* (8:30).[14] Kermode might have added that immediately after that exchange Jesus' proclamation that he is the suffering Son of man is followed by Peter's order of silence (8:31–32): Peter rebukes Jesus; in turn, however, Jesus rebukes Peter (8:33). Peter's denial (silencing) of Jesus is intercalated into the story of Jesus'

Jewish trial in which Jesus acknowledges that he is the Christ, the Son of the Blessed, and proclaims that he will be the eschatological Son of man (14:53–62). The threefold denial by Peter (14:66–72) is further related to the betrayal by Judas and the flight of the other disciples (14:43–50). At the end the resurrection is proclaimed (16:6) to those who keep silent (16:8) from a place that is both inside (the tomb, 16:5) and outside (the stone is rolled away, 16:4).[15]

In chapter 3, and earlier in this chapter, I argued that the revealed/concealed scheme affects the Markan narrative structure as a whole. And it is integrally related to the central issues of Jesus' identity (1:34; 3:11–12; 8:29–30), the kingdom of God and the parables in which it is disclosed (4:11–12), the miracles and the nature of faith (3:28–30; 4:40–41). Here one more reference to the miracles is in order. The fact that Jesus' miracles are worked in public, that the demons identify him as Son of God, and that the healed spread the word about his extraordinary acts against his commands does not undermine the messianic secret. This is an essential part of the paradox: there must *be* a revelation to be concealed, and the miracles and the reports about them fulfill this necessity. It has been pointed out that the crowds take no cognizance of the demons' identification of Jesus as Son of God nor of Jesus' self-designation as Son of man (1:24, 27; 2:10, 12).[16] This shows that the concealment element is also present in the miracle stories other than in Jesus' commands of silence. The crowds pay no attention to the messianic titles and do not respond to them. The word about Jesus' miracles is widely spread (1:34, 45; 7:36–37), and the people are moved to amazement and to wonder who he is (1:27; 2:12; 7:37), but they do not penetrate his identity and grasp the significance of the titles.

A recognition of the presiding presence of the revealed/concealed scheme can shed light on difficult passages. Ernest Best has pointed out the close tie that Mark makes between Jesus' walking on the water (6:46–52, the risen Lord coming in stormy times) and the feeding of the five thousand (6:30–44).[17] This connection suggests that the risen Christ present in the eucharistic meal comes to help in the difficult times of life. If that is the correct interpretation, then the strange motif, difficult to interpret, that Jesus meant to pass by the struggling disciples (6:48) would bring to bear on this story of revealed presence the related theme of concealment. That Jesus wanted to pass them by suggests the mysterious, nonmanipulable, hidden dimension of revelation. Or to put the matter the other way around, such passages as this one point to the pervasive presence of the revealed/concealed scheme.

Second Messianic Secret Paradox:
Plain Revelation Misunderstood

The second paradox is that when Jesus' true identity—suffering-dying-rising Son of man—is *plainly* disclosed to the disciples (8:31–32; 9:31; 10:33–34) they do not understand it (8:32–33; 9:32–34; 10:35–41). What do they not understand? The discursive meaning of these sayings is clear, and Peter understands the matter quite well enough to reject it (8:32–33). The misunderstanding is an existential failure, an unwillingness to accept suffering, the way of the Son of man, as the pattern for their own existence. This is clear. Each indication of failure to understand who *Jesus* is is followed by a teaching on suffering *discipleship* and being servant of all (8:34–37; 9:35–50; 10:42–45). I have dealt with this theme in connection with the ending of the plot (chapter 3), hardness of heart (chapter 7), and the interpretation of 10:32–52 (chapter 11). Here I want only to treat one aspect of it and in relation to another text, Jesus' return to his hometown in Nazareth (6:1–6a).

The disciples' severe misunderstanding begins even before the teaching about the suffering Son of man, especially in connection with the feeding miracles (6:52; 8:17–21). I have argued that one strand in Mark's thought is that the misunderstanding (6:52; 7:14–18) and rejection (3:6; 12:12; 14:1–2; 15:1) of Jesus is willful, freely chosen, and blameworthy (see chapter 7). Here I want to raise the following question in connection with 6:1–6a: is the failure to understand Jesus and to accept the role of serving love for the neighbor *simply* the individual's freely willed rejection of suffering and risk as a way of life? Or is there an element of fatedness in the *human* situation which is, as least provisionally, distinguishable from the *divine* determination of human ignorance and failure which comes to expression in the first messianic secret paradox, according to which God (or Jesus) conceals the revelation at the point at which it is given (4:11–12).

Why do the people of Nazareth, his hometown, take offense at Jesus and fail to believe in him, according to 6:1–6a? Fernando Belo gives a Marxist answer. The home is the place of the ideological production of the codes of the social formation, and for Belo it is really wealth that determines all of these codes. The habitual repetition of the codes, the acceptance, without critical questioning, of the given social structure, prevents the townspeople from seeing the revelation in Jesus' narrative. It is the blinding power of these forms which is the object of Jesus' amazement (6:6a).[18]

I contend that Mark does not support the view that the predispositions which prevent receiving the gospel are exclusively and most fundamentally determined by economic factors (see my argument in chapter 10). As we have often observed, in this Gospel the refusal of the kingdom and of moral good, the refusal of Jesus' way, originates in the heart (3:5; 7:21–23; 10:5), not in property, however much this refusal may in particular cases fasten upon property (10:22). It is hardness of heart (8:17–18), not economic codes as such, which is the predisposition that inhibits the understanding of the mystery of the kingdom (4:11–12, 24–25). Hardness of heart is the pre-understanding as non-understanding which generates more non-understanding (4:25b) or prevents faith (6:6a). Yet given Mark's view of the circular relationship between being or character and action (9:43–48), hardness of heart, the deformation of spiritual understanding or of the self, will certainly be deepened by acts of holding on to wealth.

According to Kermode, in 6:1–6a Jesus is heard first by the townspeople with astonishment and then with resentment, apparently because of the break with his family which has already been narrated (3:21, 31–35).[19] I do not think that the text suggests any development from astonishment to resentment: they coincide. The many in the town hearing him were astonished (imperfect), saying (present participle), where did he get all of this, and so forth? What they say expresses both their resentment and their astonishment. And the statement that they took offense at him (6:3b) simply sums this up. Nor is there any indication that the people resent him because of his differences with his family. In fact, the meaning of this short narrative requires that the people of Nazareth take him to be part of his family. Yet the import of the story points to why the disciple needs to break with the natural family: it is the town and the family (3:21) which generate the predisposition to reject the new and unexpected. What the townspeople take offense at is that as a known and familiar family member he does extraordinary things; in their understanding, that ought not to be the case. In a sense they resent the mystery which they tacitly acknowledge: that the extraordinary (wisdom and miracles) occurs in the familiar. They are not astonished and then resentful but rather resent the paradoxical fusion of the extraordinary and the ordinary which astonishes them. Their predisposition or pre-understanding is challenged by the new occurrence, but the predisposition in this case is too strong for the new to break through it and create faith (6:6a). Therefore, Mark 6:1–6a in the Markan context does suggest that the misunderstanding and rejection of Jesus is not *simply* a free and willful act but is also predisposed by attitudes engendered in part by the

familiar communities. Any other attachments and commitments would
have the same effect.

The Relationship of the
Two Messianic Secret Paradoxes

What is the nature of the connection between the two paradoxes?
Werner Kelber seems to deny that there is an essential connection:
"More recently we have learned to differentiate at least between the
secrecy motif [my first paradox] and discipleship failure [my second
paradox]."[20] I argue that there is an organic relationship between the two
concepts. To make such a claim is not to imply that the Markan text
itself sets out this configuration of ideas in a precise and conceptually
systematic way. But the claim is consistent with the phenomenological
hermeneutic which I have tried to expound (chapter 1 and Appendix I).
The *text* is to be transformed into a *work* by the interpreter who, given
access to the text by a pre-understanding and then submitted to the
critical power of the text, seeks to bring coherence and solution to the
clues in the text, which are inchoate and possibly discordant or lacking
in solution. If the conflicts in the text are resolved, it will be through a
principle of reconciliation which is *not* formulated explicitly in the text
itself.[21]

Once again I present the Markan concepts that call for a coherent
solution. (1) It is the outsiders (non-disciples) from whom Jesus' identity
and the meaning of his mission are concealed (4:10–12; 8:30). Yet some
outsiders do come to faith: the Gerasene demoniac, the woman with the
hemorrhage, and the Roman centurion, for example. (2) It is the disciples
to whom the secret of the kingdom and Jesus' identity are plainly disclosed (4:11, 34; 8:32a). Yet they are uncomprehending and hard of heart
(8:17–18, 9:10, 32). This non-understanding is both freely chosen and
predisposed, predisposed by a prior understanding which has individual
(4:25b) and communal roots (3:21; 6:2–4). Pre-understanding can either
give access to new understanding (4:25a) or destroy it (4:25b), and this
pre-understanding with its power to predispose is attributed to the disciples in that it is described in a discourse to them (4:10), and Jesus
addresses them in the imperative: "take heed what you hear" (4:24). But
Mark also sees these remarks as addressed to "anyone" (4:23); and while
it is indicated at 4:10 that he is speaking privately to the disciples,
4:33–34 assumes that he has been talking to the crowd that was his
audience at 4:1. Thus Jesus is represented as saying what is the situation
generally for human beings as such. We may speak of these two sets of

ideas as the outsider and the disciple (insider) configurations. As it turns out, each of them has elements both of revealedness and concealedness. While not attempting to develop all of the possible relationships among the parts of these two configurations, I do want to pursue a couple of the relationships which will, I think, disclose an essential and coherent connection between the two complexes. I have two questions: First, what is the connection between the fact that the *disciples* fail to understand Jesus and the fact that it is the *outsiders* from whom God/Jesus conceals the truth? Second, what is the connection between the *human* predisposition not to believe and the *divine* concealment of revelation?

Turning to the first question, we note that there are terminological and conceptual parallels between the hardness of heart attributed to the disciples and that attributed to outsiders. In both cases it involves a failure to understand, an absence of *real* seeing and hearing (compare 3:5; 4:10–12 with 6:52; 8:17–20). And in the case of the outsiders (opponents) this failure is intended by Jesus. He uses parables *in order that* (*hina*, purpose clause) the outsiders might not understand (4:12). Since the conditions of the two groups turn out to be the same, there is also the suggestion that they have the same cause: God/Jesus has actually also concealed the truth of revelation from the disciples. But why would Mark have found it theologically necessary to presuppose that? Why would he also attribute divine causality to the disciples' failure?

Recall that some interpreters hold that, in Mark, Jesus conceals his identity and purpose because he does not want his narrative to be short-circuited or read prematurely; that is, he does not want to be identified as Messiah until the right time, until his suffering role is unmistakably clear. The concealment from non-disciples is only a *postponement* of the revelation of his identity until enough narrative has transpired to show in what sense he is Messiah and Son of God. The hiddenness of his identity is not a permanent and essential part of the revelation. In chapter 3, I argued that it is, and I want to continue that argument here.

It should be said that the postponement view could explain why the centurion can legitimately confess Jesus as Son of God when the demons could not: he has seen the end of the narrative and knows Jesus as Son of God on the cross. And the postponement interpretation could also explain why after a certain point Jesus' true identity as Son of God could be revealed to the disciples (9:7): it is near enough to the end to show that he is Son of God *as* suffering Son of man (e.g., 8:31; 9:9). When, however, this later point is reached and Jesus' true identity is revealed, it is still not grasped by the disciples. As we have seen, that is due in part to their not being willing to understand, to their rejection of the way of suffering and risk. But when the mystery continues into the resurrection which was supposed to clear things up (9:9) and beyond that into the life of the church (see chapter 3), then we must ask if the concealment from God's side is not more than just a postponement and if it does not in fact present God's revelation of the kingdom in the mission of Jesus as *in principle* a concealed revelation, for the disciples as well as for everyone else. But why did Mark need to suggest that? That revelation is concealed in principle is a needed explanation for the failure of the disciples to understand revelation in the light of Mark's eschatology and Christology.

As Son of man on earth with power to forgive sins and set aside the obligation to obey the Sabbath law (2:10; 2:28) Jesus is the proleptic manifestation of the eschatological Son of man (8:38; 13:26–27). His word has the power of miracle (1:25–28; 2:10–12) to produce effects, and it lasts forever (13:31). If his word has such eschatological authority, then how could the failure of *this* word and of his eschatological presence to produce fruit in the disciples, or in anyone else, be explained except by maintaining that his identity and teaching have been concealed by God or Jesus himself? Mark's correlative understanding of faith (see the next section) also bears on this issue. Discipleship failure in the light of who Jesus really is (Christology) requires the secrecy motif (concealed revelation) as an explanation. And if the open revelation to the disciples is also concealed, the concealed revelation to the outsiders is also the word with eschatological power. Because outsider and disciple are defined by the narrative in very similar ways—each of them as other than they are—the irony of the narrative virtually erases the normal difference in meaning between insider and outsider.

The reason why the disciples fail to appropriate existentially what they know intellectually is that the revelation itself is veiled or concealed. This problematical character of the revelation is further enforced by the suggestion in the parable of the seed growing secretly (4:26–29) that the revealer himself does not know how the word works, does not control its destiny. It is proper to understand Jesus as the sower in this parable because Mark presents the parable-enigmas of the Gospel as allegories. The sower (4:3–9) is interpreted allegorically (4:14–20), and this instance is taken as the model for understanding all the parables (4:13).[22] So the man who sows in 4:26–29 is Jesus and what he sows is the word, for the sower of the seed (4:3–4) has already been interpreted by Mark as the sower of the word (4:14), and it is Jesus who proclaims (sows) the word

(8:32; 13:31). Obviously the earth or ground that receives the seed (4:26–28) is the hearers of the word (4:14–15).[23] Jesus sows the seed-word upon the ground, and the seed sprouts and produces grain he knows not how.[24] This not knowing about the generative relationship between seed (word) and earth (hearer) does not prevent the assertion that the earth produces of itself (*automatē*). Yet still the confluence of the effect of Jesus' word and action with the response of the hearers is a mystery for him.[25] Mark 4:14–20 shows that there are many contextual factors involved in receiving the word or not receiving it, and various responses result from the sowing of the word. Jesus sows, and then the process of the interaction between the word and the hearers remains beyond his knowing. But that there will be a harvest he is confident (4:29; 13:31).

What is the relationship between the concealment of revelation from Jesus' side which inhibits understanding and the power of human pre-understanding which predisposes people as a fate not to believe or to understand? Can the former simply be reduced to the latter? Or must we not say that at least for Mark the two sources of non-understanding are mysteriously mixed? Jesus does not know the mysterious interworkings of the proclaimed word and the human heart (4:27). In Mark 6:1–6a we see both sides. There is revelation in that the divine presence, that which evokes astonishment, is manifested in Jesus' authority, wisdom, and mighty works. But it is concealed in one who is a familiar carpenter, son, and brother. So we have concealed revelation. But we also have the human pre-understanding of the people of Nazareth which is nurtured by the habitual familiarity of the town. Their pre-understanding is strained by the revelation; they must ask themselves where he got all of this (6:2). But the pre-understanding is finally strengthened when they reject the new disclosure and refuse to change; Jesus marveled at their unbelief (6:6a). One who has the wrong pre-understanding for proper hearing (4:25b) will have a still greater wrong pre-understanding once one has refused to hear revelation with understanding. Concealed revelation and the human predisposition not to accept the new (the *new* creation is here for indissoluble marriage, for giving up your goods for the *new* community) reinforce one another. Is it that the revelation, because it is concealed, strengthens rather than bursts the predisposition not to believe, get free of oneself, and act for the neighbor in love?

Mark 4:1–34 and the Messianic Secret: Light, Hearing, and Faith

Mark 4:1–34 deserves special attention because it contains the harshest and most extreme expression of the concealed revelation motif: Jesus teaches in parable-enigmas in order that the outsiders might not understand, repent, and find forgiveness (4:10–12). It also suggests a way out of the impasse: nothing is hidden except in order to be brought to light (4:21–23).

In interpreting this passage we will look at aspects of its concentric structure. A concentric structure is a symmetrical arrangement of introverted parallelism of four, five, or more elements that may have a single unparalleled element in the middle (a b c b′ a′) or be entirely balanced (a b c c′ b′ a′). If it has the single middle element, this member characteristically opposes the thought of the rest of the pattern.[26] First, note the concentric pattern of 4:2b–20:

a	(2b–9)	parable of the sower
b	(10)	disciples' question about the parables
c	(11–12)	purpose of the parables to prevent understanding
b′	(13)	reproof of the disciples
a′	(14–20)	interpretation of the sower

Only in the middle (c) are the parables a mystery, riddle, or enigma. Elsewhere in this section they are meant to be understood.[27]

The whole of 4:1–34 also falls into a concentric pattern:

A	(1–2a)	introduction (teaching in parables)
B	(2b–20)	parabolic material
C	(21–25)	sayings about light and hearing
B′	(26–32)	parabolic material
A′	(33–34)	conclusion (teaching in parables and explaining)

The entire text (4:1–34) stands under the dominance of the concealing or secrecy motif. That is the case because the passage *ends* on that note (4:33–34), and the ending repeats and reinforces that same theme as it comes to expression in c (4:11–12), which is the center of B. The meaning of "parable" in 4:33–34 has been determined by the meaning given it in 4:11–12, so to speak the word to the crowd in parables as they were able to hear it means to speak to them what they could not understand.[28] Over against this stands the center (C) with its affirmation that the intention of the word is revelation, to bring things to light.[29]

Thus we have seen that the center (4:11–12) of this small circle expresses concealment, while the center (4:21–25) of the large circle expresses disclosure and illumination. I will focus on these two centering segments and the pericope that connects them, the interpretation of the sower (4:13–20).

In Mark 4:11–12 the very purpose of teaching in parables is to keep the

outsiders out, to prevent their seeing and hearing from issuing in understanding. Kermode[30] speaks of uncompromising exclusion. John Meagher
takes strong exception to this motif in Mark. In his view the theme of
esoteric teaching is inconsistent with the Gospel at large and is localized
in 4:10–13 and only a few other places. Moreover, the concept that
revelation is intentionally obscured is horrendous in itself and does not
make sense in any setting.[31]

I have argued and continue to argue that concealment has a dialectical
relationship with revelation in Mark, and that concealed revelation is the
thematic counterpart to the plot as a whole and is in Mark's narrative
world the necessary explanation for the disciples' failure of faith and
understanding. This is clearly not a localized element. Whether or not it
is horrendous and senseless is for everyone to decide. But to reject it out
of hand entails a negative judgment about a tragicomic view of existence
in principle and a condemnation of any standpoint that takes fate in both
its transcendent and historical dimensions seriously.

This brings us to the interpretation of the parable of the sower (4:13–
20), which mediates between concealment (4:10–12) and illumination
(4:21–25). Paul J. Achtemeier has stated that 4:11–12 and the explanation
of the sower have the same point: that the point of the parables is how
one listens to and responds to Jesus.[32] I would say that the two passages
do deal with the same theme but do not exactly make the same point; at
least the accent is different. Mark 4:11–12 acknowledges the giving of the
secret of the kingdom to the disciples but emphasizes its intentional
hiddenness from others, while Mark 4:13–20 details the temporary de-
feats of the word but reaches its climax with the word's extraordinary
fruitfulness. This latter point prepares the way for 4:21–25, where the
purpose of concealment is revelation. But before leaving 4:13–20 we
should observe that in this passage what prevents fruitfulness is not the
intention of the revealer or the nature of the word but concrete external
circumstances and lack of resolution on the part of hearers. In considering 4:11–12 and 4:13–20 together, one ought to say that the destiny which
prevents responsiveness to the word is spun from a number of strands:
God's mysterious tendency to conceal (4:11–12), the power of Satan
(4:15), difficult historical and social circumstances (4:17b, 19), and lack
of internal staying power in the faith of individuals (4:16b, 17a, 19).[33]

What is concealed is hidden in order to be revealed (4:21–25). Mark
4:11–12 makes concealment the purpose of parabolic preaching (*hina*
clause). But 4:21–23 also contains purpose (*hina*) clauses. In this passage
Jesus' parabolic word is compared to a lamp whose purpose is not to be

put under a bushel or a bed but on the lampstand to shine. It is also stated that nothing is hidden or secret—the mystery of the kingdom— except for the purpose of being brought to manifestation. So the final purpose of the word that conceals is manifestation or unconcealment. If unconcealment is the real purpose of a concealment which is also inten- tional, then the concealment of revelation is an integral part of revelation as Mark conceives it. Both hiding and disclosing are necessary in order to say what revelation is. Faith mediates between revealed-in-order-to- conceal and hidden-in-order-to-be-made-manifest. Thus revelation and faith are closely correlated in Mark. If concealment is a necessary part of revelation and redemption in Mark, necessary because God postpones full revelation until the future, then penetrating the concealment is a necessary part of faith.

Human pre-understanding is the factor that mediates revelation and faith. Perhaps Mark presupposes that concealed revelation joins with pre-understanding to generate faith, and faith enables the disclosure pole of concealed revelation to become more actual.

We observed that in the strongest possible way Mark stresses the divine initiative in salvation (chapter 6). Salvation is impossible for human beings, but all things are possible with God (10:27). In 4:21–23 the divine initiative comes to expression by means of the image of the lamp whose purpose is to give light. But something *is* also expected of human beings: they are put under the imperative to hear (4:23, 24a), and fruitful hearing clearly involves the pre-understanding with which one hears. The *way* the *human* being hears has something to do with the effectiveness of the seed (4:15, 16, 18, 20) or light (4:24). The measure one brings to hearing conditions the measure of understanding one gets (4:24b). More understanding will be given to the one who already has understanding (4:25a). Recall that the soil or earth is also an image of the hearer in Mark 4. The earth produces "of itself" (*automatē*, 4:28). The "of itself" is the pre-understanding of the hearer; it is the measure that he or she already has and brings to hearing the word or seeing the light, the measure that enables the latter to produce an effect. Mark has attributed everything in salvation to God and consigned human beings to radical hardness of heart. But even Jesus, the revealer, the sower of the seed-word, does not know everything about the relationship between the revealed word and the heart of the hearer (4:27). That area of mystery leaves room for the measure that the hearer of the word brings to understanding (4:24–25a) from himself (4:28a), a human measure for which Mark's theology seems to have no logical place in view of 10:27. Where does this "of itself" come

from? Within Mark's frame of reference could it be other than a trace of
the nature that human beings had at the beginning of creation *before*
hardness of heart set in (10:5–9), a trace of the primordial nature which
is now being restored eschatologically? This trace is a part of what makes
indissoluble marriage or giving up all wealth and security for the sake of
the new community conceivable. But then if God is the *creator* of human
beings so constituted, perhaps Mark has not really modified "with human
beings ["men," RSV] it is impossible, but not with God" (10:27). Nor
does he suggest that pre-understanding alone leads to faith. There is light
for the eyes, word for the ears, and seed for the earth.

In discussing Mark 4:13–20 I suggested that the word mediates concealment and disclosure. The word that fails to produce fruit finally
proves to be extravagantly effective. That is clear in the text of Mark 4.
But faith is also a mediator in the same context. Faith's seeing through
the surface turns the concealing word into the revealing. Proper hearing
brings the hidden and secret to open manifestation (4:21–25). Mark
speaks of the mediating factor on both its objective (word) and subjective
(faith) sides. Since both word and faith are mediators of the same opposition, Mark's presupposition must be that the word enlivens faith. In fact,
we noted (chapter 4) that it is Mark's explicit belief that the narrative-
word about Jesus creates faith (1:28, 45; 3:7–12; 5:27, 34; 10:47, 52). Even
though the word may be met with repeated misunderstanding or rejection, as in the first three seed episodes (4:14–19) and in the experience
of the disciples throughout the plot, it is also finally fruitful, as in the final
seed episode (4:20) and in the suggestion that some of the disciples were
responsive after the resurrection (10:39; 13:9–11). But how, when, or
whether the word will evoke faith remains a mystery. Just what the
relationship is between seed and fruit, between word and faith-love, the
sower does not know (4:27).

Faith in Mark is responding to the gospel, the heart of which is the
saving death and resurrection of the Son of man. Therefore it is the
existential experience of losing one's life to find it, the death of the old
self, the abandonment of securities, which gives freedom from the self *to
be* for God and the neighbor/other. The disciple with faith is on the *way*
to salvation (10:52), and the way image reflects Mark's dual eschatology,
that the kingdom has both come and not come. The kingdom overlaps
a segment in the history of hardness of heart. The disciple lives after and
in the light of the resurrection of Jesus, because Jesus' powerful word has
proclaimed it, but also before the resurrection. Since faith is given by the
uncompleted eschatological salvation event (10:27, 45, 46–52), the disci-

ple both has faith and does not. Having it and not having it at the same time is, then, not just the situation of the *would-be* disciple or the natural human,[34] but the condition of the *disciple*. All disciples must say, "I believe; help my unbelief!" (9:24).

Since the concealment of revelation will never be fully broken through from God's side until the end of the world, faith will always be like looking through the veil. God's revelation as hidden beneath the surface of ordinary existence and faith as penetrating the surface are complementary sides of the same reality. Mark portrays the ministry of Jesus as the key to this correlation. Who Jesus really is, for Mark, is concealed beneath the fact that he is an ordinary carpenter, son, and brother who dies a cruel and ignominious death. So a disciple must be able to see through the veil and beneath the surface and acknowledge that it is the Son of God on the cross (15:39) and to understand himself or herself as the follower of *this* Son of God.

Yet somehow and in some measure the true identity of Jesus does break through the concealment (1:27; 2:12; 6:2): the ordinary man does extraordinary things and this offends people's expectations. Thus faith is being able to see through this offense. Since Jesus does the unexpected and transgresses the principles of traditional piety (2:1—3:27), having faith is to see through the offense and to encounter in Jesus, not the presence of demons, but the Holy Spirit as the disrupter of human expectations (3:28–30).

Mark's understanding of faith may be further clarified by showing how it differs from religious faith as defined in a very prejudicial way by the literary critic Murray Krieger. According to Krieger, a poem is not an emptiness with no center as deconstructionists would say, but a presence, even if that ordering presence falsifies reality. This presence is constituted by the closed system of the poem in which the poem's own unique meaning is brought forth from within ordinary words. Krieger acknowledges with some admitted embarrassment that his view of the poem as presence is analogous to Mircea Eliade's concept of sacramental presence. In Eliade's view, there are sacred times and places because an ordinary time or space is invested with the sacred and thus becomes something else but without ceasing to be itself.[35] Krieger then proceeds to claim that despite this similarity between the poem and the sacred there is a crucial difference between them. An object or moment of faith is arbitrarily chosen as such; its choice is determined by fiat from outside and not by elements intrinsic to its own makeup. It is not chosen because of resources within the object or moment. The poem, on the other hand, which is experienced by the critic as presence is not chosen because of the arbitrary command of an outside faith. Rather, the critic responds because of the internalizing directions within the poem, directions that come from the transforming play of language with language in which presence emerges from ordinary generic discourse.[36]

While Krieger's view of religious faith doubtless corresponds with certain moments in the history of religions, it is completely discordant with the understanding of faith in Mark or in any other major segment of the New Testament. In fact, faith in Mark is more like the experience that Krieger attributes to the literary critic than it is like Krieger's definition of faith. The reader of Mark is not expected to accept the narrative as the revelation of divine presence, because one has been told in advance that it is there regardless of any intrinsic relationship between presence and the story. Rather, it is the narrative itself that is regarded as evoking faith, and any experience of power that would lead one to a sense of the divine presence and action will come from the particular content of this story as it is shaped by plot, ironies, tensive parallelism, and so forth. Faith, then, is seeing the world through the particular form of this story.

There is an important way, however, in which Mark's understanding of faith differs from Krieger's "literary faith." According to Krieger, it is our humanistic triumph that we can create myth and metaphor, but it is fact that wins out in the end. We can see life more acutely through our literary figures. But we must be able to see around the creations of our literary vision to the bedrock of existential fact, not making any final commitment to the vision as if it were the only reality.[37]

The Markan text, on the other hand, has a very different view of commitment. What it seeks from the reader is total commitment to *life as viewed through the narrative*. At the same time, life envisioned through the narrative world of Mark is always the way into the open future.

The Meaning of the Mystery

What is the content of the secret that faith is supposed to understand? That the meaning of the gospel which is to be grasped *is* a mystery is underscored not only by the plot and the broad messianic secret paradoxes but by specific words: mystery (*mystērion*, 4:11), secret (*kryptos*, 4:22), hidden (*apokryphos*, 4:22). Exactly what is the secret that the disciple is to penetrate?

Some interpreters of Mark think that the mystery has a definite content which can be identified. One of the focal points for the discussion is the two related passages, Mark 6:52 and 8:14–21. In both cases the disciples are accused of hardness of heart because they do not understand about the loaves multiplied in the feedings of the multitude. What exactly should they have understood? According to Kelber, what they fail to grasp is the meaning of the "one loaf" (8:14)—Jesus as the unifier of Jew and Gentile in one community.[38] For Howard Clark Kee, the mystery is not that Jesus is the Messiah but the nature of his messiahship. It is the insight that contrary to appearances there is no hopeless incongruity between Jesus' eschatological claims and the death he died.[39] In the judgment of Quentin Quesnell the mystery of the kingdom, knowledge of the parables, freedom from the purity laws, and the understanding of the loaves all belong together; and Quesnell assumes that this comprehensive mystery is something that can be identified and understood. He states that in the first part of the Gospel we are not sure what the disciples do not understand, but in the second part it is Jesus' approaching fate and its meaning for would-be disciples. The mystery is the content of the gospel, what is revealed as an object of faith. Or it is the theme of the resurrection. It is everything associated with the bread of the Eucharist—the meal itself; its announcement of Jesus' death as saving and his future coming; the disciple's share in Jesus' death; the union of believers, including Jew and Gentile, through participation in the one loaf; the experience of the presence of the resurrected Lord.[40]

There are other interpreters of Mark who think that when we arrive at 8:14–21 the disciples are expected to understand something about the kingdom of God but have never been told in a straightforward way what it is. We do not know what it is that they are to understand.[41] The mystery is impenetrable, and its content cannot be identified. Those who see the matter in this way will evaluate it differently. According to Meagher, the disciples do not catch the significance of the twelve and seven baskets full of bread left over from the two feedings, and the reader senses uneasily that she or he does not get it either. The story seems self-defeating unless the point is that proper insight is beyond us all but is still required. Nor does Mark understand the secret. From Mark's opacity and mystification a mystery is born.[42] Kermode also sees the mystery as impenetrable, to the disciples, to Mark, and to us.[43] But in contrast to Meagher, Kermode sees the unfathomable and irreducible mystery in Mark as pointing up in a striking way the element of secrecy in narratives generally, the dimension that makes them really interesting, valuable, and perpetually to be interpreted.[44]

Can we reach a synthesis? What is it that is to be understood but remains perpetually a mystery? In Mark 4:10–12 it is the kingdom of God. And the prominence of language about understanding in relationship to the death and resurrection of the Son of man (9:10, 32) suggests that this is also the mystery. In view of the close relationship between *Jesus* and the *kingdom* in Mark[45] they are really the *same* mystery. And in the light of the strong parallelism between the language of eyes and ears, the language of seeing, hearing, and understanding, in both 4:11–12 and 8:17–18 the mystery of the *kingdom-Jesus* is the same as the mystery of the *loaves*. Recall also that the same language of not understanding is used not only of outsiders (4:10–12) but also of the disciples (8:17–18). James M. Robinson's interpretation of 8:14–21 points toward a possible synthesis between specific interpretations of the secret and the view that the secret is unfathomable. According to Robinson, what is to be understood is the quantity of broken pieces left over from the two feedings: the twelve and seven baskets signify the inexhaustibleness of the eschatological reality.[46] The significance of the loaves is unfathomable, and this attaches to any specific interpretation of the secret. It may be that the kingdom or christological or eucharistic content of the mystery can be named, but the named content cannot be fixedly specified. What it means for the individual disciple and the Christian community must be discovered all along the way. The meaning of the kingdom of God and the suffering-death-resurrection of the Son of man can never be exhausted and is subject to endless interpretation, but that which cannot be exhausted is named and qualified. A disciple cannot know in advance all that might be entailed in following on the way of the Son of man, nor can the disciple know how far beneath the surface he or she has seen. But it *is* the way of the Son of man as defined by the narrative that is being followed. The meaning of the mystery is neither totally specifiable nor totally open.[47] That the kingdom remains a mystery for the disciple is congruent with the fact that Jesus himself does not fully understand the relationship between the word of the kingdom and the faith of the hearer.

Conclusion: Ethics

The disciples of Jesus in the middle of Mark's plot are moving along a *way*. And those who become disciples through their encounter with the Gospel let its story shape that segment of the middle of world time which they occupy. The time *along the way* is one of overlapping: the time of hardness of heart is penetrated by the time of eschatological salvation. The kingdom of God has both come and not come; faith is both given and withheld. Faith is seeing and hearing aright, an understanding of oneself formed by the narrative in which life emerges from death. Finding one's life by losing it gives freedom from the self and openness to the neighbor. Faith so understood defines the character of the disciple as Mark understands it. This character or being is enabled by the kingdom's coming, and out of it flow acts of love, which in turn shape character. Mark would agree with Stanley Hauerwas that one is as one sees. The disciple, in order to do what is required, must be what one comes to be by *seeing* the reality hidden in Jesus (4:10–12; 6:52; 8:17–18; 8:22–26; 9:9, 32; 10:52–53; 15:39). But our whole discussion, and the passages just listed, show how hard the seeing on which conduct depends is: "do you not *yet* understand?" (8:21) is the question asked of the disciples halfway through the story. And they do not see throughout the remainder of the plot. But sooner or later some of them do: the capacity for right hearing belongs to them as human beings. And other people are reached by the word of and about Jesus: the Gerasene demoniac, the woman with the hemorrhage, blind Bartimaeus, and the Roman centurion.

Mark's ethic makes a total demand upon the disciple, but the plot and its themes are a warning against the expectation of perfection. A person is put *on the way,* a way which surprisingly affords new beginnings. It is always the way with the suffering Son of man, who is yet the rising Son of man who will appear at the end as eschatological judge and redeemer. But what exactly does the latter vindication mean if victory is risk, loss, and servanthood (8:34–37; 9:35; 10:43–44)? That is what has to be discovered along the way in relation to spouse, property, and the complexities of communal relationships. The one who leads the way and enables following (Jesus) knows resolutely where he is going. Yet as sower of the seed-word, everything is not without its mystery for him. There are definite things to be done (stay with your wives and husbands; give up your property), but the will of God for the disciple is always more than the traces it leaves in the form of principles and rules, traces of ethical direction. Yet the traces are not traces of traces, but traces of what God's will requires.

If Mark is to be considered as one authoritative source for constructive Christian ethics, not only must the Markan norms be taken into account but also the paradoxical, ironical, presentation of ethical enablement must be an element in the Christian understanding of existence with its moral project. The norms make a radical demand, a demand that not only impinges on the heart, the hidden inner core of a person (7:15–23) but also requires concrete action (9:33–50; 10:1–31). It is perhaps a token of Mark's realism, however, that Matthew's positive term "the pure in heart" (Matt.

5:8) does not actually appear in Mark. It is only implied by its opposite, the hard (Mark 10:5) and defiling (7:20–23) heart. The radical norm, which assumes realized eschatological fulfillment, has no place to be obeyed except the middle of time in which the kingdom of God and the fallen age overlap. The time of the Christian community's life is woven from processes of both amelioration and degradation. God's eschatological power is manifested in the narrative to give sight and to overcome imprisoning demonic evil and to enable indissoluble marriage and a community sharing houses and lands, composed of persons freed from the self for others. All things are possible for believers (9:23), as all things are possible for God (10:27). But believers also disbelieve (9:24), for in terms of both plot and theme Mark's narrative world is one in which revelation is concealed at the source, understanding has difficulty seeing beneath the surface, and hardness of heart is fated. Both the radical norm, which expects obedience, and the paradox of the time belong to the same whole narrative world; and it would be an unwarranted abstraction to disengage the norm from its narrative matrix and texture.

It is the *disciples,* who have responded to Jesus' call and left their jobs (1:16–20; 2:13–14), who have been encountered by the powerful language event of the crucified and risen Son of man (8:31; 9:31; 10:33–34), who have actually preached, healed, and cast out demons (6:12–13). It is *these disciples* who do not and cannot understand what the dying and rising Son of man means for them (8:32–37; 9:32–37; 10:35–41) and thereby do not and cannot grasp the ethical principle of moving themselves from first to last and being servants of all (9:35; 10:42–44). And the women at the tomb, to whom the resurrection has been announced, go away in fear and trembling without carrying the message to the disciples. But it is also the case that the word of resurrection has been spoken (16:6), and while the word experiences many failures (4:14–19), it is finally extravagantly fruitful (4:20). So the Gerasene demoniac is delivered from stagnating time by the word (5:8, 13), sitting there now clothed and in his right mind, sent to tell about the mercy of the Lord/Jesus. And once-blind Bartimaeus is following on the way.

NOTES

1. John Dominic Crossan, "A Form for Absence: The Markan Creation of Gospel," *Semeia* 12 (1978): 44–45, 50–53.

2. For an elaboration of this view, see Via, *Kerygma and Comedy,* 90–94.

3. Petersen, *Literary Criticism for New Testament Critics,* 80.

4. See Appendix II for my critique of the structuralist tendency to dissolve the chronological. On the tension between the chronological and the logical, see Roland Barthes, "Introduction à l'analyse structurale des récits," *Communications* 8 (1966): 12; Greimas, *Sémantique structurale*, 196–97, 205, 207, 212; Paul Ricoeur, "The Narrative Form," *Semeia* 4 (1975): 48–50.

5. William Wrede, *The Messianic Secret*, Eng. trans. J. C. G. Greig (Greenwood, S. C.: Attic Press, 1971), 124–28, 213, 218, 220, 223, 227–29.

6. On the "feel of lived time," see Stephen Crites, "Angels We Have Heard," in *Religion as Story*, ed. J. Wiggins (New York: Harper & Row, 1975), 26.

7. Käsemann, *Commentary on Romans*, 13.

8. Kee, *Community of the New Age*, 95.

9. Bilezikian, *The Liberated Gospel*, 69, 75.

10. Belo, *A Materialist Reading of the Gospel of Mark*, 107, 127, 139, 154–55. In Belo's view, the present (later) Markan narrative in which Jesus goes to Jerusalem to die as Son of man overlies an earlier narrative in which he went to Jerusalem for two purposes: (1) to take over the temple and proclaim the transfer of the vineyard to other owners; (2) to go forth to the pagans with his mission of sharing bread with the poor. His death was no part of this earlier narrative, but it occurred because his original strategy failed. The later narrative tries to justify the failure and give meaning to his death. The messianism of the earlier narrative is neither Zealot nor "spiritual" in type. Thus for Belo the factor which the earlier narrative does not want to short-circuit is not Jesus' death but his social mission to the pagans (*A Materialist Reading of the Gospel of Mark*, 206, 208, 210, 211). One must question how the Markan author around A.D. 70 could have been dealing with a narrative, even an unwritten one, in which Jesus did not intend to die, *unless* such a narrative had a claim to be the real story of the historical Jesus. Such a narrative might theoretically still have been in competition with the church's focus on his death as intended by God through Scripture. But Belo denies (ibid., 157) that his distinction between the earlier and the later narrative has anything to do with the bourgeois problematic about the historicity of the narratives of Jesus. Yet the way Belo states his case necessarily brings in the historical question. Why would the earlier narrative as Belo reconstructs it ever have generated the later one had not the actual death of Jesus intervened to make this necessary?

11. Rhoads and Michie, *Mark as Story*, 84, 87, 112.

12. Kermode, *The Genesis of Secrecy*, 16.

13. Ibid., 139–41.

14. Ibid., 139–40.

15. Ibid., 114–15, 143.

16. See Dewey, *Markan Public Debate*, 177.

17. Best, *Following Jesus*, 232.

18. Belo, *A Materialist Reading of the Gospel of Mark*, 7, 134, 173.

19. Kermode, *The Genesis of Secrecy*, 142.

20. Kelber, *The Kingdom in Mark*, 142–43 n. 37.

21. See Iser, *The Act of Reading*, 46–48.

22. See Rhoads and Michie, *Mark as Story*, 56.

23. Such an interpretation will not seem strained once it is granted that the

language of a literary text functions primarily poetically. That is, the language refers primarily to itself internally, plays off against itself, and only indirectly refers to phenomena outside the text or to some possible extra-textual intention of the author.

24. After verbs of saying, thinking, and so forth, *hōs* means "how." See Vincent Taylor, *The Gospel According to Saint Mark,* 267.

25. For this approach to 4:26–29, see Belo, *A Materialist Reading of the Gospel of Mark,* 123. Belo argues that Jesus' knowing that he must die in Mark contradicts the not knowing of 4:27, but the cry of forsakenness on the cross accords with it (ibid., 156). But I would say that (the Markan) Jesus' knowing that he must die is not in conflict with his not knowing how the word of his suffering interacts with the hearts of hearers. Nor would his sense of a destiny toward a violent death necessarily be in conflict with a subjective feeling of forsakenness when that event occurred.

26. See Dewey, *Markan Public Debate,* 33, 148. James M. Robinson has sketched the tradition history of Mark 4:1–34 from an oral stage (4:3–8, 10, 13–20) through a pre-Markan written stage (4:3–10, 13–20, 26–32) to the present Markan form, a history governed by a concern about the hermeneutical problem of understanding (4:3, 9, 10–12, 13, 34b). See James M. Robinson, "Gnosticism and the New Testament," 43–45.

27. Dewey, *Markan Public Debate,* 149, 151. See James M. Robinson ("Gnosticism and the New Testament," 46–47, 50) on the view that in this chapter Mark programmatically presents Jesus' whole teaching as enigmatic in nature.

28. See Dewey, *Markan Public Debate,* 150–51; Quesnell, *The Mind of Mark,* 85–86.

29. Dewey, *Markan Public Debate,* 150–51.

30. Kermode, *The Genesis of Secrecy,* 31–32.

31. Meagher, *Clumsy Construction in Mark's Gospel,* 87, 89, 120–22. Étienne Trocmé denies that in this passage or elsewhere Mark develops a theory of the esoteric nature of the Gospel. Mark 4:11–12 refers to the unfruitfulness of Jesus' family and the scribes. The things of Jesus' mission happen to them in parables; that is, they do not understand what is happening. Trocmé seems to think that in 4:11–12 Mark is simply describing the case of the family and the scribes, despite the fact that in 4:12 Jesus specifically speaks of the purpose (*hina*) of the parables as being to prevent understanding. Trocmé's position leads him to the somewhat puzzling conclusion that only in 4:33–34 does Mark speak of the reason for the use of parables: parable is a form of teaching adapted to the spontaneous ability of the *crowd* to understand, but the *disciples* find parables more difficult, and they need special explanations. See Trocmé, "Why Parables? A Study of Mark 4," 461–63, 465.

32. Paul J. Achtemeier, "Mark as Interpreter of the Jesus Traditions," *Interpretation* 32/4 (1978): 345.

33. Also see Jean Starobinski, "The Struggle with Legion: A Literary Analysis of Mark 5:1–20," Eng. trans. D. Via, *New Literary History* 4/2 (1973): 348.

34. As suggested respectively by Best (*Following Jesus,* 69) and Quesnell (*The Mind of Mark,* 264).

35. Krieger, *Theory of Criticism,* 210–12.

36. Ibid., 212.

37. Ibid., 243.

38. Kelber, *The Kingdom in Mark,* 53, 57–58, 62.

39. Kee, *Community of the New Age,* 96, 173.

40. Quesnell, *The Mind of Mark,* 125, 161, 188–89, 219–20, 232, 257.

41. Rhoads and Michie, *Mark as Story,* 90–91.

42. Meagher, *Clumsy Construction in Mark's Gospel,* 77–81.

43. Kermode, *The Genesis of Secrecy,* 28, 47, 143.

44. Ibid., xi, 2, 14, 45, 143.

45. For parallels between them, see Via, *Kerygma and Comedy,* 134.

46. James M. Robinson, *The Problem of History in Mark,* 85.

47. Evidently deconstructionism would opt undialectically for the complete undecidability of meanings. See Herbert N. Schneidau, "The Word Against the Word: Derrida on Textuality," *Semeia* 23 (1982): 15, 19, 23.

APPENDICES

Appendix I

Structuralism and
Phenomenological Hermeneutics

Before taking up the relationship between the two approaches, I wish to comment on some of Daniel Patte's constructs. Here are the narrative functions as he presents them:[1]

> arrival vs. departure
> > departure vs. return
>
> conjunction vs. disjunction
> mandating vs. acceptance (or refusal)
> confrontation
> domination vs. submission
> communication vs. reception
> attribution vs. deprivation

A few comments about this approach to the narrative functions are in order. First, the oppositions among the functions are not all of the same kind. In some cases it is a matter of a logical either/or. The same hero in the same battle cannot both win (domination) and lose (submission). Winning would cancel out losing. But in the case of mandating versus acceptance, it is a matter of both/and with chronological separation, however slight. Mandating does not cancel out acceptance but is the necessary precondition for it. A mandate can be both given and accepted, but it cannot be accepted until it has been given.

According to Patte, when a character refuses a mandate, the sequence aborts and the following steps do not take place.[2] The story thus must come to an end or begin again. We have seen something of this in Mark 10:32–52 where the four subdivisions are (1) mandate (10:32–34); (2) refusal (10:35–42); (3) mandate (10:42–45); (4) acceptance (10:46–52). The first sequence aborts because the mandate is refused, and the following functions are not manifested. But the story does not end, because the mandate is reissued to begin a new sequence. Aborting and beginning again, however, are not the only possibilities. It is possible for a refused mandate to generate a confrontation which interprets the refusal and issues in submission and consequence. That is in fact what happens in the parable of the talents (Matt. 25:14–28).

In Patte's view, movement (disjunction/conjunction) normally occurs after a character has accepted a contract, the movement being the first stage in the realization of the contract.[3] This means that the disjunction/conjunction comes more or less in the middle of the sequence. But Patte also states that a second movement may occur after the completion of a contract, and this introduces a new sequence.[4] This means that the movement is on the boundary between two sequences. But Patte also says that this second movement is the disjunctional statement of another sequence,[5] which would have to mean that it is in the middle of the sequence. Both in the light of natural logic and because functions are defined not only by content but also by their relationship to the whole of a sequence[6] a disjunction/conjunction cannot be both in the middle of a sequence and also on the edge of it. The inconsistency is largely solved by Robert Funk's observation that arrival and departure (or conjunction/disjunction) are sometimes basic functions and at other times only a part of the "narrative scaffolding," a distinction that should be regarded.[7] I judge that the notations of movement in Mark 10:32, 35, 46, for example, are more nearly a part of the scaffolding, while Bartimaeus' leaving his seat and coming to Jesus (10:50) is a functional disjunction/conjunction.

What is the relationship between structuralism and phenomenological hermeneutics? A synthesis between them could be fruitful, but in exactly what fashion can they be joined? Can they be combined in such a way that each has equal force? If it is true that structuralist thinking is not totally dominated by logical and objective thought but itself contains a hermeneutical core,[8] we must still assess this fact. What are the defining features of the two approaches, beginning with structuralism?

Frederick Jameson[9] argues that the very distinction between causes external to a phenomenon and intrinsic causes represents a definition of the idea of system itself: a system has only intrinsic causes. Applied to a narrative text, this would mean that its meaning is its relationship to the formal structures of narrative in the abstract and not its relationship to patterns in the situation of the interpreter. Interpretation in this mode has been guided by the presupposition that if language is about anything, it is about itself.[10] Jonathan Culler[11] states that a structuralist poetics, rather then discovering or assigning meanings, strives to define the conditions of meaning. Culler[12] then represents Roland Barthes as maintaining that the task of structuralist poetics is to make explicit the underlying system which makes literary effects, actual narratives for example, possible. Its object will not be the full meanings of particular works but the empty meanings which support the variety of full meanings. For Tzvetan Todorov, the goal of structural analysis is not to describe concrete works but to understand the abstract structures of which the work is one possible manifestation. It wants to construct a theory of the spectrum of literary possibilities. Structural analysis deals with real works, not to portray their specific meanings but to display them as particular instances or realizations of the underlying, abstract structure and to show what they have in common with other works.[13] Patte, in his translator's preface to Jean Calloud's *Structural Analysis of Narrative,* observes that structure as a relational network is semantically empty and is manifested only when invested in variable semantic features. The analyst must *reduce* (my italics) the variables in order to uncover the structure.[14] Calloud[15] then states that analysis begins with the text and ends when the system or immanent structure is brought to light. There is a passage from the concrete text to abstract units which can be elements of a system. At the level of abstract structure everything is rigorously logical. These few illustrations, reveal, in my judgment, what is essentially structuralist in structuralism. It is defined by the analytical movement away from the text toward those abstractions from the concrete text which are the deep structures of structuralism.

In hermeneutics, on the other hand, the thrust is from the text toward the reader-interpreter understanding himself or herself in the world through the interaction of the text and his or her own horizon. Is it not true, then, that structuralism and hermeneutics move from the text in opposite directions? And this dual movement is not a dialectic within hermeneutics itself such that the meanings uncovered by structural analysis can then be used to relate the interpreter meaningfully to the world. It is not such a dialectic, because the meanings discovered by structuralism are empty, abstract patterns. Having expressed the antithesis between the two approaches in such a stark and unqualified way, let me now disclose more fully my understanding of phenomenological hermeneutics.

I suggest that for phenomenological hermeneutics there is one reflective question: What is the nature of understanding? How does it occur?[16] Since understanding is always understanding of something, in our case texts, the question becomes: how are texts understood? Many different answers can be given. A text is understood by grasping its language in context and defining the author's individuality; comprehending its unknown pattern through one that is known; viewing it in relation to its historical context and antecedents; analyzing its own informed content; bracketing out all everyday presuppositions and describing it as experienced; looking through its surface to the abstract underlying structure; asking what psychological phenomena are manifested; probing its understanding of existence; and so forth. Some of these are more formal than others, and many of them are not mutually exclusive. Each of the answers can be elaborated theoretically at length, and each of them gives rise to a correlative method of interpretation: historical, literary, structuralist, existential, and so forth. Thus there is one reflective hermeneutical question and a multiplicity of hermeneutical methods.[17]

Yet there is one element at the reflective level of phenomenological hermeneutics which, if true, affects all the methods, and that is the idea of the hermeneutical circle. When everyday presuppositions are bracketed out in order to describe the text as experienced, some presupposition(s) is also bracketed in, through, and in terms of which we see the text. This is not a negative factor, because we can understand our tradition and its texts *only* when they are seen in the light of our questions and language. To perceive is to understand something *as* something.[18] Certain aspects of the hermeneutical circle are tacitly acknowledged even if the concept is neglected as such. Historical criticism recognizes the circular relationship between text and context, and literary criticism, that between the whole and parts of the text. Perhaps it is existential interpretation that has most self-consciously acknowledged the circular relationship between text and interpreter. What is the text's understanding of existence as a possibility for me? How does my prior understanding enter into what I see? I would submit that the circular connection between text and interpreter affects all methods, because it is impossible to understand something new and other except *as* something that I already understand. But the circle is not vicious, because pre-understanding is always subject to correction and reversal from the new.[19]

Phenomenological hermeneutics is an effort to describe *how* the *understanding* of texts *occurs*. And it is an effort to describe the *text itself* in the light of the methods of interpretation that emerge from the various possible answers to the reflective question (What is the nature of understanding?). It recognizes the play of the hermeneutical circle (pre-understanding) in elaborating the various answers to the reflective question and in the employment of the methods that emerge from these reflective answers. It is description which is critically self-conscious about the hermeneutical circle. Thus it wants to clarify what presuppositions are at work, and it knows that no interpretation is final. Phenomenological hermeneutics seeks to describe and understand the text in its ever-widening contexts; therefore it sees the interpreter and his or her world as involved in interpretation, and it grasps the need for a multiplicity of methods. It is the phenomenon of interpretation itself which requires this expansive statement of what it is. I have defined phenomenological hermeneutics in formal terms and have made it virtually identical with hermeneutics as such. It is the formality which makes possible a plurality of legitimate methods. The formal or phenomenological element in hermeneutics is simply description within the hermeneutical circle. The material element, which governs the kind of subject matter that can be grasped by means of the questions asked, is the methods that emerge from the various answers to the question about how understanding occurs: historical criticism, literary criticism, existential interpretation, structural analysis, and so forth. It turns out, then, that the method that defines the subject matter to be seen is both answer and question. Take the historical method as an example. It is an *answer* to the question about how a text is to be understood, by examining it in the light of its context and antecedents. It is a *question* to put to the text: what does it tell me about the events and issues of the time in which it was written or the time to which it refers?

The interrelationships among text, interpreter, and world can be further illuminated by reference to Paul Ricoeur and Wolfgang Iser. For Ricoeur, discourse has sense—immanent, repeatable meaning—which is grounded in the synthetic relationship between identification (subject) and predication in the sentence. But discourse also has reference because people speak and write in the first place because they have experience they want to bring to language.[20] The world that is referred to in spoken discourse is the situation common to speaker and hearer. This here and now of ostensive reference is lost in written discourse and becomes more and more remote as time passes, but that does not mean the end of reference. Rather, the world referred to is a "pro-ject" for the reader, a possible way of being in the world.[21] For religious language, or at least for the parables of Jesus, the projected world is the limit-experiences of life. The task of hermeneutics is to clarify mutually the limit-expressions of religious language and the limit-experiences of life.[22] Mark has its share of both.

According to Iser, proper interpretation is an interaction between subject (reader) and object (text) which overcomes the division between them and thereby constitutes the reader by bringing about a change in

him or her.[23] Meaning is not just within the text but in the interaction
between text, reader, and context. The reader constitutes the meaning
out of his or her subjectivity, but is guided by the verbal structure of the
text, which sets up the dialectic between text and reader.[24] The operation
of the hermeneutical circle is clear.

It should be pointed out that the subjective element in the reader's
construction is his or her experience, decisions, and attitudes in a social
and cultural context.[25] Thus the subject's contribution involves his or her
relationship to the world; interpretation brings text, self, and world together. Fiction, in Iser's view, tells us something about reality, although
a reality that is defamiliarized and changing.[26]

What is it about the nature of the text that enables it to set up the
dialectic with the reader, that enables it to affect the reader and change
the reader's existence, that makes it what some theologians have called
language event? (1) Response is elicited from the reader to deal with the
fact that the text both reveals and conceals.[27] (2) What is revealed is a
multiplicity of perspectives and layers of meaning which creates indeterminacy. The reader constitutes the meaning by bringing about a convergence of the perspectives, a convergence that was not articulated in the
text itself.[28] (3) The unfamiliarity in the text calls on the reader to make
it familiar. In order to do this, the reader must bring to light a layer of
his or her own personality which could not previously be made conscious.
The old and the new are merged.[29]

We have seen that structuralism relates the text to an underlying
system of abstractions, while hermeneutics relates it to the reader-interpreter in his life-world. How can these opposite movements of interpretation be related? One may point out, of course, that structuralism is never,
or not usually, so narrowly practiced as I have suggested above (pp.
200–201); there are other elements in it. But to the extent that this is
true, are those other elements really structuralist? Do they not reflect
some other point of view? There may be non-structuralist elements in
structuralism, especially as practiced, but this still leaves open the question how the structuralist and non-structuralist elements are related to
each other. Both may be present in a given scholar, but they may nevertheless be logically incompatible or their relationship may not really be
defined.

The work of Daniel Patte (and Aline Patte) is an instructive example.
Clearly for this scholar a full interpretation does not involve just the
search for deep structures but also traditional exegesis, a concern for the
specific meaning of a given text, and the matter of the text's relationship

to the contemporary experience of the interpreter.[30] But how are these elements related, especially the structuralist thrust and the concern about the contemporary experience of the interpreter? Patte can more or less balance them, because he separates exegesis, which he regards as "rigorous" (at least in structural exegesis), from hermeneutic, as two distinct stages of interpretation.[31] Exegesis, with the emphasis on structural exegesis, gets most of the attention in practice, but in principle it is balanced by the issue of contemporary hermeneutical appropriation. Yet because the two parts of interpretation are separated, their opposite tendencies do not come into clear view. Also the conflict is moderated somewhat by not taking the natural abstracting tendency of structuralism as far as it could be taken. Because structural exegesis and hermeneutical appropriation are kept relatively separate it does not have to be decided which is to dominate.

I would argue, however, that because of the operation of the hermeneutical circle they cannot be discretely separated. My present subjective stance, what I take to be significant, inevitably affects what I see *in* the text. I do not first interpret the text and then decide what its significance is. Exegesis and hermeneutical appropriation interpenetrate each other; therefore structural exegesis and hermeneutics meet head on; the quest for an underlying abstract system and the pursuit of the text's relationship to the phenomenal world collide. And it does have to be decided which will govern interpretation.

If it is claimed that structural exegesis and contemporary hermeneutical appropriation are separable, then the hermeneutical circle is denied, and in principle structuralism is brought into conflict with phenomenological hermeneutics. But in actual practice the hermeneutical circle is at work in structural interpretation. Something to be known is seen *as* something already known. A judgment about significance is made. If I grasp Jesus' prediction of the suffering, death, and resurrection of the Son of man in Mark 10:33–34 as a *mandate* (recall the test sequence in chapter 3, excursus) to the disciples to suffer, then I have assimilated a stretch of text that I want to understand to a system of meaning that I already have in my mind. Thus structural analysis is *formally* congruous with phenomenological hermeneutics. It is at the material level that it comes into conflict with it, that is, with phenomenological hermeneutics in the *existential* mode. Interpretation cannot be equally guided by the question, what logical, abstract system is being manifested in this text? and by the question, what way of being in the world does this text project for me? The phenomenology of both Ricoeur and Iser has an existential orientation and so does my own. My material question is: what is the text's understanding of existence in a social and cultural world? But that cannot be answered apart from careful attention to literary form, historical context, and other contextual horizons. When I have said that structural analysis is in conflict with hermeneutics or phenomenological hermeneutics, I have meant phenomenological-existential hermeneutics, and that is what I mean by hermeneutics in what follows.

In view of the fundamental conflict between structuralism and hermeneutics one needs to be subordinated to the other. I value hermeneutics more highly than structuralism and thus would favor making the latter bend. One could, for example, use deep structures (functional patterns, actantial relations) simply as a means for organizing the surface phenomena which are to be treated hermeneutically. What structuralism per se discovers (abstract patterns) may not be directly useful to hermeneutics, but these patterns can be used by aesthetic literary criticism to organize concrete surface elements which in turn can be used by hermeneutics. It is in this way that I have tried to use structuralist categories in this book. So employed, structuralist narrative units and relationships may be more heuristic than generative of meanings which could not have been gained from the use of other methods. However, a structuralist approach used with circumspection does require the interpreter to be explicitly aware of narrative as narrative. And the difference between such an approach and one that is hardly literary-critical at all may represent a difference in degree so decisive as to be almost a difference in kind.

In at least one other way, structuralist abstraction may be hermeneutically significant. By showing that biblical narratives manifest the same deep structures that other narratives use the hermeneutical gap is partially bridged. The universality of biblical thinking is pointed up, the participation of biblical revelation in general revelation. Attention to surface structure will reveal possible differences between the biblical and other views of reality. Differences may also be indicated not just by *how* deep structures are manifested but by *whether* particular ones are manifested at all.

NOTES

1. Patte, *What is Structural Exegesis?* 41.
2. Ibid., 39, 42.

3. Ibid., 45.

4. Ibid.

5. Ibid.

6. See Alan Dundes, "From Etic to Emic Units in the Structural Study of Folktales," *Journal of American Folklore* 75 (1962): 101-4.

7. Robert W. Funk, "The Form of the New Testament Healing Miracle Story," *Semeia* 12 (1978): 70.

8. As suggested by Edgar V. McKnight, *Meaning in Texts: The Historical Shaping of a Narrative Hermeneutics* (Philadelphia: Fortress Press, 1978), 267.

9. Frederick Jameson, *The Prison-House of Language* (Princeton: Princeton Univ. Press, 1974), 8.

10. See Gerald Graff, *Literature Against Itself* (Chicago: Univ. of Chicago Press, 1979), 79.

11. Jonathan Culler, *Structuralist Poetics: Structuralism, Linguistics, and the Study of Literature* (Ithaca, N.Y.: Cornell Univ. Press, 1975), viii.

12. Ibid., 118-19.

13. Tzvetan Todorov, "Structural Analysis of Narrative," *Novel* 3/1 (1969): 70-71.

14. Calloud, *Structural Analysis of Narrative,* xii.

15. Ibid., 3.

16. See Gadamer, *Truth and Method,* xviii, xix, xxiv, 263, 465; F. D. E. Schleiermacher, *Hermeneutics: The Hand-Written Manuscripts,* ed. H. Kimmerle, Eng. trans. J. Duke and J. Forstman (Missoula, Mont.: Scholars Press, 1977), 41, 96.

17. This way of putting it obviates the problem raised by Robert Detweiler, "After the New Criticism: Contemporary Methods of Literary Interpretation," in *Orientation by Disorientation,* ed. R. Spencer (Pittsburgh: Pickwick Press, 1980), 16. Detweiler speaks of hermeneutics as a method of interpretation and expresses some puzzlement that it is so rarely seen in operation among secular literary critics, though it functions as a theory of understanding. I would argue that the reason for this is that hermeneutics *is* reflection about understanding, but there is no such thing as *the hermeneutical* method alongside other methods of interpretation. I would judge that what Detweiler cites as examples of the hermeneutical method are really instances of phenomenological hermeneutics with an existential and/or literary twist.

18. See Gadamer, *Truth and Method,* 80-81, 358, 429-30. For Heidegger, interpretation works out the possibilities projected by understanding, and that which is understood in interpretation has the structure of something *as* something. The "as" constitutes the interpretation, and such interpretation is always founded upon fore-having and fore-conception. It is never presuppositionless. See Heidegger's *Being and Time,* 188-92. "Seeing as" is similarly a theme in Wittgenstein's philosophy. One sees x as y by placing x in a particular system, frame of reference, setting in life or context. See Thiselton, *The Two Horizons,* 417-20.

19. Hans Frei is suspicious that interpretation guided by preunderstanding will undermine the history-likeness of biblical narrative. See Frei, *The Eclipse of Biblical Narrative* (New Haven and London: Yale Univ. Press, 1974), 322-23. But if the circle is operating properly, the interpreter's preunderstanding will be modified so as to see that existence can be understood only as a history-like narrative or so as to see at least the possibility of such.

20. Ricoeur, *Interpretation Theory,* 9–12, 20–22.
21. Ibid., 34–37.
22. Ricoeur, "Biblical Hermeneutics," 34.
23. Iser, *The Act of Reading,* 9–10, 150, 152.
24. Ibid., 14–15, 17, 19–21, 25, 30, 38, 135, 141.
25. Ibid., 19, 93.
26. Ibid., 53, 65–68, 70, 112.
27. Ibid., xi, 22, 45, 169.
28. Ibid., 35, 36, 38, 47–49.
29. Ibid., 43, 50, 132, 152, 155, 157.
30. Daniel Patte and Aline Patte, *Structural Exegesis,* 9–10, 92, 97–111.
31. Ibid., viii, 1, 94, 111–12; Daniel Patte, *What is Structural Exegesis?* 3–4.

Appendix II

The Problem of the
Truth Value of Plotted Time

The Ordering of Chronological Time
as the Ground for Ethics

We have seen that in Mark time passes; there is movement, and different things happen before and after each other. Mark certainly has no interest in presenting a connected chronological account, but notations of chronology are not absent. After a busy day in Capernaum, Jesus is said to have gone out "in the morning" to pray (1:35). The transfiguration is dated six days (9:2) after the Caesarea Philippi teaching, and in 11:12 Jesus came into Bethany "on the following day." Mark 14:1 presents a precise chronological note—two days before—and also refers to one of the basic time-structuring institutions of the Jewish year, the Passover. In Mark 15:1—16:8 there are five subsections, each of which contains a time notice[1] —morning, the third hour, the sixth hour, evening, the passing of the Sabbath. The use of the adverb "immediately" some forty times gives great urgency to the passing of time.

But the time of the Gospel is not just chronological, for it is ordered and shaped by the threefold plot. There are repetitions, correspondences, and interpenetrations. Things hold together because expectations are generated and fulfilled. These formal patterns give the times content and meaning because meaning resides in relationships. So time does not just pass but is divided into segments that have meaningful relationships to each other. Time is structured.

The middle of Mark's plot, as we have seen, is defined by the interweaving of redemptive and oppositional processes. This interweaving gives the time its content, and the processes are what they are because of their relationships to the beginning and the ending of the plot, and the beginning and the end of the world. Mark's ethic—the nature of the ethical norms or requirements, the motives, the nature of ethical enablement, the possibility of fulfilling the norms—rests on the content of time in the middle as defined by the structure and patterns of the plot, by the surface structure of the story. The very telling of the story and what is grounded upon it assume that the narrative relationships—the surface structure—and the meanings resting upon them are valid and are not a falsification of the temporality of the real world. Since the meaning of Mark's ethic rests on the meaning of the surface structure of the narrative, if the validity of surface structure as such—time formed into a meaningful pattern—could be overthrown, then Mark's ethic would be seriously compromised. Mark's ethic is intended for a real world, the world structured by his story. If plot structure as such were shown in principle to be a falsification of the real world, then the ethic would have no place. Since the truth value of surface structure has in fact been radically questioned in recent times, I need to construct an argument in support of it. In doing so, I will look at several positions that have attacked it. By necessity I must be brief and selective. But I trust that I will not have misrepresented the main thrust of each of the positions as it pertains to my concerns.

The Structuralist Attack
on the Order

I begin with structuralism and take Roland Barthes as my representative. For Barthes, structural activity is to decompose the real and recompose it so as to disclose its general intelligibility. With regard to narrative texts this means decomposing the chronology in order to show that it is secondary to logic. The task of analysis is to let the chronological succession be resolved in a nontemporal structural matrix, to "dechronologize" the narrative continuity and "relogify" it, to give a structural description of the chronological illusion.[2] This means that chronological order is discounted as inferior to logic, inferior to the deep structure of logical abstractions which underlies the narrative. The suggestion is that the chronological itself cannot really be meaningful.

The Deconstructionist Attack

The basic difference between structuralism and deconstructionism may be marked by Barthes's account of his change from one to the other. In a conversation published in 1971[3] Barthes stated that between 1966 and 1970 he changed from a position that regarded each text as the manifestation of a transcendent structure to a view that denied this structure and saw each text as its own model and insisted that each be treated in its "difference" (in the sense of Jacques Derrida) from all others.[4] According to G. C. Spivak, the translator of Derrida's *Of Grammatology,* Derrida's own fundamental criticism of structuralism is that the latter postulates a general law,[5] the transcendent deep structure of which individual texts are manifestations. Once the deep structure is abandoned, each text becomes one of a myriad of entrances into the totality of writing, with each entrance being a perspective whose vanishing point is indeterminate.[6]

In an early essay, Derrida announced a program of de-centering, the impact of which we must grasp by trying to understand what he means by center. Center is any orienting, governing principle which organizes structure and limits the free play of meaning. It is a fixed origin, which, while it is in part involved in the structure of reality, is primarily above the play of differences in that structure.[7] For Derrida, center is presence, which seems to be the state of something being fully present to itself.[8] The clue to presence appears to be the linguistic distinction between signifier (vehicle of meaning) and signified (mental construct), and the ultimate mode of presence is God. God is a transcendent signified irreducibly separate from a signifier and from the play of differences, not fallen into the sensible world—the face of pure intelligibility immediately united to, present to, an absolute logos (rationality). Such an infinite, creative subjectivity is God.[9] Center or presence also appears in less ultimate modes. It manifests itself as being, substance/essence/existence, temporal presence as the point of the now, the presence of the self to itself in the *cogito ergo sum,* intersubjectivity, subject, human-being, truth, beginning, end, the presence of the thing to sight as *eidos* (form, outward appearance), and *morphē* (form, outward appearance, shape).[10] Center, then, is a fixed, unchanging origin; a governing principle; that which gives order and coherence to anything, form or *morphe.*

De-centering apparently is both a cultural event and a subjective response to that event. A rupture has *occurred* in our world which has made it necessary *to think* that there was no center. This rupture is language's invasion of our universal realm of problems. Everything has become discourse, a system of differences in which there is no transcendental signified outside the differences. The signified is already a signifier and is originally and essentially a trace. It is never present in itself, referring only to itself. There is no presence before or outside of difference.[11]

This brings us to Derrida's concept of difference, perhaps his master concept.[12] We could say that de-centering is the recognition of difference. Derrida begins with Saussure's view of difference and notes that the verb to differ (*différer*) has two meanings, which he combines by means of the new spelling *differance.* To differ is to be distinct or other, but it also suggests delay, interposing, deferring.[13] A word signifies by means of its differences (distinctions) from other words. Thus its meaning, being dependent on its relationships to an indeterminate number of other words, is deferred until those relationships can be grasped.

Since the meaning of an element is always deferred beyond it, the element is a trace, another and closely related concept of Derrida. People or objects are as much traces as are linguistic elements. A trace might ordinarily be thought of as a mark or vestige left by the presence or existence of something else. A textual element is a trace of the organizing form or center of a narrative and has its final meaning in relation to that form. A person is a trace of God, "in the image of God," and has his or her ultimate meaning in relation to God. But for Derrida there is no origin or center of which the trace is a mark. To think that there is such would be an illusion. The trace has no origin; rather, the presumed origin (center, presence, form) is an epiphenomenon upon the trace. There are only traces and no origins. Alleged origins are simply traces of traces.[14]

What are the implications of Derrida's position for the relationship between narrative and the temporality of the world? First, let me say a word about its hermeneutical consequences. De-centering has extended the domain of the free play of signification infinitely, for there is no origin or structure to which interpretation must be related.[15] At least two tendencies in deconstructive interpretation, not mutually exclusive, may emerge from this position. The American development takes a small stretch of text and separates it from its immediate context and extends its meaning by relating it to an indeterminate number of external contexts. According to J. Hillis Miller, the proper context for interpreting a bit of language is the ever-widening one which includes all the Indo-European languages with their literatures, concepts, and social institutions. In such an extended milieu apparently univocal language becomes richly equivocal.[16] A second tendency consists of what Derrida calls the moments of reversal, or inversion and reinscription. Reversal turns upside down the hierarchy of meanings in the text; it subordinates what was prominent, and vice versa. Reinscription leads to an irruptive new concept which could never have been included or understood in the previous regime.[17] We see Derrida practicing this kind of deconstruction in an interpretation of the New Testament Apocalypse. He takes the imperative in the Book of Revelation to *come* and see the visions of the end and be nourished by them (Rev. 4:1; 6:1; 17:1; 21:9; 22:17–20), a relatively subdominant theme, and makes it dominant, but with a reversal of meaning. It is now a summons to *come* away from apocalyptic, to renounce it and recognize the futility of its expectations. Thus apocalyptic undermines itself; it contains its own outside.[18]

What does deconstruction or de-centering entail with regard to the relationship of plot to the real world? If *morphē* or form is to be rejected[19] as a center holding things together and governing interpretation, then it is natural that the legitimacy of the epic model or linear time is also undermined.[20] The beginning, middle, or end of a given plot is no more inherently related to the other parts of that plot than to various other elements in the totality of writing. Texts are systems of traces,[21] and the elements of lived experience in time *and* of narrative order are traces. The implication of Derrida's position is that a clear and correct view of things would say that both world and text lack form or organizing center; therefore text and world correspond. In this radical way, then, Derrida's position is mimetic. But for him it would be a mistake for either author or critic to think that a narrative has coherent order and a double mistake to think that there is narrative order which reflects the order of the world. Although I would argue that the larger implication of Derrida's position is this mimeticism in which de-centered text corresponds to de-centered world,[22] nevertheless his own self-conscious standpoint is that a text does not relate to a nonlinguistic world. It is a transgression of the text if a reader turns it toward a referent (metaphysical, historical, etc.) or signified whose content could take place outside of language. There has never been anything but writing.[23]

I agree that in some sense we do not have cosmos or reality apart from language. But rather than saying that language does not refer to a nonlinguistic world I argue that reality is a confluence in which nonlinguistic "stuff" is shaped and made intelligible by language. And despite the extremity of his terminology at points, that may also be Derrida's position. "Flesh and bone" comes into our existence only as interpreted by language.[24]

Against this dissipation of the surface structure which we have been considering, it may be affirmed that surface structure does have integrity, by which I mean that it is neither merely epiphenomenal upon the deep structure (as structuralism says) nor unreal (as deconstructionism says). Against structuralism the point is that the *surface structure* has order and against deconstructionism, it *does have* order—center as form.

The Attack of Radical Existentialism

Murray Krieger has affirmed that the surface of a literary work is a tight, compelling, finally closed context, a unifying enclosure of internal relations. These relations are composed of such figures and elements as ambiguity, irony, paradox, plot, metaphor, and character. Nothing in the work comes casually or at random, but rather every element serves the purpose of the whole, as everything is locked into everything else. Krieger's tacit argument for the integrity of this unifying formal structure is that it is necessary to account for aesthetic experience,[25] the experience of intransitive or enraptured attention. Apart from the internal cohesion of the surface, which is not reducible to something else, the attention of the beholder would be referred beyond the work to another object.

But one may affirm the integrity of the surface structure and still rejoin that this very order is purely a fiction, a falsification of the randomness and disorder of the real world in which we actually live. This is in fact Krieger's position,[26] a position that might be called radical existentialism and that has been developed with particular penetration by Frank Kermode.

According to Kermode, time as such, the time of reality, is inhuman, disorganized, simply chronological, merely successive, coarse, and chaotic. We compose stories because we cannot face time as it is. We want to make our lives more tolerable and not be caught in the indeterminate interval between the tick of birth and the tock of death.[27] We agree that the clock says tick-tock, two different sounds, because we want a beginning that is different from an ending. Tick and tock represent the beginning and ending of a plot. "Tick is a humble genesis, tock a feeble apocalypse." Perception of the present, memory of the past, and expectation of the future are bundled together in a common organization in which everything is in concord with everything else. The interval in the middle is purged of mere chronicity and becomes *kairos,* a time of significance. But this giving of order to what is essentially disordered is an imposition, a falsification of reality, which expresses what we wish rather than what really is.[28]

Thus, for Kermode, we tell stories because we wish to escape an intolerable reality. But apparently we also impose order because it is inevitable. At least it is inevitable when the novel form is used. A novelist, like Jean Paul Sartre, may believe philosophically that time is a discontinuous, unorganized middle, a series of disparate *kairoi* without causal relationships. But the very form of a novel makes it impossible to represent such a view, for as soon as it begins to speak, it imposes causality, concord, development, and so forth. Thus not only does the novel lie in relation to reality, but it may also lie in relation to the philosophy of time held by the novelist.[29] Kermode has suggested that giving form or order to life is inevitable for the novel. But is it inevitable absolutely?

In his more recent work, *The Genesis of Secrecy,* Kermode still holds to the fortuity and incoherence of the time of the world.[30] But he also stresses the inevitable presence of elusive mystery, the concealed, the obscure, in all *narratives.*[31] Rather than maintaining, as he did in *The Sense of an Ending,* the impossibility of a narrative without order, he now seems to hold that fortuities and disconnections do in fact fracture the surface of a narrative and that these reflect the fortuities of life itself.[32] But he also notes that we resist resigning ourselves to the ultimately insoluble and suggests that in the modern era the quest for an orienting center is inescapable,[33] even if having one entails falsifying the world. Does Kermode assimilate Mystery to the merely fortuitous or see fortuity as a sign of a genuine depth of mystery? I suspect that it is the latter.[34] He may not answer the question.

In a recent essay by Kermode the tension between the positions in the two books seems to have been modulated into a synthesis. Narrative as such has two processes. The first gives order and clarity by interweaving sequence, causality, thought, and character. The second process generates distortions which cover secrecy and elicit interpretation. Narrative tends to foreground the former and to background the latter.[35] There is no indication of Kermode's having abandoned the view that the orderly process falsifies the temporality of the real world.

However reactionary it might seem, I should like to consider the thought of Nicolas Berdyaev. He is pertinent for my purposes because he self-consciously addresses the problem of eschatology—beginning and end—from an existential standpoint and arrives at conclusions very different from mine. He is therefore an illuminating dialogue partner. Moreover, Berdyaev in a forceful way states the philosophical-theological position which is being presupposed, more or less, by more recent tendencies to discount the chronological element in the New Testament understanding of eschatological salvation.[36]

For Berdyaev,[37] as for Kermode, the time of the world is an endless middle without beginning or end. But there is a difference between the two which would probably point to still other differences of a theological sort. Apparently Kermode regards successive, unstructured time as *simply* the way things are, while Berdyaev sees this condition as a sign of the *fallenness* of reality.[38] In Kermode's view, the telling of stories with ordered beginnings, middles, and endings is a kind of finite or penultimate salvation, but for Berdyaev it would not be helpful at all to offer a vision of structured time as a solace, because he views temporality as such—the separation of time into past, present, and future—as indicative of fallenness.[39]

For Berdyaev, God is the noumenal, Spirit, the eternal. He is the *Urgrund* who is freedom and creative act; he is supra-being or the potentiality of meonic (from the Greek *mē* [subjunctive negation] plus *ōn*, the present participle of the verb "to be") non-being; he is the first and the last.[40] There are certain moments when God or the noumenal breaks through into historical time.[41] These moments can be projected backward and imagined as a golden age, or they can be projected forward as the eschaton. Since both ultimate terminals are projections of the same reality, they would seem to be identical, a conclusion which Berdyaev specifically draws.[42]

The golden age and eschaton are not events that happen. There is no beginning or end of time in time; time therefore is an endless middle.[43] This time, broken into past, present, and future, is fallen, objectified, and alienated from the core of existence.[44] Berdyaev can speak of being in a similar way. It is reality turned into an object by thought. It crushes the individual, for it is congealed or coagulated freedom, a substance like nature, a system locked up in itself.[45]

Beginning and end do not structure the temporal process. Rather, they "symbolize" the transcendent world. We have seen that for Berdyaev the transcendent world breaks into this one at moments. How do those breakthroughs affect the endless middle? The breakthroughs take place in existential time, which is outside the time of this world and is nontemporal. Yet these existential moments intersect historical time or are projected onto it.[46] How, then, does existential time affect the historical? There are points at which Berdyaev seems to say that existential time has a positive effect on historical time.[47] But that runs contrary to the overall logic of his position and to specific things which he says. The existential times belong to the vertical, not to the horizontal.[48] The breakthroughs do not order or shape the history of the world. Their fire cools down, they are borne down by the load of the world, and the world is not transformed. After these moments occur I pass on in my fallen temporality, and the existential moment remains in eternity.[49] The effect of the vertical does not remain in the horizontal. How could the eternal have any temporal extension in Berdyaev's thought, since for him temporality as such is fallen and existential time is nontemporal?[50] Since for Berdyaev existential time is not extended in chronological time, a threefold plot, suggesting past, present, and future, can only represent the fallenness of the world and not offer a new possibility for salvation.

The Claim That the Temporality
of the Real World Has
a Narrative Quality

To the claim that the time of the world is chaotic, disorganized, and merely successive and that an ordered plot is therefore a wishful (and/or misguided) lie, it may be said: no, plot is not a lie, because our experience of the time of the real world has a storylike character. Long ago Augustine spoke of the meaningful coherence of past and future with present experience through memory and anticipation.[51] Stephen Crites[52] has developed this position in an insightful way to affirm the narrative quality of existence itself. Memory at the fundamental level has a sense of succession from past through present to future which the imaginative consciousness re-configures. And many other thinkers have developed variations of the same point of view.[53] But to the affirmation that existence itself has a narrative quality it may be rejoined: you are only *seeing* it that way because you are imposing the stories you have heard on life; pre-understanding is operating uncritically.[54]

Therefore it is imperative to present an *argument* that would show the *necessity* of seeing existence itself as storylike, and I take Alasdair MacIntyre as an example. His position is that we cannot characterize human behavior independently of short- and long-term intentions grasped in their causal and temporal relations. Intentions belong to settings that have a history of change, and we can live as individuals and with others only with a sense of the future, which always presents itself as a telos. All of this involves writing a narrative, for an element in a sequence is intelligible as an action only as "a-possible-element-in-a-sequence," by finding its place in a narrative. Narrative is not first of all something created by artists but something that is lived.[55] MacIntyre's basic point is that life itself has a narrative form prior to writing and telling stories. Otherwise it would be unintelligible, and significant action would be impossible.

To this it may be replied that life in fact is, in MacIntyre's terms, unintelligible. It lacks the configuration of intentions, the sense of interrelated causes and consequences, which MacIntyre attributes to it. This is essentially the position of Hayden White. According to White, real events do not have the coherent form of a story, the order of meaning associated with a well-marked beginning, middle, and end. Real events occur as mere sequence.[56] White thus suggests that the chronicle form is a truer representation of reality than is the historical narrative with its plot and sense of significance. He cites the eighth-century *Annals of Saint*

Gall as a proper model. These annals *are* referential and contain a representation of temporality. But they are not a story as we normally think of it: there is no central subject, beginning-middle-end, peripeteia, narrative voice, or necessary connection between events.[57] If this is the way things (real events) fundamentally are, simply happening one after the other without connection, then a plotted narrative can only be seen to belong to the realm of wish, fantasy, and imagination.[58]

It is widely assumed, by White, Kermode,[59] and Krieger[60] for example, that ordered plot belongs to the sphere of subjective fantasy, while the merely successive and discontinuous defines the real world of objective temporality. I have a question about this assumption: on what ground is the latter position taken to be more objective and less falsifying than the former? If those who take existence itself to have a narrative quality are charged with imposing plotted stories they have heard or read on it, why may not those who see existence as chaotic and discontinuous be charged with imposing on existence a narrative that is annal-like, fractured, and merely successive? Or could the latter position not simply be abstracting the chaotic and discontinuous from the configuration of the narrative quality of existence?

Another and related question that poses itself is: how do Kermode, White, and others escape from the subjectivity of beginning-middle-end in order to identify another kind of temporality which is so qualitatively different? According to Frank Lentricchia, Kermode understands fictions as lenses that we are free to discard because we have made them in the first place.[61] I agree with Kermode that any given fiction, as a perspective on existence, can be discarded. But I would not agree that we can discard all perspectives so as to see objective temporality as it is. One can disengage oneself from one perspective only by taking on another. Each one is a probable opinion. Yet as one perception replaces another, we do not have a succession of hypotheses about an unknowable being but perspectives on the same familiar being.[62]

Thus we can argue that varying and opposing interpretations of the temporal world are still to some degree objective because they are about the same world and arise from the subject's involvement in it. So both the view that the temporality of existence is merely successive and unordered and the view that it has some narrative shape are both subjective *and* objective. The question, then, is: which takes account of the larger number of factors, which is the more comprehensive? A point of view which can grant that life itself can legitimately be experienced both as ordered and as chaotic and that plotted narrative is not necessarily a subjective falsification is more comprehensive than one that sees only the possibility that life is chaos and shaped narrative necessarily a falsification.

In sum, structuralism suggests that the chronological or temporal surface structure is neither as meaningful (intelligible or logical) nor as true (free from illusion) as the logical deep structure. For Derrida and deconstruction the surface structure lacks meaning in the sense in which I am using that term. That is, it lacks a coherent pattern centered in form; it is a set of traces without inherent connection. Whether a narrative surface structure is true is not so easy to say. According to Derrida, if the surface is mistakenly thought to have coherence or meaning, then it is a falsification of reality, for the latter has no center of meaning. But it would appear that if the surface is correctly seen to have no center or meaning, then it is a true representation of reality. In the view of radical existentialist critics like Krieger and Kermode the narrative surface structure has meaning, continuity, and centered coherence. But this meaning is untrue: it falsifies the real world. One way to argue for the truth of the surface structure is to describe how we actually experience time, to compare this with narrative plotting, and to point to the necessity of this narrative shape of existence if intelligible action is to be possible. MacIntyre and others have taken this route. But it can be argued that even these penetrating analyses of our experience of time are skewed by a pre-understanding shaped by stories and that life is really merely fragmentary succession. We need, then, a phenomenology of perception which would show that our perception of life as having a narrative quality is necessary and is as objective, and as subjective, in principle as is the perception that it is composed of discrete, unordered fragments. It is necessary to give a philosophical analysis of how we understand, of what goes on when we describe our experience.

A Phenomenological Argument for the Truth of Plotted Time

I am not trying to remedy the lack of an up-to-date jargon for talking about the referential values of literature cited by Gerald Graff.[63] I also recognize that philosophical arguments generally do not amount to proofs.[64] The claim, however, that the plot or surface structure of narrative corresponds in a flexible, unfixed, and indeterminate way to the temporality of the real world as we experience it—a soft mimeticism—can be supported. This means that ordered narrative does not falsify the real world (*contra* radical existentialism). And if both world and plot are shown to have a center, then the deconstructionist attack fails. And if the configuration and shaping of time in the surface corresponds to our experience of time in the real world, then chronology as a meaningful construct hardly needs to be subordinated to the deep structure (*contra* structuralism).

At first glance it might seem a little embarrassing to appeal to a philosophical position that has been around as long as Maurice Merleau-Ponty's. But on second thought, given the fact that "major" movements in literary theory have lasted from four to ten years during the last couple of decades,[65] making substantial use of a philosophical position with a twenty- or thirty-year history seems positively promising. I will adapt Merleau-Ponty's view of the relationship of subject to object in perception to state a position about the relationship of narrative text to the world. In this context the text is the subject (an implied author's— subject's—vision of reality) and the world is the object. Lentricchia in his chapter on phenomenological literary criticism quotes J. Hillis Miller, who quotes Georges Poulet to the effect that there is a consciousness on this side of and protected from any object, a subjectivity that exists in itself, withdrawn from any power that might determine it from outside.[66] The phenomenology of Merleau-Ponty is quite different from this.

Is the formal element in narrative art which confers coherence and order a falsification of reality, or is it the case that we cannot experience reality at all without some formal principle which is not simply imposed by the subject? I have suggested that we cannot avoid viewing the world from some (subjective) perspective, but I do not want to argue that we see time as storied simply because we cannot escape our subjectivity. Neither do I want to argue that we can talk about an objective world which is independent of our subjective figuration. What we can talk about is the world-as-experienced.

According to Hans-Georg Gadamer, reality may be defined as what is unstructured or untransformed, and art is the raising up of *this* (my italics) into its truth. Whether one interprets the truth of art as its correspondence with reality or as the giving of a new recognition of how things really are, as is the case with Gadamer,[67] there is concord between art and reality. The reality of the world is experienced through art, and it is implied here that reality does not become truth until it is structured by art. The truth of reality encounters us in art as the occurrence of unconcealment.

Merleau-Ponty argues in effect that we cannot experience individual items in isolation from form. To perceive is not to experience a host of impressions which can be clinched by memory. It is to see standing forth from data an immanent significance without which no appeal to memory is possible.[68] The world is perceived as significant, as formed, and both subject and object contribute to that. It is not the case that consciousness constitutes everything, nor is it that empirical reality simply imprints itself on our minds. If consciousness constituted everything, we would already know everything and would not need to pursue knowledge. On the other hand, if empirical reality contributed everything, how would we know where to look and what would enable things to be related?[69] In actuality there is a subject-object dialogue in which the subject draws together the meaning diffused through the object, and the object draws together the subject's intentions.[70] It should be observed that at least in his later reflections Merleau-Ponty intended the position which he developed in *Phenomenology of Perception* to be understood as having an ontological and not just a psychological bearing.[71]

The reason why subject and object are inextricably linked in perception is that it is not the mind which experiences but the body, and the body combines subject and object within itself. It is both touching and touched.[72] Subjective mind and objective world meet in the body and are fused. This is so because the body is made of the same flesh as the world, and thus the body extends into the world. At the same time the mind is the other side of the body, so the body, which extends into the world and brings the world with itself so to speak, cannot be described objectively in itself but only in terms of its other side, the mind, which overflows into it.[73] Or put still another way, inscribed within the visible body is the invisible act of seeing or vision which is meaning.[74]

Subject and object are fused at the most fundamental level of perception. For our purposes this means that narrative as subjective vision and the real world as object are inseparably fused. Both subject and object inevitably leave their imprint on understanding. Understanding does not take place apart from form, some principle of order and significance. And both subject and object are involved in generating form, in giving a literary interpretation of reality. Therefore the plot which informs a narrative is not a subjective falsification of our experience of the time of the real world but is in principle a true but indeterminate representation of that experience which has necessarily incorporated the imprint of the world as well as the subjective figuration of the author, and then of interpreters. Since both interpretation through narrative and interpreted world are joined in the plot structure, both do have center. There is no perception without it. And if plot is in principle a meaningful interpretation of reality, one need not look to the deep structure as the only source of true meaning. I am not denying the relative autonomy of the literary text or its final irreducibility to anything else. Nor am I denying the subjective element—the circular play of pre-understanding—in both narration and interpretation. But I am denying that plot or narrative order as such is merely epiphenomenal, unreal, or falsifying.

The plot of the Markan narrative has integrity in principle. This does not mean that the ethic which rests on its meaning is proved to be necessarily true. But it does mean that it is not necessarily false.

NOTES

1. T. A. Burkill, *Mysterious Revelation: An Examination of the Philosophy of St. Mark's Gospel* (Ithaca, N.Y.: Cornell Univ. Press, 1963), 243–44.

2. Barthes, "Introduction à l'analyse structurale des récits," 12; idem, *Critical Essays,* Eng. trans. R. Howard (Evanston, Ill.: Northwestern Univ. Press, 1972), 213–15. Similarly for Tzvetan Todorov the succession of events in narrative is dependent on a logical order as *parole* (an individual utterance) to *langue* (language system). Changing the order would not much change the meaning. See Todorov, "Les catégories du récit littéraire," *Communications* 8 (1966): 132, 138, 148.

3. See "A Conversation with Roland Barthes," *Signs of the Times* (Cambridge: Granta, 1971), 44, quoted in Jonathan Culler, *Structuralist Poetics,* 242.

4. Frank Lentricchia states that Barthes's account of his change is too dramatic to be historically accurate. See Frank Lentricchia, *After the New Criticism* (Chicago: Univ. of Chicago Press, 1980), 163–64. I think that Barthes nevertheless succinctly indicates the difference between the two.

5. See Derrida, *Of Grammatology,* lvii.

6. See Lentricchia, *After the New Criticism,* 143.

7. Jacques Derrida, "Structure, Sign, and Play in the Discourse of the Human Sciences," in *The Languages of Criticism and the Sciences of Man,* ed. R. Macksey and E. Donato (Baltimore: John Hopkins Univ. Press, 1970), 247–49.

8. Derrida, "Structure, Sign, and Play" 248–49; idem, *Of Grammatology,* 12–13.

9. Derrida, *Of Grammatology,* 7, 10–14, 18, 20, 53, 71; idem, "Structure, Sign, and Play," 249; idem, "Difference," *Speech and Phenomena,* Eng. trans. D. Allison (Evanston, Ill.: Northwestern Univ. Press, 1973), 139–40. If Christian thought observes the distinction between and relationship between mysterious depth and logos (word) in the being of God and also takes into consideration the developing changes in the word of God as Scripture, then it cannot be said that God is irreducibly separate from a signifier and from the play of differences.

10. Derrida, *Of Grammatology,* 12–13; idem, "Structure, Sign, and Play," 248–49; idem, "Form and Meaning: A Note on the Phenomenology of Language," *Speech and Phenomena,* 108.

11. Derrida, "Structure, Sign, and Play," 249; idem, *Of Grammatology,* 7, 73; idem, "Difference," 140–41.

12. See G. Spivak in Preface to Derrida, *Of Grammatology,* xliii.

13. Derrida, "Difference," 129, 139–40; idem, *Of Grammatology,* 53.

14. Derrida, *Of Grammatology,* 61–62, 73.

15. Derrida, "Structure, Sign, and Play," 249, 264.

16. J. Hillis Miller, "The Critic as Host," in *Deconstruction and Criticism,* ed. G. Hartman (New York: Seabury Press, 1979), 223. Lentricchia (*After the New Criticism,* 120–21) accounts for this tendency as a preference for paradigm (a grouping of words based on various kinds of associations) over syntagm (the chain of words as it appears in the text).

17. See John P. Leavey, "Four Protocols: Derrida, His Deconstruction," *Semeia* 23 (1982): 50, 51.

18. Jacques Derrida, "Of an Apocalyptic Tone Recently Adopted in Philosophy," *Semeia* 23 (1982): 91–95. Gerald Graff sees this tendency as an extension of new criticism's emphasis on irony and indeterminacy of meaning. See Graff, *Literature Against Itself,* 145–46.

19. Derrida, "Form and Meaning," 108.

20. Derrida, *Of Grammatology,* 87.

21. Ibid., 65.

22. Alain Robbe-Grillet had a similar point of view though expressed with different vocabulary and concepts. See Alain Robbe-Grillet, *For a New Novel,* Eng. trans. R. Howard (New York: Grove Press, 1965), 19, 21, 32–33, 58, 73, 151–54, 163.

23. Derrida, *Of Grammatology,* 158–59. Graff (*Literature Against Itself,* 21) sees this tendency as an extension of literary autonomy from the single text (new criticism) to the whole of writing.

24. Derrida, *Of Grammatology,* 158–59. For examples of biblical scholars who take a deconstructionist approach, see Crossan, *Raid on the Articulate,* 27, 34, 39–40, 42, 44, 91–93, 114; Peter D. Miscall, *Workings of Old Testament Narrative* (Philadelphia: Fortress Press; Chico, Calif.: Scholars Press, 1982), 1–2, 4, 102, 141–44.

25. Krieger, *Theory of Criticism,* 17, 18, 32–33, 100.

26. Ibid., 61, 103, 195, 243.

27. Kermode, *The Sense of an Ending,* 4, 44–46, 57–58, 145, 160.

28. Ibid., 4–5, 43–46, 173.

29. Ibid., 137–40.

30. Kermode, *The Genesis of Secrecy,* 54, 64.

31. Ibid., xi, 14, 25, 45, 47, 125.

32. Ibid., 54, 64.

33. Ibid., 53–54, 64, 71–73.

34. Ibid., 143–44.

35. Frank Kermode, "Secrets and Narrative Sequence," *On Narrative,* ed. W. J. Mitchell (Chicago and London: Univ. of Chicago Press, 1981), 79–84.

36. For examples of this tendency, see Philipp Vielhauer, "Apocalyptic in Early Christianity: Introduction," *New Testament Apocrypha,* ed. E. Hennecke and W. Schneemelcher, Eng. trans. ed. R. McL. Wilson (Philadelphia: Westminster Press, 1964), 2:608–9; Robert W. Funk, "Apocalyptic as an Historical and Theological Problem in Current New Testament Scholarship," *Journal for Theol-*

ogy and the Church 6: *Apocalypticism,* ed. R. Funk, Eng. trans. J. Leitch (New York: Herder & Herder, 1969), 182–83; Thomas J. J. Altizer, *Total Presence* (New York: Seabury Press, 1980), 3, 10, 52; Scott, *Jesus, Symbol-Maker for the Kingdom,* 87–88, 137–38.

37. Berdyaev, *The Beginning and the End,* 207.

38. Ibid., 163, 240, 241.

39. Ibid., 163.

40. Ibid., 100, 103–4, 105–7.

41. Ibid., 113, 155–56, 161–63, 166–68, 207, 209, 222.

42. Ibid., 112, 207, 232, 239.

43. Ibid., 207, 231–32.

44. Ibid., 103, 169, 183, 203, 207, 209, 240–41.

45. Ibid., 93, 98, 99, 111, 114, 143.

46. Ibid., 163, 181, 207.

47. Ibid., 207, 229–30.

48. Ibid., 163.

49. Ibid., 155, 184, 209–10.

50. Ibid., 181, 207.

51. Augustine, *Confessions* XI.28.

52. Stephen Crites, "The Narrative Quality of Experience," *Journal of the American Academy of Religion* 39/3 (1971): 298–301.

53. See, for example, Frei, *The Eclipse of Biblical Narrative,* 13–14; Eleanor N. Hutchens, "The Novel as Chronomorph," *Novel* 5/3 (1972): 219, 223–24; Roy Pascal, "Narrative Fictions and Reality," *Novel* 11/1 (1977); 46–49.

54. See Kermode, "Secrets and Narrative Sequence," 83.

55. MacIntyre, *After Virtue,* 192–201. I briefly point to two other similar arguments. Ricoeur shows that the configurational element in plot makes time meaningful; therefore it is not necessary to look to the deep structure to find meaningful order. Moreover, he does a philosophical analysis of time in the Heideggerian mode and demonstrates that narrative form does not falsify this analysis but rather confirms and corrects it. See Paul Ricoeur, "Narrative Time," *On Narrative,* ed. Mitchell, 165, 166, 172, 174–76, 180, 184. Hans Meyerhoff argues that the three unities—time, the self, narrative—are all functions of significant associations. The constitution of the self with temporal continuity through artistic creation seems to be an intensification of the ordinary organizing and synthesizing powers of the self. See Hans Meyerhoff, *Time in Literature* (Berkeley and Los Angeles: Univ. of California Press, 1968), 33, 40, 43–44, 48.

56. Hayden White, "The Value of Narrativity in the Representation of Reality," *On Narrative,* ed. Mitchell, 2, 4, 5, 13–14, 23.

57. Ibid., 7, 20, 23.

58. Ibid., 4, 23.

59. Kermode, *The Sense of an Ending,* 4-5, 43–46, 57–58, 145, 160, 173.

60. Krieger, *Theory of Criticism,* 61, 195, 243.

61. Lentricchia, *After the New Criticism,* 36–37.

62. Merleau-Ponty, *The Visible and the Invisible,* 41.

63. Graff, *Literature Against Itself,* 13.

64. MacIntyre, *After Virtue,* 241.

65. See Lentricchia, *New Criticism,* 29, 30, 65.

66. Ibid., 65–66.

67. Gadamer, *Truth and Method,* 101–2. Also for truth as unconcealing, see Martin Heidegger, "On the Essence of Truth," in *Existence and Being* (London: Vision Press, 1956), 333–34; "Plato's Doctrine of Truth," Eng. trans. J. Barlow, *Philosophy in the Twentieth Century,* ed. W. Barrett and H. Aiken (New York: Random House, 1962), 3:254, 257, 259–62, 265, 267, 270.

68. Maurice Merleau-Ponty, *Phenomenology of Perception,* Eng. trans. C. Smith (New York: The Humanities Press; London: Routledge and Kegan Paul, 1962), 22.

69. Ibid., 28.

70. Ibid., 132.

71. Merleau-Ponty, *The Visible and the Invisible,* 176.

72. Ibid., 133–34, 137, 205.

73. Ibid., 248, 259.

74. Ibid., 146, 215.

Select Bibliography

The Gospel of Mark

Anderson, Hugh. *The Gospel of Mark.* Greenwood, S.C.: The Attic Press, 1976.

Belo, Fernando. *A Materialist Reading of the Gospel of Mark.* Eng. trans. M. O'Connell. Maryknoll, N.Y.: Orbis Books, 1981.

Best, Ernest. *Following Jesus: Discipleship in the Gospel of Mark. Journal for the Study of the New Testament,* Supplement Series 4. Sheffield, England: JSOT Press, 1981.

Cranfield, C. E. B. *The Gospel According to Saint Mark.* Cambridge: At the University Press, 1959.

Dewey, Joanna. *Markan Public Debate.* Chico, Calif.: Scholars Press, 1980.

Kee, Howard C. *Community of the New Age.* Philadelphia: Westminster Press, 1977.

Kelber, Werner H. *The Kingdom in Mark.* Philadelphia: Fortress Press, 1974.

Kermode, Frank. *The Genesis of Secrecy.* Cambridge, Mass.: Harvard University Press, 1979.

Robinson, James M. *The Problem of History in Mark and Other Markan Essays.* Philadelphia: Fortress Press, 1982.

Rhoads, David and Michie, Donald. *Mark As Story.* Philadelphia: Fortress Press, 1982.

Schweizer, Eduard. *The Good News According to Mark.* Eng. trans. D. Madvig. Atlanta: John Knox Press, 1970.

Taylor, Vincent. *The Gospel According to Saint Mark.* London: Macmillan and Co., 1966.

Via, Dan O., Jr. *Kerygma and Comedy in the New Testament.* Philadelphia: Fortress Press, 1975.

Ethics and Theology

Berdyaev, Nicholas. *The Beginning and the End.* Eng. trans. R. French. New York: Harper & Row, 1957.

Birch, Bruce C. and Rasmussen, Larry. *Bible and Ethics in the Christian Life.* Minneapolis: Augsburg Publishing House, 1976.

Braaten, Carl E. *Eschatology and Ethics.* Minneapolis: Augsburg Publishing House, 1974.

Furnish, Victor Paul. *The Love Commandment in the New Testament.* Nashville and New York: Abingdon Press, 1972.

Gustafson, James M. *Theology and Christian Ethics.* Philadelphia: Pilgrim Press, 1974.

Hanson, Paul D. *The Dawn of Apocalyptic.* Philadelphia: Fortress Press, 1975.

Hauerwas, Stanley. *A Community of Character.* Notre Dame, Ind.: University of Notre Dame Press, 1981.

Houlden, J. L. *Ethics and the New Testament.* Harmondsworth, England: Penguin Books, 1973.

MacIntyre, Alasdair. *After Virtue.* Notre Dame, Ind.: University of Notre Dame Press, 1981.

Sanders, Jack. *Ethics in the New Testament.* Philadelphia: Fortress Press, 1975.

Schrage, Wolfgang. *Ethik des Neuen Testaments.* Göttingen: Vandenhoeck & Ruprecht, 1982.

Hermeneutics and Critical Method

Bremond, Claude. "Morphology of the French Folktale." *Semiotics* 2 (1970).

Bremond, Claude. "The Narrative Message." Eng. trans. A. Johnston, Jr. *Semeia* 10 (1978).

Derrida, Jacques. *Of Grammatology.* Eng. trans. G. C. Spivak. Baltimore: The Johns Hopkins University Press, 1980.

Douglas, Mary. *Purity and Danger.* London: Routledge and Kegan Paul, 1979.

Gadamer, Hans-Georg. *Truth and Method.* Eng. trans. and ed. G. Barden and J. Cumming. New York: Seabury Press, 1975.

Iser, Wolfgang. *The Act of Reading.* Baltimore and London: The Johns Hopkins University Press, 1980.

Kermode, Frank. *The Sense of an Ending.* New York: Oxford University Press, 1966.

Krieger, Murray. *Theory of Criticism.* Baltimore and London: The Johns Hopkins University Press, 1976.

Lentricchia, Frank. *After the New Criticism.* Chicago: The University of Chicago Press, 1980.

Merleau-Ponty, Maurice. *Phenomenology of Perception.* Eng. trans. C. Smith. London: Routledge and Kegan Paul; New York: The Humanities Press, 1962.

Miller, David L. "Images of Happy Ending." *Eranos Yearbook* 1975. Leiden: E. J. Brill, 1977.

Patte, Daniel. *What is Structural Exegesis?* Philadelphia: Fortress Press, 1976.

Petersen, Norman R. *Literary Criticism for New Testament Critics.* Philadelphia: Fortress Press, 1978.

Ricoeur, Paul. *The Conflict of Interpretations.* Ed. D. Ihde. Evanston, Ill.: Northwestern University Press, 1974.

Theissen, Gerd. *Sociology of Early Palestinian Christianity.* Eng. trans. J. Bowden. Philadelphia: Fortress Press, 1978.

INDEXES

Index of Scripture References

Index of Names

Index of Subjects